NOVEL I

Animated images of literature are never ideologically neutral, inevitably they present a specific political or cultural agenda and are designed to encourage a particular set of responses, yet rarely are we aware of these hidden systems of meaning.

Written specifically with the student in mind and focusing on a number of well-known texts, including *Les Liaisons Dangereuses, Nicholas Nickleby, Nice Work* and *The Color Purple*, the contributors to this book demonstrate how we can look critically at literary adaptations and learn to distinguish between mythical images and the reality of the processes that constructed them. They argue that adaptations must not be marginalised, as through them we can enter into an exciting debate with the literary text itself. Essential reading for students, teachers and specialists interested in literature, film, theatre and television as well as cultural studies.

NOVEL IMAGES

Literature in performance

Edited by
Peter Reynolds

London and New York

First published 1993
by Routledge
11 New Fetter Lane, London EC4P 4EE

Simultaneously published in the USA and Canada
by Routledge Inc.
29 West 35th Street, New York, NY 10001

Phototypeset in 10/12pt Bembo by Intype, London
Printed and bound in Great Britain by
Clays Ltd, St Ives plc.

British Library Cataloguing in Publication Data
Novel Images: Literature in performance
I. Reynolds, Peter
791.4

Library of Congress Cataloging in Publication Data
Novel Images: Literature in performance/[edited by] Peter Reynolds.
p. cm.
Includes bibliographical references and index.
1. Motion pictures and literature. 2. Film adaptations.
I. Reynolds, Peter
PN1995.3.N68 1993
791.43'015–dc20 92–24807

ISBN 0 415 09102 0
0 415 09103 9 (pbk)

CONTENTS

NOTES ON CONTRIBUTORS

John Collick lives in Tokyo, where he teaches English literature and cultural studies. He is the author of *Shakespeare, Cinema and Society* (1989). He is currently doing research on the grotesque in the nineteenth century and the politics of English literature in Japan.

Jim Davis is Head of the Department of Theatre and Film Studies at the University of New South Wales, Australia. His publications include a biography of the nineteenth-century actor, John Liston, an edition of H. J. Byron's plays, an edition of the diaries of F. C. Wilton, stage manager of the Britannia Theatre and articles in numerous books and journals.

Joan Digby is Professor of English at Long Island University, USA. Generally interested in popular expressions of culture, she has published numerous articles and co-edited three anthologies of literature: *Permutations: Readings in Science and Literature, Food For Thought* and *Inspired by Drink*.

Spencer Golub is Associate Professor of Theatre and Comparative Literature at Brown University Rhode Island, USA. He is the author of *Evreinov; The Theatre of Paradox and Transformation* and of *The Recurrence of Fate: Staging Modern Russian Culture*. His essays, articles and reviews have appeared in numerous anthologies and journals. He is also a theatre director.

Harriett Hawkins is a Senior Research Fellow at Linacre College, Oxford, UK. Her previous publications include *Classics and Trash: Traditions and Taboos in High Literature and Popular Modern Genres* (1990) and the Harvester New Critical Introduction to *Measure for Measure* (1987).

Graham Holderness is Professor of Humanities at the University of Hertfordshire. He is the author of numerous books and articles including *The Shakespeare Myth* ed. (1988), *Shakespeare: Out of Court* (1990) and *The Politics of Theatre and Drama* ed. (1992).

Christopher Innes is Professor of English at York University, Ontario, Canada. He is the author of several monographs and numerous articles on political and avant-garde theatre, modern German and Canadian drama, as well as on stage directors such as Erwin Piscator and Gordon Craig. He is also General Editor of the Cambridge 'Directors in Perspective' series and of a series on 'The Canadian Playwright': Co-Editor of *Modern Drama* and of the 'Lives of the Theatre' series; and on the editorial board of *The Cambridge Guide to World Theatre*. His most recent work is a critical study of *Modern British Drama: 1890–1990*.

David Lodge is Honorary Professor of English Literature at the University of Birmingham, UK. He is both a succesful novelist and a widely read critic of English literature. His first play, *The Writing Game*, has been produced in Britain and America and was published in 1991.

Jan McDonald is Professor of Drama at the University of Gasgow, UK. She is actively engaged with current Scottish theatre particularly at the Glasgow Citizens' Theatre and at the Royal Scottish Academy of Music and Drama where she is a Governor. Her recent publications include *The New Drama*, 1900–1914 (1985) and *Glasgow Citizens' 1990*, co-edited with Claude Schumacher (1991).

Peter Reynolds is Head of the Department of Drama and Theatre Studies at the Roehampton Institute, London, UK and a member of the editorial board of *Critical Survey*. He has published several monographs and numerous articles.

Grahame Smith is Senior Lecturer in English Studies at the University of Stirling, UK where he also teaches a course in film authorship focusing on Orson Welles. He is the author of *Dickens, Money and Society*, *The Novel and Society: from Defoe to George Eliot* and *The Achievement of Graham Greene*.

Neil Taylor is Dean of the Faculty of Arts and Humanities at the Roehampton Institute, London, UK and a theatre critic for *Plays International* and *The Times Literary Supplement*.

ACKNOWLEDGEMENTS

I am grateful for the help and advice I have received from Sarah Dann, Paddy Page, Talia Rodgers, Val Taylor and Sarah Turvey. As usual I could not have done without the editorial tact and skill of my wife, Kimberley Reynolds. Most of all I am grateful to the contributors to this volume, all of whom gave their editor nothing but pleasure by submitting their work on time and allowing him the luxury of not having to submit their texts to a prolonged process of adaptation.

INTRODUCTION

Peter Reynolds

Animated images of literature in performance are seldom produced by accident or chance, nor are they natural and ideologically neutral. They have been designed and built (consciously or unconsciously) by their author(s) in order to project a specific agenda and to encourage a particular set of responses. Camera-angle, lighting, the use of space – theatre space and the space framed by the camera – casting, gesture and editing are all part of the grammar and syntax of performance. Understanding how and why this language is employed is more likely to occur (and to prove more productive, useful and intellectually satisfying) if, to paraphrase Brecht, the spectator not only looks, but learns how to look critically.

Many consumers of texts in performance absorb what they consume without having digested it because they are critically constipated by the predominantly illusionistic conventions used in their making. Most adaptations of literature in performance do not draw attention to the fact that they are fictional rather than real, or that the point of view from which the action is observed is not the only one available. Illusionism deliberately masks the subjective nature of the performance text and presents it instead as an objective reality. What the spectator sees and hears is what he or she is allowed to see, and to set the agenda by foregrounding one issue or set of issues is to marginalize others. To use a camera, for example, to create a dominant series of images of the head and upper body of individual characters may invite a reading of the text that is mediated through conventions of psychological naturalism – the spectators are drawn into speculation focusing on individuals, often in isolation, and on their personalities and personal characteristics. The problem arises not because this is necessarily an illegitimate form of dramatization, but because it is the dominant means of representation. Often highly manipulative, it can anaesthetize critical judgement and almost invariably foregrounds individuals at the expense of issues. Spectators who want something more lasting than the fleeting pleasure of narrative seduction have to learn to be active readers, not passive consumers of other people's novel images.

The contemporary spectator and student of literature in performance has at least one great advantage over his or her predecessors: the invention and mass production of relatively inexpensive video cassette recorders. The proliferation of recordings of performances that are now sold or hired has made the systematic and close study of these works possible for the first time. There are approximately 7,500 video-software shops in the UK and many more than that in the USA. Most of them have for sale or hire copies of adaptations of novels made for screening in the cinema or on television. Surveys undertaken in 1991 by the British Videogramme Association reveal that 70 per cent of households owned – that is, owned outright or rented – a video cassette recorder (the figure is even higher in the USA). This accessible library of tapes – coupled with the mechanical means to read them – is an increasingly important cultural phenomenon. In the United States, for example, Alice Walker's novel *The Color Purple* is on the syllabus of almost every High School and Junior College (causing the cultural right to cry out in protest that more students are now reading/seeing Alice Walker than are studying *Hamlet*). The Dutch screenwriter Menno Meyjes's adaptation of Walker's novel, filmed by Steven Spielberg, is available across the USA for less than fifteen dollars. In Britain and America English literature students studying the novels of the literary canon – Jane Austen, Dickens, Hardy, Lawrence – can just as easily pick up a video cassette and watch the novel images as pick up and read the novel itself.

Good! Through a process of comparative analysis that sets out to examine adaptations without prior prejudice students can be encouraged to become aware of systems of meaning that are not necessarily recognized as such; they can learn to distinguish between mythical images of the past and present, and the reality of the processes that constructed them. The student is encouraged to recognize that meanings in novels are fluid and un-stable, made and not given, and that their study may involve exploring parallel texts (such as paintings, film and television, and theatre) without a dominant hierarchy that assumes literature as origin. However, even the so-called enlightened student of literary texts sometimes inadvertently confuses the material solidity of printed books with the true nature of what they contain, and mistakes fictional characters for real people. What the symbolic language of the printed word is constructed by its reader to mean is, of course, the result of a dialectical process in which the reader continually makes and re-makes the text according to his or her cultural, social and historical circumstances. Students of literature in performance must learn (or be reminded) how the conventions of performance operate in the construction of meanings. The concrete reality of novel images on stage and the photographic reality of those on screen is literally more than meets the eye, and far from unproblematic. Like reading, spectating involves a complex interaction between the spectator and the performance in which what has been encoded by the author(s) is decoded by the spectator. What the author/performer encodes may not always be the result of a conscious process, nor can the author(s) entirely control the reception of the text by the spectator – but they will try.

Inexpensive paperback novels and cheap videos are available now as never before, and teachers in schools, colleges and universities can, and frequently do, integrate the study of adaptations with the study of the novels on which they are based. Certainly, there is no lack of material to work with: it is hard to think of a well-known work of fiction that has not at some time been adapted for performance on the stage, television or film. From the earliest days of silent film the cinema industry has displayed an enormous appetite for screen adaptations of novels. According to Morris Beja,[1] 'of the top twenty box-office successes of all time, the four that were not adaptations have all been turned into serializations'. The film rights to best-selling novels are bought by film executives, often for massive sums of money, although the fact that a novel has been a best-seller is no guarantee of a commercially popular film, as the critically disastrous adaptation (USA, 1990) of Tom Wolfe's *Bonfire of the Vanities* proved. But unlike television and the theatre, where, until quite recently, there was a marked tendency to serialize or stage novels that came from the literary canon as opposed to popular fiction, the cinema has never been limited to what its studio bosses judged to be good or even popular fiction. Many highly commercial films have been made from novels that few people have read and even fewer remember.

Adaptations of novels originally made for the cinema are almost always eventually shown again on television. The British Broadcasting Corporation (BBC) has a long and well-documented track record of its own, beginning with radio broadcasts in the 1930s, of producing adaptations of classic texts by authors such as Jane Austen, Dickens, Thackeray, George Eliot and Thomas Hardy. They were part of that institution's commitment to national public broadcasting, programmed at a time – usually a Sunday, in late afternoon or early evening – when family members could be supposed to be gathered together and thus able to share in the infusion of morally uplifting doses of their cultural heritage. British television, especially in the last decade, has displayed an increasing appetite for screening the novel, and not just those from the literary canon. In the first two years of the 1990s adaptations constituted approximately 30–40 per cent of the output of drama. Even relatively obscure novels of vast length, and presenting massive potential problems to an adapter (such as Samuel Richardson's *Clarissa*), have been screened. But it is not only in public-service broadcasting that drama producers have been quick to commission adaptations of novels. British independent television has also established itself as a rival to the BBC as provider of novel images, often based on adaptations of twentieth-century fiction such as John Mortimer's serialization of Evelyn Waugh's *Brideshead Revisited* and the hugely popular (on British television) serialization of H. E. Bates's *The Darling Buds of May* which turned the actor David Jason (Pop Larkin) into a folk-hero, and made the re-issued Penguin books edition of the novels (complete with the obligatory production 'still' on the front cover) into best-sellers.

In British theatre, perhaps under the inspiration of the critical and economic success of David Edgar's adaptation of Dickens's *Nicholas Nickleby* for the Royal Shakespeare Company (RSC) in 1980 (it played to full houses in both the UK and the USA and a video version was recorded and sold extensively), the rest of that decade saw a tremendous expansion in the number and frequency of adaptations of novels into theatrical performances. There is nothing new in the fashion for adapting novels for the stage, but the scale of activity is new. According to statistics released by the Arts Council of Great Britain, between 1980 and

1985 adaptations from novels amounted to 5 per cent of live theatre performances, but by 1986 the figure had risen dramatically to 13 per cent and, at the time of writing (1992), it is running at around 17–20 per cent. Although, of course, it is arguable that those responsible for adapting novels into stage plays – David Edgar, Christopher Hampton, Liz Lochhead *et al.* – are known primarily as dramatists, and are creating a form of new drama, the percentage of new plays not derived from literary sources dropped to only 13 per cent of performed work. It has never been easy for dramatists, even relatively established ones, to get a professional performance of a new play; the fashion for commissioning adaptations that gathered pace in the 1980s made it seem even more difficult than usual.

The momentum established in British theatre in the 1980s continued unabated into the early 1990s when nearly one in five productions in the subsidized theatre was likely to be an adaptation of a novel or short story. In 1991, for example, the repertoires of the two leading British theatre companies – the Royal National Theatre (RNT) and the RSC – contained four adaptations: of Kenneth Grahame's *The Wind in the Willows* (which generated the highest box-office revenue and most demand for seats in the history of the RNT), Kafka's *The Trial* and Bulgakov's *Black Snow*; and, at the RSC's main house at the Barbican, the year ended with David Edgar's adaptation of Robert Louis Stevenson's *Dr Jekyll and Mr Hyde*.

The popularity of adaptations amongst theatre managements in the 1980s had as much to do with economics as it did with aesthetics. Despite the short-lived so-called Thatcherite 'economic miracle' of the mid-1980s, theatrical life throughout the decade seemed characterized by financial crisis. Unemployment amongst actors was higher than it had been for a very long time, and state funding of even the major national companies was barely more than minimally adequate. The RNT was forced temporarily to close the smallest of its three auditoria, the Cottesloe (ironically, the space most frequently used to present new writing), and even the internationally prestigious RSC was partially kept afloat by the box-office takings of its musical show *Les Misérables* (itself an adaptation of the novel by Victor Hugo) which had been transferred to the West End. Indeed, at one stage in the winter of 1990, even this additional enterprise income was insufficient and the RSC was forced to take drastic action in order to make economies: it closed both theatres in its London base at the Barbican.

In such strained and difficult financial circumstances, not helped by an Arts Council policy of linking future financial assistance to increased box-office revenue, theatre managements were even more cautious than usual in their choice of repertoires. The willingness to take the inevitable risks involved in commissioning new plays (most new plays that get produced are commissioned rather than sent in on speculation) – risks so essential for a healthy theatrical culture – was severely constrained by the increased fear of the consequences of a hostile reception and therefore a possible box-office 'failure'. By choosing a play based on an existing text (usually, though not always, a well-known one) something of the risk involved in commissioning new writing for the stage could be removed, or at least moderated. If the text to be adapted was a novel, especially one already established as popular fiction or with a place in the literary canon, then, to an extent, a potential audience might be supposed already to exist, one that might be curious enough to pay to see the novel familiar in their mind's eye animated in live performance.

Not all the consequences of management's infatuation with adaptations were negative for aspiring playwrights. It was, after all, the playwrights themselves who were doing the adapting. Not only that, but the work they were required to do was often very different in style to that they had grown used to producing. For example, Edgar's adaptation of *Nicholas Nickleby* had a cast of forty; most new plays seldom include parts for more than a handful of performers. Dramatists simply do not produce large-scale spectacular plays of their own, perhaps in part because they know that the spaces in which they will be performed are not suitable (small studio theatres are invariably where new work is premièred); partly also because many of them lack the confidence and experience to write big plays; and, above all, because they know that managements will never be able to afford to stage them. However, a novelist such as Dickens was already established, as far as predominantly middle-class British theatre audiences of the 1980s were concerned, not only as a novelist, but also as a favourite progenitor of film, television and radio dramas and musical entertainments. Adaptations of his work, such as that commissioned by the RSC, provided a rare opportunity for a dramatist such as David Edgar to construct a large-scale work, designed for a big theatre and with a large cast of actors. The work on *Nicholas Nickleby* also afforded an opportunity to experiment with staging. This work eventually convincingly demonstrated how complex narratives could be successfully staged without automatic recourse to large-scale and expensive spectacle, thus freeing theatre managements at a stroke from one of their perennial preoccupations in considering the financial viability of such projects. The cast, the directors and writer worked collaboratively throughout, and David Edgar found the experimental workshop approach liberating: 'it was possible to use Dickens' narrative in a vast number of ways, and, particularly, that characters could step out from themselves and narrate their own feelings about themselves or other people, in the third person'.[2]

With so much evidently going on one could be tempted to think that all was well and that adapters busily constructing novel images had never had it so good. But our culture venerates originality, and the process of adapting an original work of fiction is often thought – even if it is an unspoken thought – to be an inferior creative activity. Although the practice of adapting novels into films, television dramas and stage plays is widespread and growing, the artistic status of those responsible for creating the adaptations is relatively low, and the status of the texts they produce remains, at best, marginal. Such texts are rarely published, and even more rarely studied, and, especially in the case of television and film adaptations, the names of their creators rarely figure largely in production credits. Even when they do, as in the case of Steven Spielberg's film (USA, 1987) of J. G. Ballard's novel *Empire of the Sun*, which the cover of my video copy announces as the creation of the playwright Tom Stoppard, the credit may be misleading: only if you had access to a final draft of the shooting script would you know that the screen adaptation went through at least four major revisions before shooting began, and that only the first two were by Stoppard. The adaptation was completed by Menno Meyjes, the Dutch screenwriter and adapter of two other major movie hits, Alice Walker/Steven Spielberg's *The Color Purple* (USA, 1985) and George Lucas's *Indiana Jones and the Last Crusade* (USA, 1989). In the editing room Spielberg's film of *Empire of the Sun* departed again from Meyjes's shooting script, leaving open the question 'Who *is* the author?' – Ballard? Stoppard? Meyjes? Spielberg? the film's editor? Indeed, the whole process of the adaptation of literary texts into performance texts de-centres the original author and makes the attribution of authorial responsibility problematic.

The sense that the work of an adapter is an inferior occupation to that of a novelist or playwright is compounded by the perception of the adaptation process itself. Theatre, television and film, unlike the activity of writing a novel or play, are all semi-industrialized; they are also collective activities in which the responsibility for making and re-making meanings is to some extent shared. Ultimate authorial responsibility is obviously more easily attributed in literary texts than in performance texts, and critics are usually more at ease when authorial attribution does not seem problematic. But whatever subtext lies behind the general uneasiness and prejudice towards adaptation, most of the specific arguments raised against adaptations of novels into live or recorded performances seem to revolve around questions of fidelity. Was the spirit of the original communicated or distorted? Were the original author's intentions violated or respected?

Leaving aside the debate as to whether or not it is important or even possible to discover what an author's intentions were, the arguments concerning fidelity to an original work are as old as performance itself. Even today in the theatre when a play is produced that is thought to overstep the invisible boundary that separates interpretation from adaptation, then critical hackles usually rise, and the higher the cultural status of the original author, the louder the clamour.

Most novels were probably not originally thought of as sources to be subsequently animated in live or recorded performance; and, of course, in a literal sense it is impossible for a specific work like a novel, conceived by one individual for one particular medium, to be adapted by another for an entirely different medium without major changes in form and, possibly, in content. But whether those changes result in a violation of the original is a more complex question. It is arguable that a piece of narrative fiction of 100,000 words and more, taking two or three days to read, can indeed be compressed into two or three hours in a narrative medium that communicates primarily through visual images; such transformations do not automatically result in a loss of the intellectual and emotional impact of the original, and do not necessarily compromise its integrity. On the other hand, such compression can distort the original. A 1992 BBC television adaptation of George Eliot's *Adam Bede* (adapted by Maggie

Wadey) was squeezed into a single 135-minute episode with the unfortunate result that, as the *Observer*'s television critic crudely but accurately said, we saw 'an episode of *Neighbours* in Period Costume'.[3]

Certain major changes are inevitable in order to accommodate the different demands made of the reader and those expected of the spectator. Spectators hear words spoken in performance at a slower pace than that at which most of us read them. The sheer number of words required to construct meanings in an adaptation for performance is therefore considerably less than that employed in the original work of fiction. This fact alone makes it possible and necessary to cut a lot of purely descriptive prose.

Arguments arise not only because of disputes concerning the fidelity of adaptations, but also because there is little or no agreement on what the adapter's role with respect to the original should be. Some directors use novels, as Martin Scorsese used Conrad's *Heart of Darkness* as the inspiration, the starting-point for an entirely new fictional work, *Apocalypse Now* (USA, 1979). Does it matter? Clearly in the above case the answer must be 'No'. Scorsese explicitly stated that his film was only very loosely based on Conrad's novella, and the title was changed. But should the adapter of a work of fiction have any responsibility towards the original author, and if so how much and for what? There are those – for instance, the playwright and screenwriter Christopher Hampton (who adapted Laclos's novel *Les Liaisons Dangereuses* for the stage and the screen) – who believe that the adapter's role is, as it were, to serve the original author, and to be as faithful to the spirit of his or her work as possible. For Hampton, the task should mirror that of the translator (and arguably of the author of realist fiction on which so many adaptations are based) and the adapter should aim for what Michael Meyer, translator of Ibsen and Strindberg, has described as a clear glass screen that is held up against the original work and through which the audience are permitted to gaze with an undistorted view.

Whatever the arguments may be regarding what should or should not be regarded as legitimate, and whatever the merits of a particular adaption, it would be a very primitive view to wish to prohibit the practice entirely. However, although a novel is not physically destroyed when it is adapted, it is possible that its reputation as a novel (and even that of its author as a novelist) may suffer. It is certainly the case that more and more people are watching adaptations on stage and screen who have little or no knowledge of the original work. For example, the television mini-series, co-produced by the American Public Broadcasting Service (PBS) and the BBC, and based on novels by Dickens, Thackeray, George Eliot, Jane Austen and others become, for many viewers, indistinguishable from what those authors actually wrote. A mass audience confronted with novel images that they do not, for whatever reason, find satisfactory may never subsequently find reason to turn back to the original and discover it for themselves. On the other hand, there is a considerable body of evidence to suggest that novel images that prove popular with audiences, if not with critics, can and do send people out on to the streets to hunt down the original and claim it for themselves.

Despite the potential to increase the sales of fiction, there is also a risk that in the adaptation of novels into novel images some of the issues and arguments contained in the original may be diminished and even sacrificed to the demands of the new medium. Audiences – certainly film and television audiences – are thought by many producers to demand (having, of course, been educated to demand) fast-moving narratives, glossy settings, rich costumes, spectacle and famous faces – demands that may conflict with the presentation of a complex web of interlocking moral, social, ethical and political issues. And if there is a conflict between issues and spectacle, spectacle usually wins.

Although visual texts can be constructed to articulate complexity, they also can be, and often are, used as simply decorative. Thus the reality of, for example, the social conditions of nineteenth-century urban or rural life, or the subtleties that characterized its social composition (both of which may have been realistically and accurately described by the novelist, and which were intended to supply the context in which the actions of characters are understood), can effectively be flattened and betrayed in adaptations that show a false and sanitized environment where historical reality has been sacrificed to the demands of the picturesque. *A Room with A View* is not about the view! But to many (for example, the viewers of American PBS's 'Masterpiece Theatre series'), the English literary landscape must sometimes resemble a collage made up of the Cotswolds, Oxford colleges and Castle Howard.

The movement towards more and more lavish novel images is driven by finance. Spectacle may be expensive to produce, but it is considered an indispensable asset by programme makers attempting to market adaptations both at home and, more importantly as far as the British are concerned, abroad. Indeed, many adaptations would never have been made were it not for the availability of co-production finance, usually from North America, finance which is sometimes only made available on the understanding that filming will take place in exotic and lavish period settings. But the real value of imaginative literature lies not in its ability to describe landscapes; nor is its role solely to provide the emotional satisfaction and pleasure that comes when the aesthetic sensibilities of the reader are satisfied. Its true value lies in its ability to act as a forum in which the reader can debate and contest social and moral issues. Those who are ultimately responsible for making and re-making novel images, therefore, carry a heavy social and cultural responsibility. They are mediating their audience's relationship with often highly complex and problematic work, and if the resultant literature in performance – the novel images – is pretty but bland and unproblematic, then that audience, especially if it is a mass audience with no knowledge of the original with which to contest the fidelity of the adaptation, will invariably lose one of the significant means of challenging the social construction of reality.

This collection of critical essays deliberately focuses on texts and performances most of which have been widely read and seen in the last two decades. All the novels are, at the time of writing, still in print, and most of the performances based on them either have been staged relatively recently or are available on commercial video. The huge growth over the last few years in what could be called the adaptation industry makes this a cultural phenomenon that cannot be ignored. If the observant student reads and spectates with an informed knowledge of the conventions of live and recorded performance, as well as those that influence reading, and then applies that knowledge to the scrutiny of adaptations, she or he will be primed for an important, useful and interesting dialectical debate.

That debate is begun by Graham Holderness who looks at Christopher Hampton's adaptation of Laclos's eighteenth-century epistolary novel *Les Liasions Dangereuses*, first as a stage play and later as a screenplay (*Dangerous Liaisons*, USA, 1988). Both adaptations enjoyed very considerable commercial and critical success but, for Holderness, it is the stage adaptation by the RSC that is the least satisfactory performance text. He argues that the moral critique contained in the novel must inhere in an epistolary convention, a convention that, he claims, Hampton found it impossible to realize in theatrical terms. David Lodge in his later chapter documenting his adaptation of his own novel *Nice Work* for television, asserts that 'letters, so at home in prose fiction . . . are, however, clumsy devices in film'. But for Holderness this problem was overcome on screen by the realist convention of the film, particularly its use of real and lavish locations, which made possible for the spectator an awareness of the existence of their opposite, in a way that the stage play failed to do.

John Collick also explores a well-known novel but in a cultural context unknown to most in the West. He looks at how Emily Brontë's *Wuthering Heights* is relocated in medieval Japan by Japanese avant-garde film director Yoshishige Yoshida. His film (*Arashi ga oka*, Japan, 1988) is not only a critique of William Wyler's 1939 Hollywood movie version of Brontë's novel, but also a narrative in which Romantic radicalism is worked into a discourse of the avant-garde left in modern Japan. According to Collick (who interviewed the director), Yoshida links the fictional Cathy with the historical Emily Brontë whom he regards as having prophetic and mystical powers, powers that enabled her to realize in the novel a revolutionary vision. It is this vision that Yoshida hoped to communicate in order to inspire contemporary Japanese spectators to acknowledge the oppression of women and the lower classes, and, at the same time, to facilitate what Collick describes as 'a celebration of the disruptive and violent iconoclasm of the individual'.

Dickens was greatly enamoured of the theatre and adapted some of his own work for the stage. He often wrote idiosyncratic but rich dialogue that transposes with relative ease to the stage or screen and is seized upon gleefully by actors looking for 'character' parts. He possessed a highly developed pictorial sense, using language to create a visual text to engage and delight the mind's eye and afford an opportunity for spectacle in live or recorded performance. In common with almost all other commercially popular writers of nineteenth-century fiction, Dickens wrote powerful realist linear narratives. The presence of 'characters', strong linear narrative and the opportunity for spectacle have especially endeared the works of Dickens to film and television producers. However, with a few notable exceptions, the adaptations that were made were usually picturesque, often sentimental, and lacking what was invariably present in almost all Dickens's work – the reality of the poverty and squalor of Victorian England, and the general attitude of complacency that allowed it to continue.

There are two chapters in *Novel Images* that focus on adaptations of novels by Dickens. In the first, by Grahame Smith, Dickens's literary work is contextualized in a highly sophisticated, visually literate culture. Smith claims that Dickens's use of structural imagery and parallel action are essential elements of his genius and that any successful adaptation must recognize these elements and seek to reproduce them. Christopher Innes argues that David Edgar's stage adaptation of *Nicholas Nickleby*, by deliberately drawing attention to its theatricality, managed to involve the audience emotionally whilst at the same time encouraging an objective critical perspective on the action. Innes also discusses Christine Edzard's film of *Little Dorrit*. He argues that Edzard foregrounds the medium of film just as Edgar does theatre, using the camera to mirror Dickens's experiment with narrative viewpoints – encouraging the spectator to identify with the viewpoints of either Arthur or Amy. For Innes, in these adaptations 'the form of representation itself becomes as central as the ostensible subject of Dickens's story'.

D. H. Lawrence also experimented with the then-dominant conventions of fictional narrative by intruding apparently authorial comment. Yet, as Neil Taylor argues, film adaptations of Lawrence's work, such as those of *Lady Chatterley's Lover*, do nothing to break what Taylor refers to as 'the sealed world of its fiction'. Taylor also points out that Lawrence often challenged naturalistic and realist conventions of the novel by refusing to give the reader a realist individual characterization. Yet when the director Ken Russell made a version of *Women in Love* (UK, 1969) his casting of actors already well-established in the public consciousness (Oliver Reed, Alan Bates and Eleanor Bron) inevitably made the characters they played distinctive individuals.

Some film directors and their financial backers have chosen to use Lawrence's novels (and Lawrence's reputation in the popular consciousness – a reputation for explicit sexuality, built up by the tabloid press in the immediate aftermath of the *Lady Chatterley* trial and subsequently) in order to construct exploitative images of women designed by, and to appeal to, the voyeuristic male gaze. Novel images of women by women are focused on by two other contributors: Harriett Hawkins and Jan McDonald.

Hawkins celebrates the continuing existence of *Gone with the Wind* as a hugely popular film. She points out that women were professionally and emotionally involved in the adaptation of Margaret Mitchell's book at every stage in its genesis and claims that it has portrayed as no other book or film before or since, the bonding, solidarity and parity between women of various types, classes and races. However, Hawkins's view of the film as non-Romantic and feminist, because its 'strong woman' overcomes obstacles without a happy ending, may seem to some readers to propose an unproblematized identification with the stereotypical trope of the suffering woman, by which female virtue is directly proportional to the amount of pain endured.

Liz Lochhead's adaption of Bram Stoker's late-nineteenth-century Gothic-horror novel *Dracula* (for the Royal Lyceum Theatre, Edinburgh, in 1985) was, according to Jan McDonald, a radical and feminist reconstruction of the Dracula myth. It made the hero into a dramatic agent for the psycho-sexual liberation of his so-called victims rather than an archetype of Victorian sexual repression. McDonald considers the way in which the myth is enlarged by Lochhead in a powerful performance text that graphically shows a positive transformation of women by the influence of a secret subversive impulse.

Another text that locates as its primary focus the oppression of women – specifically black women in the USA – is Alice Walker's *The Color Purple*. Joan Digby's chapter acknowledges that a white, male director (Steven Spielberg) chose to soften a black woman novelist's approach to sex and religion in order to produce a mass-audience Hollywood film (it grossed 94,175,854 dollars on its first run in the USA). However, she praises the sensitivity of Spielberg's work, drawing particular attention to the spontaneity achieved by the actors and the use of the camera – for example, in the use of lenses that elongated and deepened rooms. Spielberg also used lighting to foreground an important element in the novel to which many readers may have been blind: he used it to emphasize the expressive significance of eye-contact between the women, contact that assumed great importance in a culture that encouraged women, and black women in particular, not to speak, but to be silent.

Evelyn Waugh's waspish novel of English manners was transformed by John Mortimer and British independent television into a series of fabricated images of a mythic Englishness in which youthful and pretty aristocrats cavorted camply in exotic and lavish locations. *Brideshead Revisited* proved popular with middle-class television audiences not only in England, but also in the USA, where it was shown on public television as part of the 'Masterpiece Theatre' series. Spencer Golub looks back at the impact of a serial that succeeded in titillating the largely homophobic, puritan New World spectators with voyeuristic, soft-focus and softly-lit images of the Old World's attractive and decadent young men. Sebastian Flyte achieved cult status, and the comings and goings filmed at carefully chosen locations in Oxford and Castle Howard resulted in enormously profitable commercial spin-offs ranging from fashions based on costumes worn by the actors in the serial to the production of personalized teddy bears and a demonstrable growth in enquiries to the English Tourist Board.

In Timberlake Wertenbaker's adaptation of Thomas Keneally's novel *The Playmaker* the adapter chose, among other issues, to foreground the oppression of women in a patriarchical and transactional society. However, as Jim Davis points out in his chapter, her work on the text (like that of David Edgar working with the RSC on *Nicholas Nickleby*) was done as part of a collective workshopping process of playmaking. Perhaps partly because of this, Wertenbaker's adaptation of Keneally's novel marginalized the novel's concern with the subjugation and virtual elimination of a host culture by an alien colonialist ideology, and instead foregrounded the idea of theatre itself as a model for a better society in which the appetite of the individual was subjugated to the needs of the community. English audiences greeted her adaptation with universal acclaim, and also a sense of relief at what was perceived at last to be an optimistic drama in a deeply pessimistic age. The performance was developed, as its director Max Stafford-Clark subsequently pointed out, at a time of government hostility to theatre and to the state subsidy of the arts, and, he might have gone on to say, at a time when the British Prime Minister had proclaimed that there was no such thing as society. The play was gratefully received by audiences, especially those on the progressive left, many of whom felt more than usually powerless. It was read as an affirmative statement that the theatre retained the power to act, as Davis puts it, as an 'agent of transformation and education' by visibly demonstrating an alternative, collectivist view of the world.

Finally, David Lodge reminds the reader of a simple but fundamental truth about adaptation – the difference in status of the writer in the production of the artefact. The production of the text of a novel is controlled often right down to the final full stop, by the author. But a novel that is to become a performance is, as Lodge puts it, 'a basis for discussion, negotiation and revision'. He also notes that being involved in making a performance is a lot more exciting than the solitary pursuit of writing a novel!

NOTES

1 *Film and Literature* (London, 1979), 87.
2 David Edgar, *The Second Time as Farce* (London, 1988), 153.
3 John Naughton, *Observer* (5 January 1992), 23.

1

DANGEROUS LES'S LIAISONS

Graham Holderness

My title is possibly the one remaining permutation of this phrase, whose changing fortunes, from *Les Liaisons dangereuses* (via *Fatal Attraction*) to *Dangerous Liaisons*, register a peculiarly rich and illuminating process of cultural reproduction. It began in 1782 with the publication of what we now confidently recognize as a novel, but which was originally printed, if only in jest, as a collection of private correspondence – Choderlos de Laclos's *Les Liaisons Dangereuses*, subtitled *Letters Collected in One Section of Society and Published for the Edification of Others.*[1] In 1985, under the same main title, appeared a dramatized version, *Les Liaisons Dangereuses: A Play by Christopher Hampton, Based on the Novel by Choderlos de Laclos.* The performance text corresponding to this printed adaptation was a production by the Royal Shakespeare Company, which opened at the Other Place in Stratford in 1985, shifted to The Pit in London's Barbican Centre in January 1986, and later that year, by way of a commercial transfer, moved to the Ambassadors Theatre in the West End. The production then transferred to Broadway, opening at the Music Box Theatre in April 1987. The published text represents 'the text of the play as it stood on the first day of rehearsal; and the various minor cuts and abrasions (and improvements) sustained and effected during rehearsals are therefore not included'.[2]

In 1989 Hampton published a screenplay from the film version released in the previous year, the printed text now bearing the title *Dangerous Liaisons*. This text was designed to correspond exactly to the completed film-text: Hampton wanted it to 'resemble the final cut as closely as possible'.[3] Penguin Books, who had published a translation of Laclos's novel in 1961, promptly re-issued the book, with a re-designed cover carrying an illustration from the film, and bearing a multiplicity of titles, a practice reminiscent of the title pages of Elizabethan plays:

Choderlos de Laclos
Les Liaisons Dangereuses
Now a superb film starring
Glenn Close · John Malkovich
Michelle Pfeiffer
Dangerous
Liaisons

What's in a name? The objective of this chapter is to examine the relationship between these various written and performance texts; to analyse the process of cultural production entailed in the various transformations of a single narrative source; and to throw some light on the relations between the internal structures of 'narrative' and the conditions of cultural production.[4]

NOVEL

Published in 1782, Laclos's *Les Liaisons Dangereuses* appeared only a few years before the French Revolution. Laclos was a soldier and amateur intellectual who attempted writing in various different kinds – comic opera, poetry, sociological treatises, including one on the education of women – but wrote only the one novel. Laclos was a man of the Enlightenment, and in politics a Jacobin. His political affiliations seem a source of embarrassment to one of his English translators, who glances casually at Laclos's political career, defined as a matter of 'chicanery' and 'intrigue', and concludes that 'there is no room here to explore some of the obscurer passages and back-alleys of history'.[5] In fact, Laclos was an active Jacobin, in the service of the Duc d'Orléans (the king's liberal cousin, known as 'Phillippe-l'Egalité'), a speech-writer for Danton, and imprisoned twice for political reasons. This would seem in retrospect to constitute a rather closer connection to the central political currents of the age than a bit of chicanery in a back-alley.

It is certainly as such an Enlightenment liberal, sympathetic to the Revolution, that Laclos appeared to Christopher Hampton:

> In the Revolution he was a Jacobin, not prominent but

> assiduous, a friend of Danton and the associate and secretary of the Duc d'Orléans . . . [6]
>
> At the time of Danton's execution he was in jail at the very same prison and expected to die, even wrote farewell letters. . . . Nobody knows to this day how he escaped death, but extraordinarily he did, and ended up as a general in Napoleon's army.[7]

Les Liaisons Dangereuses is an 'epistolary' novel, in the same genre as Rousseau's *La Nouvelle Héloïse* or the novels of Samuel Richardson. Constructed entirely of letters written from one of the characters to another, it displays a completely impersonal narrative, with no overt or explicit indication of an authorial point-of-view. Laclos appears in the guise of an 'editor', earnestly protesting the veracity of his sources; and in the persona of a 'publisher', ironically questioning the authenticity of the book's contents.[8] Of course, the 'Publisher's Note' and 'Editor's Preface' are exercises in ironic imitation, typical eighteenth-century spoofs, like those prefaces of Defoe and Fielding which assure the reader of the morally unexceptionable character of the novel he or she is about to read. That point in the narrative where the author, through a particularly sharp ironic mode, manifests his presence with greatest clarity, is paradoxically the point where the doubleness of his ironic style defeats any effort on the reader's part to make connections between Laclos's life and his novel. Ultimately, the novel must, like a play, speak for itself.

The chief critical problem raised by the novel is precisely this question of authorial perspective. What sort of attitude towards its protagonists does the novel appear to encourage? Is it an Enlightenment critique of the frivolity and corruption of the French aristocracy, as they appeared to a detached observer's eye shortly before the Revolution that destroyed them? Or is it rather a piece of 'high pornography', a genre much favoured by writers of the time, designed to provoke voyeuristic fascination rather than moral outrage at the sexual intrigues depicted? The novel could certainly be read in the latter way earlier in its history, and there is little doubt that in its new manifestation as *Dangerous Liaisons* it is offered, at least in terms of media representation, as a narrative of sexual adventure.[9] Its subtitle – *Letters Collected in One Section of Society, and Published for the Edification of Others* – suggests the detached moral stance of an outsider, comprehending in a clearly defined moral perspective the corruption of the ruling class. The novel was certainly viewed in the nineteenth century as a particularly dangerous book, defended by Baudelaire, condemned to destruction in 1824 by the *cour royale de Paris*, and feared as much (perhaps) for the subversiveness of its class analysis as for the salaciousness of its sexual intrigues.

Christopher Hampton was clearly confident in his understanding of the relationship between author and novel (his view here expressed by Jason Best, in a published interview with the dramatist):

> The bourgeois Laclos, contrary to what many readers may have imagined, was writing a condemnation of the *ancien régime*'s depravity, not a celebration of its erotic Machiavellianism. Beneath the architectonic brilliance of the novel's design, the almost mathematical precision of its pointing, there was, for those readers prepared to look between the lines, an excoriating attack on the codes and values of the upper class.[10]

Hampton suggests that the author's bourgeois viewpoint emerges in the novel through the character of Mme de Tourvel: 'I do think Madame de Tourvel is the repository of decent feelings in the story, the character that was most sympathised with by Laclos himself.'[11] That bourgeois consciousness, condemning the aristocratic code of *mariage de convenance* and extramarital adultery, constitutes for Hampton a kind of proto-feminism:

> I think Laclos was certainly a feminist. At the time of the Revolution he said there can be no revolution without a proper education for women. The fact that these poor girls are stuffed away in convents and then brought out at the age of 15 to be sold to the highest bidder is something he disapproved of very strongly.[12]

There, of course, Hampton is able to invoke Laclos's published views on the education of women in support of his own attempt to construct a distinct authorial viewpoint, which in turn appears as a mixture of the moral and the political: Laclos's 'disapproval' of the objects of his artistic representation takes the form, it is assumed, of a self-evidently critical perspective, linked with a continual predictive adumbration (made explicit at the end of the play) of the shadow of revolution ('You can't read the novel without thinking all this has got to stop'[13]). That sense of an imperative need to arrest the process of decadence and corruption is both an articulation of moral outrage, and a retrospective confidence in the almost providential pattern of history, taking revenge through the Revolution on the effete and luxury-loving aristocracy. Hampton used a comment from André Malraux as epigraph to his play:

> Comme devant tant d'oeuvres de notre temps – pas seulement littéraires – le lecteur des *Liaisons* eut pu dire: 'Ça ne peut pas durer ainsi.'[14]

> More than so many works of our own age – and not just literary works – the reader of *Liaisons* has to say: 'This can't go on.'

However, in the absence of any explicit authorial commentary within the novel, this (or any other) interpretation of its ideological perspective must emerge formally, from the significant interaction of the items of epistolary correspondence. Each letter is written by one character, to another, and concerns third parties connected with both: each act of communication ramifies in various directions, and performs a number of different functions – to express, to impress, to persuade, to challenge, to cause an action or provoke a reaction. Each letter tells us as much about the writer as it does about the correspondent or the other characters to whom it alludes. It is worth remembering that at this time prose fiction had not by any means reached that great generic consensus known as 'realism' and had not established any of its manifold narrative possibilities as dominant: it was a highly experimental and volatile form. The epistolary novel was, at one level, one of the means by which the novel pretended to a naturalistic imitation of life: such texts always purported (fictionally) to be actual documentary records of discovered correspondence. When read as fiction, of course, such texts operated at the furthest remove from naturalism, calling attention to their own artifice in rhetorical, typographical and narrative ways.

STAGING

The epistolary novel could in some ways be described as a particularly dramatic form, since the utterances of the characters, like the speeches of actors on stage, are offered directly to the reader, rather than mediated through some form of fictional narrative. In other ways the epistolary novel is not dramatic, or at least not like a play, at all. The basic convention of epistolary fiction presupposes distance: you would not (except in very exceptional circumstances) write a letter to someone who was actually next to you. The basic convention of stage drama is physical proximity: dramatic action needs people on stage together to secure its most characteristic effects. Proximity in representational space (on stage, on screen) need not, of course, necessarily signify proximity in space and time within the 'real-life' space represented (compare, for example, the use of split-screen techniques in television and film). In a theatre where anti-naturalistic conventions are possible on stage, there is no reason why simultaneity and physical proximity should not be read as distance in time and space, from the cosmic figures of the medieval mystery-play who converse across a stage spanning Heaven and Hell, to the stock-market whizz-kids of Caryl Churchill's *Serious Money* who communicate with one another by telephone from opposite sides of the stage. In Laclos's *Liaisons Dangereuses* Valmont and Merteuil meet only once. If Christopher Hampton had attempted in his adaptation to imitate that narrative detail, he would have had to start from a much more anti-naturalistic basis than any he did actually in practice countenance.

For reasons of this kind, the letters largely disappear from the stage version (though they re-appear, interestingly, in the film).

> Laclos' novel is composed of letters and one of the difficulties of adapting it for the theatre is that, in the course of it, Valmont and Merteuil meet only once. In tackling this problem, I lost almost all trace of the novel's letter-technique . . . [15]

In the novel, as we shall see, the epistolary technique makes possible narrative devices of simultaneity, montage and superimposition, which are lost from the stage play. In the novel whatever controlling ideological attitude or governing moral perspective there may be must necessarily be formulated in the meaningful interaction of the letters. Yet Hampton did not think these devices necessary in order to sustain, in a stage adaptation, the novel's moral critique. Even more surprisingly, Hampton obviously intended that the stage production should be a much more naturalistic production than the one that actually emerged in the Other Place. Earlier I quoted the dramatist's observation that the published play text did not incorporate the changes inevitably introduced into the production text by the processes of rehearsal and performance. In fact, the variations are considerably more substantial than this understated comment suggests. The published script contains stage directions for scene-changes and the fixing of locations, which never actually appeared on the single-set design of the production. In Scene 17, Valmont is killed in the duel with Danceny. The last scene of the production (Scene 18) presents Merteuil, Mme de Volanges and Mme de Rosemonde playing cards, with Valmont's muffled corpse surrealistically in a hump at centre-stage. The script calls for this scene to be set 'in the salon of Mme de Merteuil's hotel' on New Year's Eve, while the duel between Valmont and Danceny in the previous scene had been set 'on a misty morning in the Bois de Vincennes'.

The printed and the performance texts here diverge considerably. The script was actually written for a performance that never took place – a production on the main stage at the Barbican theatre, a space offered to Hampton by Associate Director Howard Davies. In the event that space was not available.

> If you look at the published script then you'll see that I wrote it for several changes of scene. Then the bombshell came. They said I couldn't have the Barbican because Trevor Nunn was doing some other French thing there.[16]

'Some other French thing', disguised in Hampton's cool irony, was, in fact, the hugely successful mega-musical *Les Misérables*. So the single-set basis of the stage production was not, for Hampton, an artistic choice but an institutional constraint.

> They said you'll have to have the Other Place in Stratford and you can't have any set changes because if you take a chaise longue out of the Other Place when it's raining, which you have to there because it really is just a tin hut, then when it comes back in it will be too bloody wet for anyone to sit on! This was how the studio production originated. In fact most of the other productions in Europe are being done in vast auditoria and it seems to work there.[17]

Despite this preference, Hampton obviously agreed with the director and the company that a commercial transfer of the play should preserve the 'studio' character of a production shaped in the Other Place and the Pit, and would therefore fit better into the Ambassadors, 'the smallest theatre in the West End'.[18]

It was clearly Hampton's intention that the play would translate and sustain the moral urgency and apocalyptic warning of Laclos's novel. Did the play in production actually succeed in realizing that intention? The moral critique of the novel must inhere, I have argued, in an epistolary convention that Hampton found impossible to realize in theatrical terms. If one were to look at the development of the play in its institutional trajectory, it would be quite natural to locate its critical potentialities in the intensive 'intimacy' of the studio space (especially a space famous for the moral power of Trevor Nunn's *Macbeth*, or Buzz Goodbody's *Hamlet*) or in the anti-naturalistic production devices imposed by the physical characteristics of such spaces. Yet Hampton seems, in his insistence on the appropriateness of the 'main-house' large auditorium, to regard the play's moral power as quite independent of these accumulated, accrued characteristics.

Let us consider, for example, the play's historico-political significance. Everyone from Hampton on talks about the play and the novel as texts of the French Revolution. Of course, the novel preceded the Revolution, so that context is one supplied by a retrospective historical judgement. Nothing could be further from the minds of the characters in the novel than an impending Reign of Terror. The play duplicates precisely that *closed* character of the aristocratic class, its ideological conviction that nothing of any significance lay outside it; and that sense would be confirmed by a broadly naturalistic production in an 'intimate' studio space. So if the play is haunted by the spectre of an imminent revolution, how is that context to be supplied? It can only be supplied by the extrinsic awareness of the spectator, a historical consciousness that members of the audience bring to the theatre with them.

If the play depends for a realization of its moral, historical and political meanings on the guaranteed, secure possession of such a historical sense on the part of its spectators, then it is, of course, requiring of its audience the possession of certain minimum qualifications. But what exactly is the extent of that historical competence, the nature of that historical consciousness? Certain historical traditions effortlessly prescribe that any representation of the lives of the French aristocracy in the 1780s should be viewed through a guillotine-shaped frame. But does this constitute a secure grasp of significant history? Or is this rather a historical myth, composed of fragments from Edmund Burke and Charles Dickens, and consisting largely of a fascination with the Terror? Can the historical significance of 1789 be reduced to the successful testing of an efficient instrument of execution, and the perfecting of an art of undistracted knitting? The bicentenary celebrations of the French Revolution specifically endeavoured to revise this historical myth, stressing the progressive character of the bourgeois revolution, commemorating the intellectual legacy of the Enlightenment, and invoking such testaments to the spirit of political liberty as the Universal Declaration of the Rights of Man. The potential subversiveness of this historical revaluation of the revolution can be measured by the intervention of the British Prime Minister, who made an uncharacteristic foray into political philosophy to claim that the complete charter of political liberties had been expounded long before (and by 'us') in Magna Carta!

In the film adaptation, Hampton seems to have been concerned to avoid explicit premonitions of the Terror:

> We had an enormous debate whether to contain any reference to the Revolution; and indeed we shot various things which did refer to it. In the end we decided that if the film was strong enough it would work in the same subliminal way that the book did, and just indicate a society on the brink of collapse.[19]

The stage version had no such confidence in the receptiveness of its audience to subliminal promptings, and ended with a silhouette of the guillotine plastered all over the set ('[*Very slowly, the lights fade; but just before they vanish, there appears on the back wall, fleeting but sharp, the unmistakable silhouette of the guillotine.*]'[20]). Bill Overton is surely correct in judging such an overtly external and declarative demonstration a damaging compromise: 'The sense in the play of the impending guillotine allows audiences a comfortable moral detachment, knowing the retributions of history.'[21]

FILM

The 'worlds' of novel and film, even though constructed to represent the same inward-looking, exclusive class as in the play, are quite different in this respect from the particular studio stage-world occupied by the play. In the novel the letters, although all written from one member of the aristocracy to another, have to travel to reach their destination, and therefore inhabit a more open spatial world. The choice of location rather than studio for the film immediately transfers the action to a material world of actual buildings, parks, rooms, where an overwhelming sense of opulence automatically provokes in imagination an awareness of its opposite. Valmont's ostentatiously charitable and philanthropic assisting of the poor family (calculated to impress Tourvel) is literally described, by Valmont himself, in the novel,[22] and literally represented in the film.[23] In the play it is merely alluded to in a conversation between Valmont, Tourvel and Rosemonde.[24]

In the next stage of its development, from stage production to screenplay, the narrative of *Les Liaisons Dangereuses* began to circle back towards its novelistic ancestor.

> The theatre and the cinema speak two quite different languages . . . . The devices of the theatre – rhetoric, a certain artifice, the slow unfurling of a tightly-knit argument, the pleasures of language – are not merely different from those of the cinema – sensuality, speed, unexpected juxtapositions, the eloquence of images – but to a large extent antithetical.
>
> It has always seemed to me that film has far more in common with the novel than with the specialized codes of the theatre; so in accordance with that theory, the first step in adapting for the cinema a play, which had itself been adapted from a novel, was to close the circle and go back to the original.[25]

Theatre and cinema are both media of 'performance', yet the technological and theoretical differences between them are radical and profound. Performance studies often pose a familiar distinction between a play as literary textualization, and the play-in-production as a living enactment. On the one hand, there is the printed text, apparently fixed and immobile, resistant to intervention or participation, inviting the kind of reading that seeks to locate the intended coherence of authorial meaning; and on the other, the ephemeral medium of theatrical performance, an experiential form obviously concerned with the shaping of a malleable material, open to contribution from performers and spectators alike, a collaborative enterprise of production and interpretation.

In fact, as Hampton argued, the medium of film, at least in terms of the social and cultural uses to which the technology has traditionally been put, has more in common in this context with literature than with drama. Clearly the processes of theatrical and film adaptation have equal liberty to interpret and reconstruct a dramatic text – both theoretically 'free', both subject to the pressures and determinants of any socio-cultural situation. The process by which a 'text' is turned into a 'performance', through analysis, discussion, interpretative experiment, improvisation and rehearsal, may be very similar in each case. Yet, although in a film a drama is being enacted by living performers, that concrete human realization is overridden by the finality of the finished product: the enactment is ultimately fixed and frozen in a perpetually mobile immobility. In a theatrical space actors may be empowered to continue interpreting the dramatic text in an experimental process of exploration and discovery; in a film, whatever procedures of rehearsal and exploration may precede the final shooting, the entire product of the actors' communication is arrested at the point of editing. In a theatre an audience is present at the dramatic event, participating in the performance in whatever manner may be permitted by the nature of the theatrical space and the relations between actors and audience; in a cinema the spectator is present at the image of an absent event, illuminatingly shadowed by the two-dimensional phantasmagoria of the screen.

> It's in the editing room where the final, fundamental difference between theatre and cinema becomes clear. Whereas a play is a kind of metaphysical idea, a random collision between a text, a group of actors, a set and a director, and thus endlessly potential and open to change; a film is an object, a submarine, say, where one by one the hatches are battened down until you break the bottle of champagne over it and let it dive and roam the world, unalterably itself.[26]

Of course, this general distinction deals with potentialities rather than with innate and inevitable characteristics of the respective media. A theatrical performance can be conventionalized into rigidity, choreographed to the point of fossilization, or starched into conformity by institutional pressures; and can thereby approach as closely to the resistant fixity of literature as a naturalistic film. A more experimental filmic medium can realize in concrete form some of the pluralistic potentialities still present in the discourses of 'script' and 'screenplay'. It is perhaps more important to distinguish between conservative and experimental discourses within each medium, than to attempt to estrange the media utterly from each other.

The point in Christopher Hampton's formulation where our theoretical reservations ought to be alerted is where he talks of the theatrical performance as 'endlessly potential and open to change'. Is the theatrical 'text itself' completely open to the influence of those contingent determinants? If so, then any given production will be entirely shaped by them – shaped, in the terms I am using, by the institutional factors operating within the given context of production. However, if the text is also conceived of as (in his phrase) 'a metaphysical idea', then clearly it must be possible to identify and isolate, within the diversified and pluralistic possibilities of interpretation to which any play script is open, a solid core of existence that remains fundamentally unchanged. If the text itself is open and iterable, no individual production would ever be a direct incarnation of this core-text, but a 'random collision' of determinants, a temporary and provisional stabilizing of various focused but potentially centrifugal energies. Yet, we must consider if the stage performance text is in reality more likely in its passage to be changed by the cultural processes through which it evolves. Is it in truth more open and pluralistic than either of its counterpart texts in prose and film?

DIFFERENCES

I have space for only one example of the kind of detailed comparative analysis that should ideally accompany this general theoretical evaluation. Letter 47 of Laclos's novel, written by Valmont to Merteuil, describes how Valmont finds himself in the arms of a courtesan Emilie,[27] whose body is employed not only for sexual satisfaction, but as an aid to his correspondence with Tourvel:

> I have been using her as a desk upon which to write to my fair devotee – to whom I find it amusing I should send a letter written in bed, in the arms, almost, of a trollop

> (broken off, too, while I committed a downright infidelity), in which I give her an equal account of my situation and conduct.

The letter to Tourvel (which is actually enclosed together with Valmont's letter to Merteuil, accompanied by instructions to the latter to post it for him!), is an accomplished essay in facetious *double entendre*:

> I come, Madame, after a stormy night during which I never closed an eye, after suffering without cease now the turmoil of a consuming passion, now the utter exhaustion of every faculty of my being, I come to you to seek the peace I need, but which as yet I cannot hope to enjoy . . . . But I must leave you for a moment to calm an excitement which mounts with every moment, and which is fast becoming more than I can control . . .

The letter is written, therefore, for two separate readers, and constructed so as to bear two distinct readings. That ironic ambivalence, holding together the discourses of ardour and flippancy the satirical and the romantic, is there to be decoded as ambivalence by the reader of the fictional narrative. But it is designed within the narrative to be deconstructed between two readers, each of whom privileges one dimension of its doubling style: with Tourvel reading the tormented accents of unrequited love, and Merteuil perceiving the libidinous sarcasm of an easy cynicism. The letter carries therefore a double purpose: to entertain and provoke Merteuil and to convince Tourvel of the authenticity of Valmont's passion.

Within the fictional world of the novel, the letter functions as communication, albeit of a complex, oblique and double-edged kind. Within the narrative, it functions as a revelation of meaning, meaning constructed by the interrelationships of writing and context. The reader is thus presented with a pluralistic discourse, capable of multiple readings, rather than a single unified intention or direction of significance. This does not imply, on the other hand, that the text displays a radical indeterminancy, offering the reader a completely free play of signifiers – only that the process of making meaning from it involves, on the part of the reader, an active participation in the narrative, a comparative weighing of evidence, a continual activity of judgement and moral choice.

If there is any movement towards a closing-off of this process, it lies in Letter 50, Tourvel's reply, which, far from being persuaded by the patina of passion that glistens deceptively along the top of Valmont's language, reads the letter almost as if she knows it was inscribed on the body of his licentiousness:

> After all, what do you do in the very moment of your setting forth, as you think, an apology for love but show the effect of its terrible ravages?

It is in the language of Tourvel's resistance that we encounter a movement of the narrative towards moral affirmation, although this is not at all the bourgeois consciousness that Christopher Hampton found speaking through Tourvel, and attributed in turn to Laclos. The full range of available meanings lies beyond the awareness of any individual character, and is embodied only in the narrative, accessible only to the reader. Tourvel's stern reproof unwittingly turns the tables on Valmont, not simply by rejecting his advances, but by reading through his ironic language to the cynical motives underlying it; she (or rather her utterance) unconsciously decodes the subtext within the text, sees (as it were) through the tissue of elegant phraseology to the prostitute's back on which it was penned.

This episode appears in the stage version[28] in a greatly simplified form. Valmont is in bed with Emilie:

> VALMONT. Now, do you have pen, ink and writing paper? . . . Now, don't move. [EMILIE *is still puzzled. But she submits graciously enough. Valmont begins to write.*] 'My dear Madame de Tourvel . . . I have just come . . . to my desk . . .' [EMILIE *understands now. She turns her head to smile up at him*] . . . . We'll finish it later, shall we?

Whereas in the novel the narrative of this event is orientated towards its two readers, on stage it is addressed directly to the audience. The device of giving Merteuil sight of the letter before Tourvel receives it, disappears from the dramatic text, as does Tourvel's response. In place of the multiple readings offered by the prose text, the stage version presents the spectator with a simply structured comic trope, enacted between the substantial (that is, physically present) figures of Valmont and Emilie, and eliminating the other characters incorporated by the fictional text. Far from being an 'open' text, the theatrical version closes off all possible readings except the obvious acceptance of Valmont's gesture as a function of the conventions of farce.

The film version[29] reverses this tendency of the stage text towards closure, and in place of the novel's deployment of juxtaposition, ironic congruity and contrast, substitutes the filmic device of montage:

INT. EMILIE'S BEDROOM. NIGHT.

[*A sheet of writing paper is spread across the bare back of* EMILIE] . . .

VALMONT. 'My dear Madame de Tourvel . . . I have just come . . .'

EXT. GARDENS OF ROSEMONDE'S CHATEAU. DAY.

[TOURVEL *sits on a bench reading Valmont's letter.*]

VALMONT. [*Voice over*] '. . . from exaltation to exhaustion and back again; yet despite these torments I guarantee that at this moment I am far happier than you . . .'

[*The letter: a teardrop falls on to the paper, smudging the ink*].

INT. EMILIE'S BEDROOM. NIGHT.

[VALMONT *lays aside paper, pen and inkwell and murmurs to* EMILIE.]

VALMONT. We'll finish it later, shall we? [*He leans in to embrace her.*]

Where the naturalistic mode of the theatrical adaptation requires a literal representation of this event, confined to a single time and place, the film can secure an anachronistic effect of simultaneity by intercutting the writing of the letter with its reading. The significant juxtaposition obtained is quite different from (and indeed, less complex than) those of the novel; but it clearly produces, by linking cynical manipulation with emotional responsiveness, experience with innocence, a more open text than that of the stage version.

At one level, the general theoretical contention that a theatrical text is open to change, in ways that a novel and a film are not, is irrefutable: and a different type of analysis from the one I am offering here could usefully trace, in the detail of performance, the play's trajectory of development from the Other Place to the West End. Yet the procedure of comparative analysis applied to the printed texts produces a perhaps surprising conclusion: that of the three versions of *Les Liaisons dangereuses* discussed here, it is the theatrical text that appears least open, least pluralistic, most self-enclosed, and most resistant to alternative readings.

NOTES

1 The translation used here is that by P. W. K. Stone, *Les Liaisons Dangereuses* (*Dangerous Liaisons*), (Harmondsworth: Penguin, 1961).
2 'Author's Note', prefatory to Christopher Hampton, *Les Liaisons Dangereuses* (London: Faber & Faber, 1985).
3 'Introduction: *My Dinner with Milos*', Christopher Hampton, *Dangerous Liaisons: The Film* (London: Faber & Faber, 1989), p. xiii.
4 The present chapter is part of a forthcoming book on cultural production and narrative form.
5 'Introduction', Laclos trans. Stone (1961), 13.
6 'A Note on Laclos', prefatory to Hampton (1985).
7 Steve Grant, 'Hampton Holds Court', *Time Out* (1–8 October 1986), 17.
8 See 'Publisher's Note' (p. 17) and 'Editor's Preface' (p. 19) in Laclos trans. Stone (1961).
9 The title *Dangerous Liaisons*, not merely a convenient translation (the other two films so far adapted from the novel, by Roger Vadim (Fr, 1959) and Milos Forman (Fr/UK, 1989), are both titled *Valmont*), was obviously calculated to subsume, via a cross-reference to Glenn Close (the actress who appeared in both), the notoriously successful *Fatal Attraction* (USA, 1987), a film as pornographically voyeuristic (in terms of both sex and violence) as it is crudely moralizing. Press reviews and feature articles on both play and film tediously ring the changes on these related titles: 'Fatal Attractions', 'French Letters', 'Bulging Trousers', even 'Close Encounters'. (A recent film comedy called *Consuming Passions* rather defies expectation, being the story of three men falling into a vat of chocolate and emerging as hard centres.)
10 Jason Best, 'Fatal Attractions', *Due South* (March 1989), 15.
11 Hampton, quoted ibid.
12 ibid.
13 Hampton quoted in Robert Gore Langton, 'An Old Liaison', *Plays and Players* (October 1986), 13.
14 Epigraph to Hampton (1985).
15 Christopher Hampton, 'Going for That Gut Feeling', *Guardian* (29 December 1988).
16 Hampton quoted in Best (1989), 15.
17 Hampton quoted in Grant (1986).
18 Hampton quoted in Langton (1986).
19 Hampton quoted in Best (1989).
20 Hampton (1985), 101.
21 Bill Overton, 'The Play of Letters: *Les Liaisons Dangereuses* on the Stage', *Theatre Research International*, 13/3 (1988), 273.

22 Laclos trans. Stone (1961), Letter 22 (pp. 59–60).
23 Hampton (1989), 14–15.
24 Hampton (1985), Act I Scene ii, p. 21.
25 Hampton (1988).
26 ibid.
27 See Laclos trans. Stone, Letters 47, 48, 50 (pp. 108–14).
28 Hampton (1985), Act 1 Scene iii, p. 28; Act 1 Scene v, p. 44.
29 Hampton (1989), 24.

2

DISMEMBERING DEVILS

The demonology of *Arashi ga oka* (1988) and *Wuthering Heights* (1939)

John Collick

In this chapter I want to examine Yoshishige Yoshida's 1988 film of *Wuthering Heights* (*Arashi ga oka*) and its relationship to the 1939 American version. The goal is not to produce a comparative analysis; such an approach can rapidly degenerate into a mere list of differences or similarities. Furthermore, I do not want to compare the film adaptations to the 'original' novel. The question of whether the Japanese or the Americans can do 'justice' to the orthodox Anglo-American literary establishment's assessment of Emily Brontë's book reinforces essentialist beliefs in the purity of the central text. It also establishes a critical hegemony in which foreign adaptations are forced to assume the position of helpless ignorance in the face of more 'accurate' British readings. In this hierarchy Japanese versions are, at the very least, hampered by the fact that they must either portray nineteenth-century Yorkshire people speaking Japanese or change the setting. Even the Americans have problems: since the book is traditionally thought of as a part-hymn to the wild moors above Haworth, the sight of a huge cardboard mountain masquerading as the Nab can appear ridiculous. Yet, as this last example shows, even orthodox interpretations of the book rapidly become entangled in their own myths. Popular images of Cathy and Heathcliff running towards each other across a stunning, Romantic heath have no equivalent in the novel or any of the films and if *Wuthering Heights* is a novel of landscape then there are very few references to the natural features of Yorkshire. Instead, I want to look at the Japanese film as a particular reading of both the novel and the American movie from the viewpoint of the Japanese avant-garde.

WUTHERING HEIGHTS IN JAPAN: THE MGM LEGACY

To understand how the story has been appropriated within Japanese culture we need to establish the way in which it was originally introduced into the country. *Wuthering Heights* came to Japan relatively late, compared to the rest of early-nineteenth-century English literature. After two-and-a-half centuries of isolation Japan was finally forced to open its borders to the west in the 1850s. Terrified of colonization, the Japanese government began an intensive modernization programme to industrialize the country. As part of the plan they established a number of universities with the aim of educating future leaders in European and American law, culture and science. Young Japanese men studied western philosophy and literature and attempted to use them to transform Japan's politics and culture. During the late nineteenth century and early twentieth century, Romantic poetry was especially popular, mainly because intellectuals identified themselves with the rebellious geniuses of Byron, Shelley and Wordsworth (as they were portrayed in Victorian literary studies). As far as novels were concerned, late Victorian fiction was read from a utilitarian point of view: that is to say, the works of writers like Dickens, Hardy and George Eliot were used as guides to the life, customs and manners of the English middle classes. *Wuthering Heights* was too early and too esoteric to be a 'useful' guide to British society. Furthermore, since most of British literature was disseminated in Japan via the English academic establishment (the first Japanese students were usually taught literature by English or American professors) *Wuthering Heights*'s uneasy position on the edge of the canon meant that its translation into Japanese was delayed. As late as 1921 British literary critics were claiming that

> critical judgement is still in suspense. It is not desirable to read; to take *Wuthering Heights* from the shelf is to prepare for oneself no pleasure. The song of love and of morning that makes *Jane Eyre* an imperishable possession is not sung here.[1]

In fact, *Wuthering Heights* did not appear in Japanese until the late 1940s and its publication coincided with the showing of the 1939 film by MGM which was released in Japan just after the war. Thus most Japanese people came to the novel via the film. In fact the majority of the Brontës' works were not published until the mid-1950s so the cultural position of *Wuthering Heights* is indissoluble from that of William Wyler's film version. Basically, the film was watched as, and the book read as, a doomed love-story. Both works were experienced in the context of a number of popular Hollywood films that have been combined into a small genre of sentimental, 'period' romances popular among young middle-class women. These include such movies as *Gone with the Wind, Waterloo Bridge, Roman Holiday*, and, inevitably, *Casablanca.* Within these films the themes that offer the strongest parallels with Japanese cultural motifs are the subjection and punishment of wayward and uncontrollable women and the image of the doomed lovers whose transgressive love disrupts the social order. To Japanese audiences in the 1940s Merle Oberon's Cathy appeared as a more extreme and vicious example of Vivien Leigh's Scarlett O'Hara. She was a woman whose impetuous and inconsistent wilfulness destroyed the lives of the men who surrounded her and, ultimately, destroyed her.

The position of *Wuthering Heights* in Japanese culture is further complicated by the fact that the American film is synthesized from popular imagery, situations and motifs from Hollywood movies of the 1930s. *Wuthering Heights* was produced in 1939, at a time when the big movie companies were seeking to establish respectability by making film versions of classic literature. Warner Brothers had already made *A Midsummer Night's Dream* based on the Max Reinhardt theatre production of 1934. Laurence Olivier, during his stay in the United States, was to be involved in a number of prestigious 'classic' movies, including a version of Daphne du Maurier's *Rebecca.* Each of the major Hollywood companies responded to the impact of Roosevelt's 'New Deal' in a variety of ways. Warner Brothers focused on social-conscience issues in its crime movies; Columbia sought to smooth over inequalities of class through the redeeming humour of 'screwball' comedy. MGM's *Wuthering Heights* also carries a strong critique of injustice and snobbery, setting up an opposition between Heathcliff the working-class gypsy (his class affiliations are emphasized when Cathy searches for his face among the farm labourers gathered at her wedding) and Hindley and the Lintons. The film's moral tone is best represented by the benevolence of old Mr Earnshaw. Heathcliff's introduction to the family is softened considerably. In the novel he is blamed for the loss of the presents that Mr Earnshaw brought back from Liverpool for his children: Hindley's new violin is shattered and Cathy's whip is lost. When Cathy teases Heathcliff in anger her father hits her.[2] In the film both gifts are intact and Cathy's bad manners earn a mild Christianly reproof. In general the early scenes are a curious mix of childhood escapism and social conscience; indeed, the young Heathcliff would not look out of place among Warner's Dead End kids.

Throughout the movie a series of binary oppositions are constructed: between the Old and New world, between the wilderness and enervating civilization and between entrenched snobbery and personal achievement. Stress is placed on the fact that Heathcliff journeys to America to make the fortune that will enable him to confront and avenge himself upon the class prejudices of the English. A further opposition is created between the natural world of Penistone Crag and the aristocratic drawing-rooms of Thrushcross Grange. Cathy's downfall is characterized as a wilful desire for material sophistication – a passion to be absorbed into the aristocracy that destroys both her and Heathcliff. Conversely, Penistone Crag becomes the symbol of liberty and expansive freedom: the ghosts are shown walking towards it hand-in-hand at the end of the movie. That the painted set bears more resemblance to the Rocky Mountains than the Yorkshire moors may not be entirely coincidental. The contrast between the wilderness and civilization is a continual theme in the American Western, especially those of John Ford. In *Wuthering Heights*, this 'frontier myth' takes on strong class elements through Hindley's and the Lintons' continual emphasis on the fact that Heathcliff is a 'mere' gypsy stable-boy.

The central motivating force of the MGM film is Cathy, specifically Cathy's desire for material wealth and social sophistication. The death of Cathy at the end of the movie can be read as a male revenge-fantasy. On her deathbed she acquiesces to the accusations of Heathcliff as he tells her that 'Misery and death and all the evils that God and man could have ever done would never have parted us. You did that alone. You wandered off like a wanton, greedy child to break your heart and mine.' To this condemnation all she replies is 'Heathcliff, forgive me.'[3] Rendered meek and compliant by her illness, Cathy is carried to the window where, after seeing Penistone Crag, she dies in Heathcliff's arms. It is then that he declares 'Leave her alone. She's mine now.'[4] In the context of the portrayal of Cathy as a fickle, inconsistent socialite Heathcliff's final curse that she haunt him until he dies takes on a significantly manipulative tone. The fact that her ghost returns to beg entrance to the Heights (as a woman and not as a child, as in the novel) signifies that Heathcliff has finally pinned her down; she is silenced by death. From then on her existence is defined and controlled by the uncouth American fortune-hunter. Attempts to entrap and control wilful women also emerge as a significant theme in *Arashi ga oka*. However, in this case, the outcome is reversed. The Japanese Cathy's association with both the supernatural wisdom of the Romantic poet and Emily Brontë herself makes her by far the most powerful character in the film. The political radicalism behind this restructuring of the Cathy/Heathcliff relationship is compounded by the fact that the latter, instead of representing the dynamic adventurism of a new frontier-society, is a demonic, alien force that intrudes into and destroys a rigidly structured, disintegrating society.

ARASHI GA OKA

The Japanese film of *Wuthering Heights* was released in 1988 under the name *Arashi ga oka* (a direct translation). Curiously enough, the international print was called *Onimaru*, which is the name of the Heathcliff character (the 'Oni' in 'Onimaru' means 'demon'). It is possible that the distributors were wary of inviting ridicule by giving the name *Wuthering Heights* to something so apparently alien to popular conceptions of the story. The renaming of films for the international market often marks attempts to enlist them under the protection of traditional Anglo-American criticism. The sight of samurai trooping across a Wuthering Heights composed of lava slopes and volcanic craters would probably have invited ridicule from a substantial number of narrow-minded western film critics.

Arashi ga oka is not a mainstream Japanese film. It may come as a surprise to many people outside the country that internationally renowned directors like Yoshishige Yoshida, Nagisa Oshima and Akira Kurosawa are not especially popular in Japan. Japanese cinema is dominated by the American film market. Roughly 80 per cent of videos available in rental stores are foreign, 60 per cent being American. The domestic film industry is dominated by mass-produced genre films. Low-budget gangster movies, samurai dramas, comedies and pornography comprise most of the output of the major film companies. The industry's main concern is money, hence the reluctance to finance big projects and the reliance on the rapid production of popular formula movies. The situation is so grim that for twenty years Akira Kurosawa, Japan's most famous living film director, has had to rely on foreign sponsors to provide finance for his films. Yoshishige Yoshida, who like many of the Japanese avant-garde is popular in France, used a substantial amount of French capital for his film version of *Wuthering Heights*.

Yoshida's *Arashi ga oka* has to be viewed in the context of the radical cinema movement of the late 1960s and early 1970s, a period when directors like Nagisa Oshima and Yoshida himself were producing independent, experimental, anti-establishment films heavily influenced by the work of people like Jean-Luc Godard and Luis Buñuel. During this period of political unrest many film directors were allied with the theatre of the left which combined traditional Japanese folk-theatre with Brechtian agit-prop. However, nowadays the depoliticization of the student body and a general reaction against the earlier movements has manifested itself in audience indifference to home-grown experimental cinema. This has meant that directors like Yoshida have found themselves playing to an international market in which traditional theatre and experimental film are often merely exotically Japanese rather than politically interventionist. A significant proportion of the Japanese audience mentally switches off when it sees beautifully made, intellectually challenging period films, adopting the attitude that such movies are produced for foreigners to watch.

Yoshida's film of *Wuthering Heights* is set in medieval Japan during the Onin period (late fifteenth century), a revolutionary era characterized by brutal civil wars between clans competing for control of the country. Most of the story takes place on the lava slopes of a volcano, scenery common to many Japanese period movies set at this time. As well as providing ample opportunity for eerie shots of bleak, mist-swept landscapes, it also has associations with the Buddhist warrior Hell where the dead souls of samurai fight eternally in a landscape littered with fires and volcanoes. The general atmosphere of the film is one of a time of misery and strife, and continual reference is made to the end of the world; trains of Buddhist monks wander through the towns praying for salvation and forgiveness. The plot of the film follows that of the novel quite closely and, unlike the MGM film, Yoshida's version spans both generations. Wuthering Heights becomes East Mansion, presided over by the elderly Takamaru (Mr Earnshaw), while Thrushcross Grange is West Mansion. There are no ghosts, and the supernatural element has been absorbed into the symbolic rituals of Japanese Shintoism. The opening sequence of the novel, when Mr Lockwood encounters the ghost of Cathy at Wuthering Heights, is gone. Instead, a blind priest, in the company of two other travellers, visits a graveyard to pray for the soul of Cathy (called Kinu, or 'silk', in the film). There they find her coffin unearthed. Onimaru appears and kills the traveller who examined the grave while the others escape. Then he takes the coffin back to East Mansion. The film then flashes back to when Takamaru first brought him to the mansion as a child and the main narrative begins.

When asked why he chose to make a film of *Wuthering Heights*, Yoshida stated that one reason was the desire to challenge what he saw as the romanticism of the Hollywood version.[5] Yoshida intended the film to be a part-tribute to the unfinished film version of Luis Buñuel, a director whom, along with Jean-Luc Godard and Michelangelo Antonioni, he regards as a major influence on his work. Given his interest in the European avant-garde, it is not surprising that he chose to evoke the transgressive element in Emily Brontë's book. The desire to retain the brutality of the original novel alienated a substantial number of Japanese *Wuthering Heights* fans who, used to the imagery of the Hollywood film, were not prepared to encounter a 'fierce, pitiless, wolfish' Heathcliff.[6] The film is, however, not merely an anti-Hollywood film. In reworking the story from a transgressive perspective Yoshida adopted a number of images and structures from traditional Japanese culture. The result is a complex insight into the way in which Romantic radicalism has been picked up and worked into the discourse of the avant-garde left in modern Japan. Yoshida himself divides the themes of the film into three areas: the relationship between a small, isolated tradition-bound community and a larger, powerful and threatening cosmos; the stranger who is transformed into a god and who disrupts the social order; and finally the traditional Shinto belief in the genii loci or spirits of nature.

Wuthering Heights and the world: the isolation of Japan

The action of the film takes place within a very narrow compass: locations are limited to the two mansions, a town street and the lava slopes of the volcano. The continual feeling is one of claustrophobia. There are no panoramas, even on the sides of the mountain. The camera inevitably points into a slope or valley. As a result, the viewer is left with the distinct impression of being trapped within a small, enclosed world. The image of a disintegrating world is accentuated by the more immediate decay of the families involved in the story. Takamaru names Onimaru as an heir to East Mansion because of the need to inject new, vital blood into the family. Their insularity is emphasized by the fact that even though both East and West Mansions use the same graveyard their inhabitants have never met. Yet at the same time there is the sense of a dynamic and rapidly changing world beyond the boundaries of the screen. The Onin period was a revolutionary and violent era, and elements of this function as impassive and wilful gods that enter, like a *deus ex machina*, into the story to disrupt and destroy the fossilized traditions of the two families. When soldiers march across the sacred slopes of the volcano the aged Takamaru, whose job it is to protect these grounds, rides out to challenge them. He is cut down without a fight by a perfunctorily fired arrow. Onimaru runs away just before Kinu leaves for the West Mansion. Much later he returns as a successful warrior. With arbitrary finality he produces an edict from the Shogun which awards him a fief that includes both houses.

It is not hard to see the relationship between the immediate world of the two mansions and what lies outside as echoing the popular self-image of modern Japan as a country isolated within an uncomprehending world. Hamstrung by a factionalized government whose decision-making apparatus depends heavily on nepotism and power-brokering, Japan is coming under increasing international criticism for its failure to create and maintain an adequate foreign policy. In the eyes of the American government especially, Japan's hesitant response to the Gulf War was seen as proof of a general unwillingness to take on 'responsibilities' commensurate with its economic influence (though what are chiefly at issue here are Japan's 'responsibilities' to American interests). In a culture that prides itself on being unique the division between Japan and the rest of the world dominates portrayals of the country throughout all aspects of the media. Japan has always felt itself to be overshadowed by the outside, especially as it adopted so much of its culture from abroad (China until the nineteenth century, then the major western imperial nations). Peter Dale, in a Freudian reading of the relationship between Japanese intellectuals and American and European society suggests that 'behind the contrived image of the "West" . . . one cannot but sense a narcissistic antagonism to the father'.[7] This theme coincides remarkably with Yoshida's introduction of the marauding stranger/god Onimaru as a representative of the intimidating external cosmos. Onimaru behaves in many ways like a parody of a westerner: he transgresses social boundaries by entering parts of the mansion forbidden to servants, he 'pollutes' a secret ritual by watching it and he cooks and eats birds sacred to the mountain. In an interview Yoshida explained the role of Onimaru as similar to that of a legendary stranger who enters a community, is killed and then returns in the form of a marauding god.[8] When considered in this light, Onimaru's presence becomes doubly threatening as he represents the continual intrusion of western society into Japan. At the same time his semi-divine nature means that he is inescapable; Japan's fear of the west is internalized as a fear of the disruptive and fantastic demons of the Japanese cultural unconscious who, like the stranger/god, are repressed only to return again in a more powerful form. At the end of the film Yoshimaru (Hareton) fights with Onimaru and cuts off his arm – a significantly Oedipal gesture. Yet Onimaru lives on, reappearing in the last few scenes where he drags Kinu's coffin across a 'Valley of Hell' (a common name for volcanic areas in Japan).

Onimaru: insanity, Romantic rebellion and the Japanese intellectual

What are the political implications of the portrayal of Onimaru/Heathcliff as a marauding outsider and what can it tell us about the relationship between the Romantic period and the Japanese avant-garde? Japanese society is renowned for its celebration of homogeneity, hence the oft-quoted phrase 'The nail that sticks out gets hit on the head.' Despite a massive range of cultural and economic groups the majority of Japanese people openly identify themselves with the middle class. The emphasis on the group above the individual in mainstream bourgeois society has meant that Japanese radicalism has tended to focus on the iconoclastic individual as the site of revolution. Japanese radicalism has its roots in the late nineteenth century. When Japan opened to the west Japanese intellectuals were faced with the problem that, although their country was desperately trying to transform itself into a western-style imperial power, it was, in the eyes of the west, just another 'oriental' nation. Notions of subjectivity and individualism were introduced to Japan via western books of philosophy and novels. However, much of the tradition of western humanism was founded on the very racial distinctions that fuelled nineteenth-century orientalism. Jonathan Dollimore has pointed out both the transcendentalism and the racism inherent in the philosophy of writers like Kant and Hume. He states that at the basis of essential humanism is the process whereby 'a specific cultural identity is universalised or naturalised'.[9] Essential 'man' was white, western and bourgeois; the Japanese intellectual was not. Thus the latter, trying to establish a new concept of self, was hamstrung by the fact that western philosophy placed Japan in the position of an oriental object, 'a phenomenon possessing regular characteristics'.[10] For this reason, in order to assert individuality the Japanese subject had to stake out an area that appeared untouched by either traditional Japanese ideology or modern, western rationalism. Insanity, sexuality and suicide were mobilized as literary motifs to express radical, personal rebellion. The psychological 'I-novels' that were so popular in the early part of the twentieth century can be seen as a reaction against the fixed ideas of the oriental character imposed from outside, and as an attempt to explore and assert a genuine concept of Japanese individual subjectivity. In reality, the revolution they offered consisted of an attempt to create hermetically sealed worlds of decadent transgression similar to those of de Sade.

This pattern conforms to that in England in the early nineteenth century. In the wake of the reactionary period of the Napoleonic wars the early radical enthusiasm of the Romantic and Gothic writers became transformed into introspective psychological angst. Even though *Arashi ga oka* places strong emphasis on the injustice of class distinctions, Onimaru is not a revolutionary. His passion for Kinu and his nihilism make him more like a cynical, Byronic iconoclast. Yet the fact that he is possessed and transformed into a god also echoes the visionary madness that was supposed to lie behind the works of Blake, Coleridge and Shelley.

The key link between the themes of *Arashi ga oka* and Romantic literature is the use of Shintoism in the film. Shintoism is the oldest religion in Japan. Despite its appropriation by the far right and its association with Emperor worship, it is in fact a shamanistic religion in which each location has its own spirit or god. Traditional Shinto festivals follow a common theme: a god descends into a sacred space where it takes possession of a human. Then it blesses the location before returning to its true dwelling-place. This ritual forms the basis for Japan's oldest dramatic form, the Noh theatre. Yoshida had the actors in his film perform Noh exercises for an hour each day under the guidance of a professional instructor. The fact that the Noh has remained unchanged as an art-form for 600 years means that it provides a direct link with the dramatic mannerisms of the period in which *Arashi ga oka* is set. Furthermore, it gives the concept of possession by the gods a self-conscious quality. Actors whose performance confirms their access to a supernatural source of power echo the claims of the Romantic poets who self-consciously set themselves up as the mouthpieces for the spirits of nature (as with Keats's nightingale, Shelley's Aeolian harp and Wordsworth's universal spirit).

In *Arashi ga oka* life at the East Mansion is dominated by the Orochi festival. In a secret ceremony the male head of the household is possessed by the god of the volcano which gives him a mystical and violent power. When Onimaru becomes lord of the mansion he must also become the god. As he runs up the mountain at the end of his dance he is confronted by Yoshimaru who fights and overcomes him. Yet, as mentioned above, the defeat of the iconoclastic outsider merely serves to reinforce his power. In the film, at least, the Romantic rebel continues to haunt the perimeters of a fragile society. There is an element of wish-fulfilment behind this portrayal of Onimaru, which is understandable given the diminishing influence of the avant-garde cinema on Japanese politics. Yet, at the same time, the iconoclastic outsider is a powerful motif for the Japanese fears of a dangerous and alienating cosmos which, like Freud's Repressed, is conquered merely to return in a more powerful form.

Kinu and Emily Brontë: oracles of the gods

The portrayal of Cathy is one of the most striking things about *Arashi ga oka*. Viewers used to traditional representations of the heroine as a spirited and wild child of nature will be surprised at the cold, almost emotionless Kinu. The fact that Onimaru is played with all the barely suppressed rage and energy of a man possessed throws his lover's passive and measured responses into stark relief. It also drastically affects the balance between the two. Onimaru's rage and passion finds no equivalent in the character of Yoshida's Cathy and it is evident that he often finds her as baffling as the audience. Before she journeys to the West Mansion she seduces Onimaru in a very cold and enigmatic way. After commanding him to undress she disrobes and insinuates herself around him. He remains transfixed, paralysed by the confrontation with a female sexuality that even he cannot control. Later, when Onimaru rides away from East Mansion Kinu does not run out into the wilderness to look for him; instead, she declares 'Onimaru hasn't left, he is still here'; then, looking into her hand-mirror she intones 'Onimaru is myself, I am Onimaru.'[11] The mirror comes to symbolize Kinu's control over her lover: from the very beginning of the film, when she is given it as a gift by her father, she uses it to dazzle Onimaru. After death it shines into his face from her coffin. Finally, Onimaru gives it as a gift to Kinu's daughter. She immediately directs a blinding light on to his face. The two women exercise the only power that can discomfit and suppress the demon.

Much Japanese culture is concerned with the 'exorcism' of women's sexuality which it frequently represents as supernatural. At weddings the bride wears a traditional head-dress which is supposed to conceal the horns of the demon that lurks inside her. Thus an emotionally and sexually independent woman poses a frightening and incomprehensible threat to many Japanese men. The villainesses in Kurosawa's movies are almost all portrayed as cold, calculating or insane. Manifestations of a mystic power in woman can shatter the fabric of society. As Onimaru continually returns to disrupt the decaying social order of the two mansions, so Kinu returns from the dead to hound him. Each time Onimaru confronts her corpse or skeleton he is powerless.

Kinu's independence and control over Onimaru not only inverts the power-relationship in the MGM film but it also takes on a strong radical quality. The oppression of women is a persistent theme in the film. At East Mansion, when women menstruate or give birth, they are confined to a small hut where a thick woven rope hangs from the ceiling like a noose. After hearing that daughters born to the family of the East Mansion traditionally enter service as shrine-maidens, Kinu remarks 'It's evil to cast women away.'[12] Partly to avoid this fate she engineers her marriage with the lord of the West Mansion. Her father, the patriarch of her family and guardian of the mountain's sacred grounds, acquiesces in the face of her resolution, remarking only that her first-born son should inherit East Mansion. His response is in stark contrast to his authority over his son which he wields with impunity.

Yoshida explained that Kinu's power, and her control over Onimaru, is due to the fact that she 'can speak the language of the gods'.[13] Yoshida draws a direct parallel between the character of Cathy and Emily Brontë. He believes that the Brontë family were in a similar situation, living within the very small, rigidly circumscribed world of nineteenth-century Yorkshire. The fact that Emily Brontë produced a radical and challenging novel has led him to regard her as a Delphic oracle whose access to a mystical power enabled her to achieve the revolutionary vision that he feels is embodied in the book. What is remarkable about this belief is that it is almost identical to the Romantic image of the poet-as-prophet. For example, Yoshida's image of Emily Brontë as a Delphic oracle is similar to Mary Shelley's association of herself with the priestess of Apollo in the first chapter of the *The Last Man* (1826).

ARASHI GA OKA AND JAPANESE ROMANTICISM

In removing *Wuthering Heights* from its role in Japanese culture as a Hollywood love-story Yoshida has managed to create a radical study of a Japanese society helpless in the face of a vast and powerful world-order. *Arashi ga oka* is also a fascinating example of the way in which the political radicalism of the English Romantic period was picked up by Japanese intellectuals at the turn of this century and transformed into a discourse that continues to influence the culture of the left. The avant-garde in Japan has been forced into a position of isolation where it can only confront the homogeneity of bourgeois Japanese culture by adopting the perspective of rebellious insanity. Hence traditional Shinto concepts such as possession by the gods have become interwoven with such Romantic themes as that of the poet as an intermediary between a realm of overwhelming truth and mystical power and the ordinary world. Inevitably, the reliance on such introspective and personal themes as madness, eroticism and death means that the film hovers between a study of the oppression of women and the lower classes and a celebration of the disruptive and violent iconoclasm of the individual. Yet at the same time that *Arashi ga oka* introduces Onimaru as the stranger/god who destroys the fossilized and insular world of the two mansions it subjects him to the control of Kinu. Onimaru's motives are destructive; Kinu, as the oracle of the gods, explicitly uses her power to control male violence. At the same time she displays a desire to transcend the narrow role proscribed for her by the society of the two mansions. Although Yoshimaru overthrows Onimaru and becomes the lord of the two mansions there is no doubt that Kinu's daughter, the 'demonic' woman who egged him on, is the motivating force behind the new order. Changes in Japanese society are causing many women to assume a more active role in politics. Yoshida's *Wuthering Heights* suggests that the radical avant-garde, in allying itself with feminism, may be finding a more valid and interventionist means of expression than the traditional angst of the crazy rebel.[14]

NOTES

1 'The Brontës', A. A. Jack, *The Cambridge History of English Literature*, vol. XIII, (Cambridge: Cambridge University Press, 1921), 410.
2 Emily Brontë, *Wuthering Heights* (London: Oxford University Press, 1963), 43.
3 *Wuthering Heights*, dir. William Wyler (USA, 1939).
4 ibid.
5 Yoshishige Yoshida, interview with the author, 19 April 1991.
6 Brontë, *Wuthering Heights*, 126.
7 Peter Dale, *The Myth of Japanese Uniqueness* (London: Routledge, 1986), 39–40.
8 Interview with Yoshishige Yoshida.
9 Jonathan Dollimore, *Radical Tragedy: Religion, Ideology and Power in the Drama of Shakespeare and his Contemporaries* (Brighton: Harvester Press, 1984), 258.
10 Edward Said, *Orientalism* (Harmondsworth: Penguin, 1985), 42.

11 *Arashi ga oka*, dir. Yoshishige Yoshida (Japan, 1988). Original scenario by Yoshishige Yoshida, trans. John Collick, 64.
12 ibid., 35.
13 Interview with Yoshishige Yoshida.
14 I would like to thank the following people for their help in the preparation of this chapter: Yoshishige Yoshida for his help and for allowing me to interview him; Ryuichi Yorozuya; Yoichi Higashikawa and Matsusugi Kimura for their advice concerning Japanese and Japanese literary history; and Mr Takahashi of Seiyu Film Company.

3

DICKENS AND ADAPTATION

Imagery in words and pictures

Grahame Smith

All views of the past are partial and limited, distorted by ideology, myth and misconception, and our late-twentieth-century responses to the Victorian era are no exception. Two of the most obvious, and related, examples are found in our confident assessment that the Victorians were hopelessly enmeshed in, first, sexual repression and, second, a generalized hypocrisy that masked the realities of nineteenth-century life in a variety of evasions. I am not concerned to unravel the truth, or otherwise, of these particular views, although it might be worth noting, in passing, that sexual repression was evidently quite compatible with the production of large families. What I am concerned to combat is a different, and perhaps more subtle, set of responses to this period, an almost unformulated sense of the visual impoverishment of the Victorian world. Of course, it is possible – inevitable, in fact – that society and individuals should have a whole series of notions of any historical period, some of which are incompatible. Saturation in the Victorian novel, especially Dickens, communicates a sensuously vibrant fictional world pulsating with the sights, sounds and smells of a novelistic image of reality. However, when we turn from fiction to 'reality' itself I believe that our responses may be somewhat different, for reasons rooted in technology.

When we look at Victorian photographs of people, for example, we must be struck by the unsmiling rigidity of pose almost universally associated with such images, a solidity that reinforces, and perhaps helps to create, our feeling that the Victorians are somehow heavy and daunting, with little of the varied richness we take for granted in images of modern people. But this inflexible vision of the past is a reflection of a technical inadequacy in Victorian cameras which required extremely long exposure times if the photograph was to come out satisfactorily. It is impossible to maintain a natural-seeming smile and flexible pose for more than a few seconds, a human factor which locks into the technical limitation and produces, for example, representations of patriarchy that comfortably confirm all our worst fears of the horrors of the Victorian family.

Similarly, when we look at the earliest cinematic images of people from the late-Victorian or Edwardian period we are usually presented with a ludicrously flat surface of tiny, jerky figures that conveys merely a parody of human existence, a black-and-white farce that, again, contrasts unfavourably with the dense, highly coloured texture of life captured by modern cinema. What we must remember, however, is that such visions of the past are usually distorted by two technical failings: poor print quality and projection at the number of frames per second required for sound, rather than silent, cinema. Anyone who has experienced the majestic beauty of silent film projected at the correct speed in a good print will grasp how our apparent experience of the past can be limited by purely external pressures.

The starting-point for this discussion of imagery in words and pictures in relation to adaptations of Dickens is the conviction that the Victorian period was a densely visual epoch in its high art, popular culture and social reality, that 'looking at the world through the medium of pictures . . . became a habit in the first half of the nineteenth century'[1] and that this habit had an enormous influence on art, entertainment and social life in the later nineteenth and earlier twentieth centuries. Demonstrating this large-scale development will require examination of such varied matters as Dickens's methods of serial publication, book illustration, entertainments such as the magic lantern and the panorama, and the spectacular effects employed in the Victorian theatre. The form and style of Dickens's novels will be analysed in relation to their visual implications and their possible influence on early cinema. Finally, a brief examination will be made of some major adaptations of Dickens's work.

DICKENS

It is well established that Dickens's novels were subjected to various forms of adaptation, or what we would today call piracy, from the very beginning of his career. The absence of copyright protection meant that all kinds of literature were liable to be appropriated in the highly commercialized world of early Victorian entertainment. Not only were works of literature translated for European consumption and published in the United States without the writer's permission being obtained or any payment being made, but various kinds of popularization were perpetrated with no regard to the wishes of individual authors. And so we find, to use the contemporary phrase, commercial rip-offs of *The Pickwick Papers* and theatrical versions of the novels appearing long before their completion in serial publication form. These practices were widespread, but there are special reasons why Dickens should have been so ready a victim. Again – using perhaps appropriate modern terminology – Dickens was a hot property from almost his first appearance in fiction. The eruption of Sam Weller in the fourth number of *Pickwick* ensured the most meteoric rise of any career in the history of English literature, and there were all too many inhabitants of the commercialized world of Victorian entertainment waiting to batten on this pre-existing success. Added to this must be the actual physical appearance of Dickens's fiction before the public, the very reverse of the intimidating three-volume format (the so-called 'three-decker') of the 'serious' novel. Against the advice of interested friends Dickens insisted on his work appearing in the format established by the accidents involved in the creation of *Pickwick*, and for the remainder of his career the novels came out in various forms of serial publication. (The fact that Dickens also wrote serially, creating the novels as they appeared in monthly or weekly parts, is also crucial to his development as a writer,[2] but too far removed from my subject to be dealt with here.)

What, then, did avid Victorian readers find in their hands when they held, say, a monthly part of one of the novels? They saw a pale green cover, the densely illustrated title page, which remained the same throughout publication. Like the overture to an opera, this engraving contained hints of the delights to come and possible clues as to how the complex narrative would be revealed over its many months of publication. Turning the page took the reader into the world of Victorian commerce with as many as seven pages of advertisements, many of them illustrated, for everything from 'Laming's Effervescing Cheltenham Salts' to an invitation to 'Reform Your Tailors' Bills!' (The advertisements were continued on both sides of the green endpaper.) Commerce gave way to two vivid illustrations, most characteristically by the brilliant 'Phiz' (Hablot K. Browne) and only then did the reader finally get to the text itself. What this suggests is an element of continuity, rather than an absolute break, between the novel and the social world from which it emerged. Looked at in this way, *Pickwick* can be seen as a commodity fiction presented in a manner not dissimilar to the 'classic' television serial, a text sandwiched between commercial breaks. On this view, Dickens is a 'great' imaginative writer, a central figure in the canon of English literature, who is at the same time a deeply popular writer consciously aware of the demands of a large and varied public and in no way disdainful of having his work operate in the market-place with maximum success. One aspect of this marketing strategy is his willingness to see his work embedded in a visual context. Indeed, it could be argued that despite the control he exerted over Phiz's illustrations, they constitute an element of adaptation from within the text itself.

The physical appearance of a monthly part can, then, give us our first clue to what I shall argue is the intensely visual quality of Victorian culture, a clue that can be followed up, first, in the quality of Dickens's own imagination. In a letter to his friend and biographer, John Forster, Dickens wrote of the difficulty he found in writing *Dombey and Son* while living in Lausanne because of the 'absence of streets':

> I can't express how much I want these [streets and crowds]. It seems as if they supplied something to my brain, which it cannot bear, when busy, to lose . . . a day in London sets me up again and starts me. But the toil and labour of writing, day after day, without that magic lantern, is IMMENSE.

Again, on one of his many arrivals in Paris Dickens took what was for him a habitually long walk at night through the city of which, Forster reports, 'the brilliancy and brightness almost frightened him'; Dickens, in his own words, went 'wandering into Hospitals, Prisons, Dead-houses, Operas, Theatres, Concert

Rooms, Burial-grounds, Palaces and Wine shops', an experience which he found a whole 'Panorama' of 'gaudy and ghastly' sights.[3] In evoking his own needs and sense of the social world in terms of the magic lantern and the panorama Dickens makes unforced use of two of the most popular forms of entertainment and instruction in his period. Once more there is a need to counter a possible modern prejudice, especially in the case of the magic lantern. The very title may summon up a hopelessly old-fashioned and technically inferior experience compared with the wonders of contemporary forms of visual communication. Again, however, it is possible to enjoy the delights of the past through modern reconstructions of a medium which, at its best, involved effects of great visual sophistication such as subtle dissolves from summer into winter, day into night, calm into storm and so on. The technical innovation of mechanically operated slides meant that ships could appear to sink and trains thunder past a landscape in a highly convincing manner. The link with the present is obvious:

> Lantern shows, like television drama today, popularized books and boosted sales so much that publishers would send copies of every book suitable for illustration to lantern slide makers. Many classics like Dickens would be boiled down to a sequence of perhaps 12 or 24 slides.[4]

If modern readers have only a distorted version of the magic lantern in the recesses of their memory it is likely that they have no conception at all of the nature of the nineteenth-century panorama. At its simplest, a panorama was a 360-degree painting housed in a temporary or permanent circular structure which used all the technical means at its disposal to give the viewer a 'successful illusion of reality'.[5] The subjects were famous historical scenes such as battles, views of European cities and more exotic views of far-away places. Great stress was laid on the panoramas' accuracy of historical detail and fidelity to nature, an emphasis that highlights the Victorian need to feel that the experience could be instructional as well as entertaining. Technical advances led eventually to the diorama, a movable auditorium which, in collaboration with effects of lighting and the use of music and transparencies, unfroze the static panorama into what may well have been a more colourfully vibrant experience than the earliest experiments in cinema. The final touch was provided by the vivid expertise of a good commentator, the most famous British example being that of Albert Smith who gave over 2,000 performances of his moving panorama lecture on the ascent of Mont Blanc in London in the 1850s. Smith and his show were well known to Dickens, and evidence of the widespread popularity of such entertainments, for those who could afford them, is provided by an article in Dickens's weekly magazine *Household Words* entitled 'Some Accounts of an Extraordinary Traveller' on the 'voyages' of a retired bank clerk by means of regular visits to the panorama. As with the magic lantern, the link between the kinds of stimulation provided by these marvels of Victorian technology and our own marvel of television is obvious. Archaeology, foreign travel, historical evocation, sport, excitement and information of many varieties were as available to the Victorians in their own visual forms as they are to us.

To find the most spectacular visual effects in the nineteenth century, and the closest approximation to the full resources of contemporary cinema, it is, however, necessary to turn to the theatre. Nothing demonstrates more clearly the centrality of the role of the Industrial Revolution in nineteenth-century life than the constant technological improvements which invested the theatrical experience with a level of spectacular realism that has never been superseded on the stage. These developments were far from controversial in the sense that for much Victorian theatre 'the eye and not the ear was the organ of appeal',[6] to the extent that some critics and theatre-goers felt that language was being sacrificed to spectacle, even in the case of Shakespeare. But since 'melodrama and pantomime were creatures of technology'[7] and the general audience appeared to have a boundless appetite for the spectacle that could be created by stage machinery this line of development proved unstoppable until challenged by the even greater spectacular realism of sophisticated silent cinema. Some idea of what could be seen on the nineteenth-century stage in anticipation of film can be derived from this description of a London production of *Ben-Hur* which had first been performed in New York in 1899:

> In this production could be seen a panorama of Jerusalem, and the interior of a Roman galley packed with slaves chained to their oars . . . . The chief scenic attraction was the chariot race in the arena at Antioch. Here twenty-two horses were

> used instead of the twelve in New York, although only four chariots could actually race together side by side.[8]

Only *four* chariots!

What I am arguing here is that if Victorian art and entertainment are understood as forms of material production in the cultural sphere then Dickens's work can be seen as part of a continuum that includes the visual media I have been describing as well as the more conventional literary contexts out of which the novels were produced. It is well established that Dickens's peculiar form of serialization in parts was only made possible by developments in the nature of publishing and distribution in addition to technical developments in engraving and printing. These facts clarify the extent to which even works of imaginative genius are not created in some ivory tower hermetically sealed off from the worlds of commerce, industry and popular culture. It is clear, of course, that the special nature of Dickens's art lies in his extraordinary command of language but, again, this does not have to mean that it exists in a realm that has no interactive relationship with the social life of which biographies prove Dickens was so actively a part. This suggests that the imagery of my title may be interpreted as a series of structural images rather than the localized vividness of language that the term more often signifies. This latter view of imagery in words and pictures in relation to adaptation can lead to a level of analysis that might be described as atomized – that is, the attempt to trace a series of one-to-one relationships between verbal imagery and its realization in visual terms. Such an approach is potentially interesting and valuable, although it does pose severe theoretical difficulties. And in practical terms it is hard to see how any adaptation of such a huge structure as a Dickens novel could attempt a point-by-point equivalence for the literally thousands of images contained in, say, *Bleak House* or *Little Dorrit*.

The concept of structural imagery I am hoping to define here may become clearer from an example; limitations of space lead me to choose only a single passage, from *Dombey and Son*, and since it has to carry a rather large weight of argument by illustration it is substantial. Chapter 47, 'The Thunderbolt', begins with an attempt to be 'just' to Mr Dombey in recognizing that he and his wife are an 'Ill-assorted couple, unhappy in themselves and in each other, bound together by no tie but the manacle that joined their fettered hands'. In examining whether Mr Dombey's 'master-vice' of pride is 'an unnatural characteristic' the narrative goes on to enquire 'what Nature is, and how men work to change her' and this leads to an examination of the horrors of nineteenth-century poverty which are 'most unnatural, and yet most natural in being so'. These narrative abstractions are followed by a justly famous passage:

> Oh for a good spirit who would take the house-tops off, with a more potent and benignant hand than the lame demon in the tale, and show a Christian people what dark shapes issue from amidst their homes, to swell the retinue of the Destroying Angel as he moves forth among them! For only one night's view of the pale phantoms rising from the scenes of our too-long neglect; and from the thick and sullen air where Vice and Fever propagate together, raining the tremendous social retributions which are ever pouring down, and ever coming thicker! Bright and blest the morning that should rise on such a night: for men, delayed no more by stumbling blocks of their own making, which are but specks of dust upon the path between them and eternity, would then apply themselves, like creatures of one common origin, owing one duty to the Father of one family, and tending to one common end, to make the world a better place!
>
> Not the less bright and blest would that day be for rousing some who never have looked out upon the world of human life around them, to a knowledge of their own relation to it, and for making them acquainted with a perversion of nature in their own contracted sympathies and estimates; as great, and yet as natural in its development when once begun, as the lowest degradation known.
>
> But no such day had ever dawned on Mr Dombey, or his wife; and the course of each was taken.

My suggestion is that this structural image of the roof-tops being lifted off by a good spirit not merely flows from the deepest levels of Dickens's imaginative life, but stems also from the vivid world of visual entertainments that I have been trying to evoke in this chapter; or, put another way, that these are one and the same thing, in that Dickens is a great popular genius, an artist with perhaps the most extraordinary command of language of any English writer, apart from Shakespeare, whose imagination is inseparable from the forms taken by the social life of his own time. This great cry of social compassion is evoked from a novelist for whom the city is the setting of his most personal and worked out responses to human degradation, whether individual or in the mass, the novelist for whom the city is a magic-lantern and a panorama, or a huge theatrical set on which the most elaborate effects can be worked out in the interests of a profound exploration of the roots of personal and social evil. It is, clearly, the theatrical implications of this passage that will most bear detailed examination. Dickens's references to magic lanterns and panoramas might be regarded as metaphorical and based on somewhat limited personal experience; the theatre, on the other hand, is like the city in being one of the worlds in which Dickens lived and had his being. A host of biographical facts prove that Dickens was saturated in the theatre from almost his earliest years. As a child he put on shows with a toy theatre for which he played many of the parts himself; as a young man there was a period during which he attended a play almost every night of the week; he was a brilliant mimic who prepared carefully for an audition that was postponed only because of illness; in his mature years one of his favourite pastimes was the production of, and acting in, a series of brilliant semi-professional performances, over the detail of which he exerted total control; and in the latter part of his career Dickens embarked on the amazingly successful public readings that made him the equivalent of a modern media personality, in America as well as Britain.

Given this level of involvement, to which yet more detail could be added, it would be strange indeed if the theatre failed to exert some influence over Dickens's work; within this context I hope it is clear that the passage from *Dombey* is suffused in theatrical elements. I have already suggested the sense in which it can be understood in relation to the tradition of spectacular visual effects and stage machinery to which I have drawn attention. But there is another key way in which this passage embodies some of the central concerns of the Victorian stage in its clear reliance on the opposing dichotomies of melodrama. We may seem far removed here from the, to us, absurdities of foreclosed mortgages, virginal innocence, hissing villains and last-minute rescues that we rightly associate with Victorian drama. But at its level of abstract social indignation exactly the same dualities are being deployed in the titanic struggle between good and evil personified in the 'good spirit' and the 'Destroying Angel'. This is yet another way in which we can see the force of the claim that Dickens is a great popular writer capable of fusing the profundities of the *Dombey* passage with the forms in which the moral atmosphere of his period struggled towards its own kinds of understanding. On the grand scale this suggests a two-way process of adaptation with Dickens drawing essential elements of his imaginative life from the theatre while simultaneously contributing to that moral atmosphere through the incalculably diffusive influence of his immensely popular writings, in his personally supervised periodicals *Household Words* and *All the Year Round* as well as through the novels.

DICKENS AND FILM

The direction of my argument so far could be summed up in two ways. First, that there is an element of continuity between the technical aspects of nineteenth-century popular entertainment and the cinema, although to our eyes moving film might seem to arrive with the force of a totally revolutionary upheaval. The point is made clearly by one expert in claiming that early cinema 'was the most sophisticated and successful of a host of late Victorian inventions . . . which projected moving pictures'.[9] Second, what I have already referred to as the moral atmosphere of some central features of Victorian culture – reliance on melodrama and its attendant sentimentality as devices for embodying the clash of good and evil – was taken over into early cinema as part of its essential inheritance. On a purely practical level, this is not hard to explain since many theatrical practitioners moved over into what they saw as the potentially more successful world of the new form, presumably bringing with them the ways of seeing and feeling that had developed throughout nineteenth-century drama. Again, adaptation entered into cinema in its very beginnings through its reliance on already-existing texts, especially plays. But these issues can be pursued at a level more interesting than the practical and more convincing, perhaps, than large generalizations. With the insight of genius, the great Russian film director and theoretician, Sergei Eisenstein, has coupled the names of Dickens and one of the (if not *the*) founders of cinema, D. W Griffith.[10] How does Griffith fit into the pattern of my argument?

A bold clarification might be helpful at this point: 'the roots were in Griffith. And Griffith thrived on the theatre of his time. And everyone's roots encircled nineteenth-century entertainments, like a convoluted piece of *art nouveau*.'[11] The force of this claim can be justified by the following:

> Between two mountains was the location chosen for the great wall against which Holofernes hurls his cohorts in vain attacks. Eighteen hundred feet long, and broad enough to permit of the defenders being massed upon it, the wall rose slowly until it was a giant's causeway connecting the crags on either side. Within, a city sprang up . . . . Beyond it, in the valley, was pitched the great armed camp of the Assyrians. In the chieftain's tent alone were hangings and rugs costing thousands of dollars.[12]

Apart from the reference to a wall eighteen hundred feet long, this might well be the set of any one of a number of American or British stage productions from the 1850s on. It is, in fact, a location for Griffith's *Judith of Bethulia* (USA, 1914), the film that marked his break into longer, feature-length work from the period from 1908 to 1914 in which he made nearly 500 short films. What we see here is the transition from stage to screen within the realm of the spectacular, but in a form that 'succeeded in eliminating the restrictions and conventions with which . . . [the] stage had been fettered'.[13]

What seems clear from a comparison of the location of Griffith's film and the passage from *Dombey and Son* quoted earlier is that they share the quality I have referred to as 'structural imagery'. In doing so they can be seen to be part of a continuum that unites technology and popular entertainment, spectacle and high culture; in other words, we are not dealing here with a simple relationship of influence from Dickens to Griffith. On the other hand, it is well established that Griffith did acknowledge his debt to Dickens in a number of ways, some of which are summed up by the eminent historian of silent film, Kevin Brownlow:

> The use of melodrama amid settings of complete reality, the exaggerated, yet still truthful characters, the fascination with detail, the accuracy of dress and behaviour, the sentimentality, the attitude toward religion, and the outrage over

> social injustice, are all points which their works have in common.[14]

Although Brownlow's common assumption about the realist nature of Dickens's work needs to be questioned, this remains an accurate description of the similarities between two major creative figures. It is not surprising, then, that Griffith did himself adapt Dickens in a version of one of the Christmas Books, *The Cricket on the Hearth*, in 1909 as one of the myriad of short films made for Biograph. But Brownlow omits from his list what might be regarded as Griffith's most important inheritance from Dickens, the technique of parallel action, which Eisenstein analyses brilliantly as parallel montage. This is the method that Griffith brought to its highest point of development in his *Intolerance* of 1916, in which four different narratives from widely different historical periods are carried forward together through a complex process of intercutting.

It is at this point that my argument on the nature of words, images and adaptation in relation to Dickens comes to a focus. I have suggested that structural imagery is crucial to the novels' success, but this large-scale and spectacular deployment of effects is also crucially dependent on parallel action in bringing together the juxtapositions that lie at the heart of the thematic and formal success of texts such as *Bleak House* and *Little Dorrit*. In the former, we see the links between the worlds of Chancery and Fashion, the hopeless degradation of Tom-all-Alone's and the empty splendour of the Dedlock place in Lincolnshire; in the latter, we move from the literal gaol in Marseilles to the metaphorical prison of London, from the Poverty of the novel's first section to the Riches of its second. If adaptations of Dickens are considered in relation to this central feature of his work, theoretically and also with regard to practical questions of relative success or failure, then I believe we are able to escape from some of the difficulties involved in the attempted one-to-one equation of the verbal and the visual to which I referred at the very beginning of this chapter. In a recent attempt to deal with these problems in a comprehensive manner, *Screening the Novel*, we encounter the following:

> But the fact is that Dickens was a writer of genius and naturally his stock in trade is words. This is the first, and totally unbridgeable, gap we face when discussing Dickens

> and film, or Dickens and television. It helps us to account for the fact that what we get on the screen is not Dickens. It may look like Dickens and occasionally it may sound like Dickens, but it isn't really Dickens at all.[15]

This is hardly a helpful comment on a difficult problem. If the gap between the media concerned is 'totally unbridgeable' then there seems to be absolutely no way forward. But since adaptations, or versions, of Dickens exist and continue to be made it seems important that we should be able to find a way of talking about them sensibly.

Progress might be made through some consideration of BBC television's version of *Bleak House* of 1984, adapted by Arthur Hopcraft. (Hopcraft scripted a brilliant version of *Hard Times* for Granada Television in 1977.) Readers may remember that the novel's opening, with its evocation of London fog and a 'Megalosaurus' on Holborn Hill, is one of Dickens's most virtuoso displays of writing. With great intelligence this is simply omitted from the television version since it clearly presents overwhelming difficulties for both production values and realism. An expensively produced (ideally, wide-screen) film could have attempted aspects of the city embodied in the text, but the presence of a prehistoric monster in Victorian London is clearly an impossibility. Hopcraft, then, avoids a simplistic equation between word and image. What this version does achieve, however, is a series of brilliant transitions, from the turmoil of the court to the tranquillity of Bleak House, from the squalor of Krook's lodging-house to the opulence of the Dedlocks' town house, and so on. (The director, Ross Devenish, may have contributed a great deal to this, of course.) Through its use of structural imagery and parallel action this version is, in my view, faithful to the spirit of the original in a way that can be said to convey something of the novel's essence even to the viewer who has never read the novel. The same cannot be said of one of the most celebrated adaptations of a Dickens novel, David Lean's *Great Expectations* of 1946, a film that has been accorded almost unanimous praise. For the writers of *Screening the Novel*, for example, it is the only adaptation that 'is universally admitted to be a great film . . . . Wherever you look you will find this film acclaimed.'[16] Well, not by Graham Petrie in his mordantly brilliant piece, 'Dickens, Godard and the Film Today', for a start.[17] Petrie's essay is required reading in this area, but Lean's film is also inadequate in relation to my criteria of structural imagery and parallel action. By stripping the novel to the bare bones of its linear narrative the film loses almost all Dickens's density of effect and thematic complexity. The removal of Dolge Orlick, to take only one omission, destroys the darker side of Pip's character which is reinforced by Orlick in his role as double. Similarly, Pip's journey to London loses the text's sombre resonances through its concentration on the quaintly picturesque. The obtrusive use of a post-horn just as the coach is commencing its journey strikes a reassuring note of Merrie England, which is reinforced by images of London at a complete remove from the crime-stained metropolis of Dickens's imagination.

Adaptation of a literary masterpiece is a dual process, an act of possession followed by recreation in the new medium, even if, to paraphrase Orson Welles's judgement of his version of *Macbeth*, it is a rough charcoal sketch of a great original. Without some gesture towards the spirit of structural imagery and parallel action adaptations of Dickens are doomed to failure.

NOTES

1 Michael R. Booth, *Victorian Spectacular Theatre 1850–1910* (London, 1981), 8.
2 See Christopher Innes, Chapter 4 in this volume.
3 Quoted in Peter Ackroyd, *Dickens* (London, 1990), 511 and 517.
4 Steve Humphries, *Victorian Britain through the Magic Lantern* (London, 1989), 49.
5 Ralph Hyde, *Panoramania! The Art and Entertainment of the 'All-Embracing' View* (London, 1988), 20.
6 Booth, *Victorian Spectacular Theatre*, 60.
7 ibid., 64.
8 ibid., 72.
9 Humphries, *Victorian Britain Through the Magic Lantern*, 170.
10 See 'Dickens, Griffith and the Film Today', *Film Form: Essays in Film Theory*, edited and translated by Jay Leyda (London, 1977), 197ff.
11 John L. Fell, *Film and the Narrative Tradition* (London, 1986), 226.
12 Quoted in Harry M. Geduld (ed.), *Focus on D. W. Griffith* (London, 1971), 76.
13 ibid., 79.
14 Quoted in Robert Giddings, Keith Selby and Chris Wensley (eds), *Screening the Novel: The Theory and Practice of Literary Dramatization* (New York and London, 1990), 47.

15 ibid., 46.
16 ibid., 52.
17 *The Yale Review*, 64/2 (Winter 1975), 237.

4

ADAPTING DICKENS TO THE MODERN EYE

Nicholas Nickleby and *Little Dorrit*

Christopher Innes

DICKENS

There has always been a close symbiotic relationship between the story-telling arts. In a sense Aristotle was already fighting a losing battle when he argued that the epic and the dramatic were incompatible, each having distinct aesthetic requirements. The history of European – and, in particular, English – theatre is a record of creative interchange, with development fuelled by cross-fertilization. Shakespeare borrowed plots and dramatic situations from Italian novellas; Tchaikovsky based ballets on Shakespeare; Jacobean masques included tableaux modelled on allegorical paintings; eighteenth- and nineteenth-century narrative pictures took the stances or groupings of their figures from the stage; and more recently there has been the vogue for publishing 'the book of the film'. However, with Charles Dickens the connections between the novel and theatre became exceptionally close – a link that extended logically into cinema, one of the earliest silent movies being a 1903 version of the school scenes from *Nicholas Nickleby*.

Almost all Dickens's fictional material is inherently theatrical. Scenes like Fagin overhearing Nancy's supposed treachery in *Oliver Twist* or the death of Little Nell in *The Old Curiosity Shop* are conceived in dramatic terms. The host of broadly drawn and strongly marked figures that populate the pages of his novels provided natural parts for the histrionic style of nineteenth-century acting. Delineated by idiosyncratic speech patterns, sharply contrasting features or extreme postures, they have the innate physical presence of stage characters, while the way Dickens sets the grotesque and the ridiculous against pure benevolence and youthful innocence echoes the clear moral conflicts of Victorian melodrama. Similarly, the continual switching between episodes of dark brutality, satiric comedy and sentimental pathos, together with the suspense called for by extended serial publication, were designed for emotional effect – the forte of the nineteenth-century theatre.

However, with the exception of the Christmas stories – which are atypical in being short and printed as a single unit – nothing could seem more alien to the standard principles of traditional drama than Dickens's novels. Their structure was conditioned by the format in which they were published. Unlike Scott, whose novels appeared complete and bound as volumes, each of Dickens's works was first issued in monthly (or in the case of *Hard Times*, weekly) instalments, following the earlier eighteenth-century practice. This naturally encouraged picaresque panoramas; and it is no accident that (like those of Henry Fielding) a large number of Dickens's plots involve extended journeys. Continually changing scenes, each with different inhabitants, were a way of injecting fresh interest over the eighteen- to twenty-month period from introductory chapter to conclusion. The loose focus that resulted from this was intensified by the usual lack of a preplanned framework since, as Dickens's letters show, particularly for his early novels, the pressure of such a timetable meant that he tended to improvise as he went along, and sometimes had little idea of the ending even quite late in the story. In addition, being published separately, each instalment had to stand as an independent unit, while at the same time picking up all the separate strands of the plot initiated in earlier instalments to preserve continuity.

To deal with these difficulties, Dickens evolved a technique of counterpoint and accretion. Each monthly section of a novel like *Nicholas Nickleby* was typically subdivided into three chapters: the first two followed the fortunes of one character or group, while the third switched to another, which then became the subject of the opening chapters in the following section. This produced a binary structure, dividing attention between two separate but interlinked stories – Nicholas's peregrinations to Yorkshire and Portsmouth and his sister Kate's tribulations in London – with each containing its own subset of minor figures. The same structural contrast carries over into the fabric of the novel. Greed for gold is opposed to the 'treasures of the heart which it could never purchase'; even the London scene is described in terms of opposites: 'Life and death went hand in hand; wealth and poverty stood side by side; repletion and starvation laid them down together.'[1] In the opening sections each chapter introduces new characters; their situations are developed over three or four instalments; then a fresh series of figures is added. This pattern is repeated for well over half the book, producing a richly varied gallery of villains and victims, egotistical poseurs and bluff benevolence, venality, roguery and brutality interspersed with simplicity and honest generosity. Only in the last third of *Nicholas Nickleby* does Dickens begin to clear his crowded canvas – killing off one character, dispatching another into exile, and sending the Crummles family off to seek theatrical fortune in America – in order to develop a tightly knit plot-sequence that culminates in multiple revelations and a dramatic denouement. As Dickens remarked, 'It is very difficult indeed to wind up so many people *in parts*, and make each part tell by itself.'[2]

Although with *Dombey and Son* Dickens began to pre-plan the plots of his novels, the same basic structural principles can be seen in *Little Dorrit*. The effect of increased organization is to bring out the binary patterning even more clearly. The thematic sequence is more continuous, as the headings of the final five chapters indicate: 'Closing in' – 'Closed' – 'Going' – 'Going!' – 'Gone'. The internal contrasts are even more explicit: the first half of the book, 'Poverty', is set against 'Riches' in the second; a chapter on 'Something wrong somewhere' is followed by one on 'Something right somewhere'. Indeed, in this late novel Dickens selects his incidents primarily for thematic resonance, rather than because they further the action. His focus is on varieties of imprisonment, the differing attitudes of the prisoners and the psychological effect of confinement. The opening scene of a murderer and a smuggler, incarcerated in a stone dungeon awaiting trial, is used as a standard to measure all the others: travellers held in a quarantine station; the debtors locked up in the Marshalsea (with old Mr Dorrit's self-deceiving degradation set against Clennam's destructive despair); the paralysis of religious intolerance and guilt that has sentenced Clennam's mother to a wheelchair in a darkened room; the entrapment of others by the governmental red tape of the Circumlocution Office, or by the constricting pretentions of a dehumanizing society; even the willing isolation of monks in a cloister high in the Swiss snows – all of which pale by comparison with the undeserved plight of the poor in London. Indeed, the city is presented as the ultimate prison:

> Melancholy streets, in a penitential garb of soot, steeped the souls of the people who were condemned to look at them . . . . Miles of close wells and pits of houses, where the inhabitants gasped for air, stretched far away towards every point of the compass.[3]

The overall effect is one of claustrophobia; and in this symbolic world, action is reduced to pointless activity.

On the economic level, the go-getters' pursuit of wealth is not only fraudulent and corrupting – whether in the suicidal high finance of Merdle, the petty graft of Amy's brother, or the melodramatic villain who is literally crushed by the house he battens on – but self-defeating. Even where the motive is benevolent, as with the engineer Doyce, attempting to get things done is frustrated by bureaucracy, leading to despair or death in exile. Similarly, in the social sphere, to rise is to sacrifice humanity for empty status, living a lie and exposing oneself to killing scorn, as with Little Dorrit's father. Carrying out strict religious principles is equally damaging, withering both body and soul in old Mrs Clennam. The society depicted deforms almost any mode of doing, inherently denying the validity of action. In such a context true virtue can only preserve its integrity by refusing to participate in the rat race or to impose its principles on others; and in comparison to those around them, both protagonists of the novel are almost completely passive. Although each performs deeds of generosity, liberating the other, their characteristic quality is self-effacing withdrawal. The reader's interest is held not by what Arthur Clennam and Little Amy Dorrit do, but by the pattern that emerges from the interweaving of the various threads of the story.

Even in Dickens's earlier novels the structural qualities developed in response to periodical publication are radically different from the principles of selectivity and compression required by conventional stage performance. The discrepancy was commented on by critics of the time, as in an 1840 review, which remarked that with any novel

> embracing so wide a sphere of action, and bringing into

> display the different passions, feelings, and pursuits of so many persons, as must of necessity form the *dramatis personae* of such works as 'Nicholas Nickleby', 'Oliver Twist', and tales of like standard, the reader can very well follow the current; but far different is it when, condensed into a very narrow compass, such works are presented to an audience, akin to their prototypes only so far as costume and scenery extend.[4]

Victorian productions based on Dickens's novels were certainly meticulous in reproducing the illustrations by Cruikshanks or Phiz, freezing the action into *tableaux vivants* (sometimes marked by melodramatic music to underline the parallel). However, there were practically no attempts to deal with the whole of a novel. Minor figures were always cut, and whole sections omitted.

When even as competent a playwright as Dion Boucicault turned to *Nicholas Nickleby*, his title – *Smike* – mirrors the radical foreshortening of the story that was typical for nineteenth-century dramatizations. After publication of the final instalments, Sterling produced a 'Sequel' to his original play, *The Fortunes of Poor Smike*, but leaves out the whole Verisopht/Hawk plot and the Cheeryble Brothers, as well as the Kenniwig circle. Most other adaptations deal with a single episode: *Doings at Do-the-Boys Hall*, and *The Savage and the Maiden: or, Crummles and his Daughter* being the most popular. There were over 160 adaptations of this sort before the turn of the century; and there was rarely a year when some material from the novel did not appear on the stage (or after 1950 in televised form) up to David Edgar's script for the Royal Shakespeare Company in 1980. By comparison, there have only been some six attempts to dramatize *Little Dorrit*, including a German and a Russian version – a measure of the problem in separating out such closely woven material and the static quality of this story, as well as the untheatrical passivity of the protagonists – although at least four film versions preceded Christine Edzard's 1987 film (double the number for *Nicholas Nickleby*).[5]

NICHOLAS NICKLEBY ON STAGE

Perhaps the main reason for the immense popularity of *Nicholas Nickleby* as dramatic material is the theatrical nature of one extended section, in which Nicholas joins up with the Crummles's acting troupe. Originally this was a satirical attack on a well-known actor-manager and his much promoted daughter, who – incredibly – performed Shylock at the incongruous age of 8 just a year before Dickens embarked on the novel. Yet the exaggerated display of Victorian coarse acting makes wonderful farce. It is also a form of metatheatre. Heightening the artifice of stage performance by self-parody has been a traditional comic technique. But this has gained a particular contemporary relevance: exposing the mechanics of stage-business by presenting the whole drama as a play or dealing with characters who are actors, expresses a doubleness of vision and self-referentiality that has become one of the defining qualities of post-modernism. In addition, it is the basis of Bertolt Brecht's dramaturgy, which has had a widespread influence on the younger generation of British playwrights, including David Edgar.

A conventional example of the exploitation of such theatrical elements is provided by a 1969 dramatization at the Glasgow Citizens Theatre. 'Faced with the apparently insoluble problem of editing . . . the rich, shapeless mass of the novel' the adapters used the Crummles's scenes as a frame, through which the story could be accommodated to the stage:

> Like so many authors tackling their first play or novel, Nicholas's answer [to the demand that he write a script] is to make it strictly autobiographical. The Crummles Company, unaware of the involvement of the two principals in the events of the real life story, play it out with gusto for a miserly speculator whom they hope will discharge their debts.[6]

However, distancing the action like this defused any possible social criticism, reducing the story to the level of a comically anachronistic acting display.

By contrast, Edgar's version emphasized the political immediacy of Dickens's material by making the production itself a prism, with the overt theatricality giving a multiple perspective to every scene. The whole cast of 49 actors was present on stage throughout the action: interjecting commentary, visibly supplying sound-effects, and (above all) observing the scenes. As Edgar put it, the central concept of the adaptation was 'that the acting company were in collective possession of an entire story, which they were then to tell to the audience'; and their silent reactions conditioned the audience's response as they stood 'watching their story unfold'.[7] Passages of narration that linked the episodes were spoken by the onlookers as a group, with the lines divided among them; apart from Nicholas and his sister, each of the actors played multiple parts; and they continually stepped out of their roles to narrate the characters' feelings about themselves or others in third-person description. They also formed the 'scenery': grouping to represent the stage-coach in which Nicholas and Smike returned to London, lining up in different configurations across the stage as the walls of various houses that Ralph Nickleby visits, or coalescing into the dark cloud of guilt and retribution that hangs over him, dogging his heels on his final flight through the streets. Thus every aspect of the performance consciously emphasized theatrical pretence, making the medium of expression as much the subject of the drama as the story itself.

Although superficially similar to Brechtian dramaturgy – in the actor stepping out of character, the objective third-person narration, the avoidance of illusion – the result was very different. The world created, being a purely human one, was psychological, symbolic, an imaginary projection. It was also shown as conditional, rather than presented as a fixed reality, by the concept of the play as a communal product. So that the actors

> – who knew how it was to end – were expressing a huge collective 'wouldn't it be good if' aspiration, as they watched and told the unfolding events. This distancing device, which in Brecht is supposed to clear the mind of emotion, had in our case the effect of directing and deepening the audience's own visceral longing for Ralph's vision of the world to be disproved.[8]

This emotional response was intensified by the physical involvement of the audience in the action. The cast entered through the spectators at the beginning of each performance, and the two-tier set extended out into the auditorium. Built out of a rough wooden scaffolding – specifically an acting-space, rather than scenery, requiring spectators to participate imaginatively by visualizing the various settings – the upper level ran all the way around the front of the mezzanine. The chase-scenes in each half of the play took place above the heads and in the middle of the audience. Compounding this, Edgar shifted the focus of the story from Dickens's hero to the pitiful Smike, the abused boy Nicholas rescues from the inhuman Yorkshire school.

Like the part of Oliver Twist, the role of Smike had traditionally been played by women to bring out the pathos of Dickens's characterization (a practice that continued up until the 1920s). In the novel Smike is described as starving, dispirited and simple-minded, his only physical impairment being a slight lameness. In order to deny Dickensian sentimentality, Edgar exaggerated his disabilities. Smike became an infantile schizophrenic, crippled almost to the point of paralysis. Although some critics felt that the bravura performance of the role (David Threlfall in the first production) unbalanced the whole dramatization, the effect was central to Edgar's thematic intentions. Smike literally embodied the deforming effects of an unjust society. The audience's initial revulsion at his grotesquely distorted and drooling figure, which associated them subliminally with the oppressors, intensified their reactions as the action revealed the victim's real humanity. Emotions evoked for the individual were thus almost automatically turned against the system responsible for his condition. Hence the spontaneous nightly applause at the point when Nicholas takes revenge on the sadistic schoolmaster, which – unusually for the theatre – signalled approval for the action, rather than appreciation of the performer.

In Edgar's view there were strong parallels between the social contexts of the 1830s and the present, both being periods in which rapid technological change and the disappearance of earlier moral standards under the pressure of capitalist expansion resulted in the exacerbation of inequality and injustice. At the same time (quoting Marx) he rejected the type of solution espoused by Dickens, whose novel incorporated an essential affirmation of existing conditions in its exuberance, and proposed idealized personal charity, innocence and the unexpected inheritance of a modest fortune (concealed by villains) as sufficient for reform. Thus Edgar's adaptation was designed as 'a play about Dickens that criticized his form of social morality, rather than a straight dramatization of the novel'.[9]

This was expressed through subtle changes to Dickens's story, even though in general Edgar's script is remarkably faithful to the novel. Through extensive doubling, practically all Dickens's figures appear, so that the list of characters includes over 120 named parts, plus various groups (and the anonymous populace of London). Although compressed, the dialogue and much of the linking narrative is produced verbatim; and the substance of Dickens's major passages of commentary is included, as well as most of his characters' main speeches. At the same time, the eponymous Cheeryble twins – paragons of charity that even Dickens's contemporaries had criticized as incredible, despite his pointing to their real-life analogues – were downplayed, as was the folly of Nicholas's mother (omitting the comic madman next-door, with whom she imagines herself in love). As a result, over two-thirds of the performance time was devoted to the first half of the novel, thus focusing on the more general depictions of inhumanity and corruption in the book – plus the theatrical parody of the Crummles Company – and de-emphasizing the positive pole of Dickens's story. Some scenes, spread out over several instalments, were reorganized into continuous units to facilitate the flow of the action. Others, separated in the novel, were interwoven in counterpoint to underline the social criticism; and this was extended by the most significant of Edgar's additions.

These additions were the drawing of political morals from the story, the inclusion of a travestied *Romeo and Juliet* as performed by the Crummles, and the final image of Nicholas holding out a 'new Smike' to the audience. What Nicholas and Kate explicitly learn from their experiences in Edgar's version is the universal corruption and destructiveness of money, declaring that even the kindest and noblest souls are inevitably 'tainted' by its touch. The conclusions of both halves reinforce this by underlining the illusory nature of Dickens's utopian solution. Transforming *Romeo and Juliet* into a travesty in which everyone but Tybalt turns out to be alive after all and Viola is imported from *Twelfth Night* as a substitute bride for Juliet's arranged husband (echoing the worst excesses of eighteenth-century treatments of Shakespeare) provides a graphic image of the spuriousness of happy endings. Similarly, the conventional image of social renewal in the marriages that crown the novel is undercut by presenting the happy couples as a sentimentalized Christmas-card tableau. Along with these false images, the audience is challenged to take action. The first half of the play closes in a parody of a patriotic Victorian Afterpiece (Mrs Crummles as Britannia) with the injunction:

England, arise:
Join in the chorus!
It is a new-made song you should be singing . . .
See each one do what he can

while the 'New Smike' cradled in Nicholas's arms is intended 'as a reminder that for every Smike you save there are still thousands out there, in the cold'.[10]

What marks Edgar's version of *Nicholas Nickleby* out from previous adaptations is partly the way such political relevance is achieved through exploiting the dramatic form itself, keeping the audience constantly aware of theatrical conventions. The presence – and consciousness – of modern-day actors, as interpreters of a 150-year-old story, simultaneously intensified the audience's emotional involvement and gave a critical perspective on the action. On a still more obvious level, what makes this dramatization unique is the way Edgar's use of overt theatricality enabled the complete novel to be staged in its entirety, although doing so still required eight-and-a-half hours playing time, so that the story was divided into two distinct halves. Exactly the same qualities characterize Christine Edzard's treatment of *Little Dorrit*, but with cinematic elements substituted for the theatricality.

LITTLE DORRIT ON FILM

All earlier film versions of *Little Dorrit* – like most nineteenth-century adaptations of Dickens for the stage – had created a conventional action by restricting themselves to very limited segments of the story. By contrast, Edzard set out to present the whole social panorama of the book. The sheer length of the whole certainly gave that impression, although there was considerably more condensation than many of the reviewers realized. The introductory section, exotic scenes such as the St Bernard mountain pass, and one whole group of characters (the blackmailing French assassin, his Italian cell-mate, a bitter female outcast and the emotionally unstable serving-girl she corrupts) are all omitted. Other episodes are telescoped together to heighten dramatic focus, as with the scene where old Mr Dorrit suffers a mental breakdown at the opulent Merdle dinner-table: here set at his social-climbing daughter Fanny's wedding-feast, instead of abroad and several weeks later.

Even so – and despite the camera's greater potential for compression, creating brief vignettes or cutting from scene to scene – the total screen-time was six-and-a-half hours. As a result Edzard was forced to adopt much the same performance-structure as Edgar. Still more unusually for cinema than the theatre, her film was designed in two halves for separate but complementary showing, although she turned this to thematic use in a way that had not been possible for Edgar on the stage.

Edzard's screen exploited the realistic impression of photography, with painstaking attention to costuming (authentically hand-sewn) and an emphasis on earth-tones in the overall colouring of the scenes. Downplaying the more grotesque characterizations in the novel, she aimed 'to make Dickens come across . . . as a journalist's piece . . . all about what you might bump into in the street'.[11] This led to some misunderstanding. In particular, the film was criticized for sanitizing Dickens's dark and malodorous nightmare city, reducing the extremes of poverty and degradation in order to make the picture more credible for a modern audience, and sacrificing imaginative truth for 'soothing' verisimilitude. Comparisons were drawn with David Lean's Gothic film treatment of *Great Expectations* and *Oliver Twist* over forty years earlier, their melodramatic expressionism being identified with socialist views and 'modernist revolt'. This led to more than one reviewer attacking the film as a picturesque (that is, Thatcherite) period-piece celebrating Victoriana at the expense of Dickens's social criticism.[12]

Some atmospheric aspects – the number of sunlit scenes, the skyline of factory chimneys that were smokeless (being a painted backdrop due to the limited budget), and (above all) the operatic opulence of Verdi as background music – certainly laid Edzard's film open to charges of sentimental romanticization. But in fact, as with Edgar, the purpose of Edzard's realism was to emphasize that 'there are great parallels in *Little Dorrit* to the Britain of today'.[13] Diverging from Dickens, the film's major theme was the destructive power of money, reflecting the Boesky and Guinness scandals – the same financial frenzy satirized by Caryl Churchill's stage hit of the time, *Serious Money* – as well as anticipating the 1987 stock-market crash, which occurred just before the film's release. The Merdle section (based, like the Yorkshire schools and Cheeryble Brothers of *Nickleby*, on actuality – the Victorian financier John Sadleir's bankruptcy and suicide) is a relatively minor part of Dickens's story. However, it becomes central in Edzard's script.

This prominence is due to her omission of the whole melodramatic element, which provides most of what conventional 'plot' there is in the novel, although such cuts are as much a response to the nature of the film medium itself. The stock villain of the sinister foreign murderer, his malevolent (possibly lesbian) accomplice, and the cliché mechanism of suppressed wills and purloined papers would have undermined the detailed realism of the social picture that is one of the camera's strengths. However, the action that was substituted for Dickens's melodrama represents a significant updating.

In the novel, the 'secret' finally disclosed is Arthur Clennam's parentage and a suppressed legacy from his great-uncle – in deathbed repentance over having forced Arthur's father to abandon his true mother for the rigidly religious woman who has raised Arthur as her son – which would have not only preserved the rejected girl's life, but also made Little Dorrit wealthy. Spurning tainted conscience-money, she persuades Arthur to burn the evidence unread, his release from the debtor's prison being due to the generosity of his engineering partner, Doyce. Edzard removes Doyce from the scene, his death being announced before Arthur's disastrous speculation that bankrupts the factory (both removing the stigma of misappropriating his partner's capital and increasing the hopelessness of his situation). Instead, Arthur's debts are paid off with guilt-money, funds that had been sent to his real mother as remittances from his father and intercepted over the years by his stepmother to provide credit for the Clennam business. The parallel with Merdle's embezzlement implies that all wealth was fraudulent – a considerable sharpening of Dickens's point that both extreme poverty and excessive riches are equally corrupting on the personality. This was underlined by replacing Dickens's ironic treatment of the Merdle crash with direct statement towards the end of the second part of the film: to the proposition that financial disasters are 'nobody's fault' (the original title for the novel and the subtitle for the first part of the film, as well as being Arthur's standard response) Little Dorrit declares them to be 'everybody's fault. Everyone who was at Mr Merdle's feast [the Establishment, including her newly enriched father] was a sharer of the plunder, everybody there assented, accepted and approved.'

Even though Edzard does not go so far as Edgar in urging political activism on the audience, her film also provides an intrinsic critical perspective on Dickens. As with *Nickleby*, the dialogue of *Little Dorrit* includes several long speeches drawn verbatim from the novel, but the type of expectations imposed by contemporary cinema automatically makes such extended statements seem overtly 'literary' – that is, artificial, self-conscious, pretentious, even false. And this distancing effect is deliberately used, almost every one of such speeches being a revelation of the disguised greed, moral hypocrisy, envious pride or egotistical materialism beneath the polite and polished surface of those characters who are presented as ornaments of society, or who aspire to such a state. Quite apart from the contrast with the conversational norm in the film, which is brief exchanges of standard cinematic dialogue, these ostentatious monologues are set against the comparative passivity of the two protagonists.

The characteristic mode of Arthur and Amy is silent observation; and it is in building on this trait that Edzard's film is most striking. Taking her cue from Dickens's experiment with narrative viewpoints – explicitly announced in the novel with 'This history must sometimes see with Little Dorrit's eyes' (a statement specifically quoted beneath the subtitle for the second, half of the film)[14] – the camera lens was identified with the vision of one or other of these main characters. Unlike the Edgar play, in which the separate parts comprised two sequential halves of a single continuous story, here each covers almost the same time-frame from two distinct standpoints.

Much praised for its originality, this was a direct extension of the narrative technique in the novel. There, the individual perspectives are always recounted in the objective, third-person voice of the author; and since Arthur and Amy are separated for much of the story (to a far greater degree than Nicholas and Kate Nickleby), the total impression is created out of the contrast that comes from continually switching between their different experiences. In the same way, Edzard's camera always shows the person whose vision serves as the focus for its lens; while the identification with the eye of the observer was emphasized by the almost complete avoidance of panoramic shots or close-ups. By concentrating on the people within talking distance, but only intruding into their private sphere at moments of intense personal involvement, the camera copied the norms of social interaction. In addition to the subliminal empathy evoked through this overlap between the character's and spectator's viewpoints, the shifts in perspective added psychological depth. In acknowledging that the structure of her film 'is suggested in the book', Edzard commented, 'What I wanted to show is that there are different perceptions of the same reality, and that Dickens' great quality is to see the characters from two angles.'[15]

Yet the effect went far beyond this. Separating out the two interwoven strands of the novel into two distinct narratives gave each half of the film a unified continuity, the only merged scenes being the final climax of the second part. At the same time, the effect – in many ways duplicating Lawrence Durrell's *Alexandria Quartet* – emphasized the partial and contingent nature of reality. It also foregrounded the artistic medium of film, just as radically as Edgar's overt theatricality.

The generally accepted convention is that the camera can never lie, that it accurately records what is before it. Edzard's adaptation played on this by diminishing Dickens's symbolic exaggeration: for instance, instead of the total destruction of the house of Clennam, only the staircase collapses to kill the odious Flintwinch.

However, the inclusion of those scenes where both Arthur and Little Dorrit are present, in each half of the film, so that they are played twice, raised questions about what spectators perceive. In one version of a scene, Little Dorrit is painfully aware of the shabbiness of her shoes; and the camera focuses on them. In the earlier treatment of the same scene, Arthur's gaze is absorbed by her face; and the shoes never appear on the screen. She sees flowers blooming even in the Marshalsea prison; for him there is nothing but a withered plant. Shot from different angles and on different days, the perspective in each replay changes and the light is never quite the same, while the background music also changes, altering the emotional tone. If sight is selective, distorted by personality or emotional state – and film is primarily a visual medium – then cinematic objectivity becomes a suspect quality. The form of representation itself becomes as central as the ostensible subject of Dickens's story.

On many levels, then, David Edgar's stage adaptation of *Nicholas Nickleby* and Christine Edzard's film version of *Little Dorrit* are comparable. Each serves as an example of productive cross-fertilization between different artistic forms; and both extend the range of their particular medium. In doing so they provide viable models for a post-modern aesthetic that has up to now been largely missing from the area of public performance. The pressure of reproducing the antithetical qualities of a nineteenth-century serial novel in the theatre and on the screen has been a catalyst for stylistic innovation. Although it is hardly to be expected that such mammoth double-decker productions will become the norm, their success has opened up new ways of handling complex material in plays and films. In particular, it is difficult to conceive of novels being dramatized in the traditional, limited manner any more. These two works have effectively moved the artistic goal-posts for their respective genres.

NOTES

1 *Nickleby* (facsimile edition, London, 1982), I: 302 and 308.
2 *Letters*, ed. M. House and G. Storey (Oxford, 1965), I: 561.
3 *Little Dorrit* (London, 1875), 34–5.
4 Cited in H. Philip Bolton, *Dickens Dramatized* (London and Boston, 1987), 34.
5 For complete annotated listings of all stage, screen and radio productions derived from Dickens's novels up to 1985, see Bolton (1987).
6 Caryl Brahms and Ned Sherrin, Programme Note, 23 December 1969.
7 David Edgar, *The Life and Adventures of Nicholas Nickleby* (New York, 1982), II: 173.
8 David Edgar, *The Second Time as Farce* (London, 1988), 157–8.
9 David Edgar, in an interview with the author, April 1986.
10 Edgar (1982), I: 164 and (1988), 158.
11 Christine Edzard, as quoted by Guy Phelps in 'Victorian Values', *Sight and Sound*, 57/2 (Spring 1988), 110.
12 Raphael Samuel, 'Dockland Dickens', in Raphael Samuel (ed.), *Patriotism: The Making and Unmaking of British National Identity* (London, 1989), 276–9; and, among others, Robert Giddings, who repeats Samuel's criticism (p. 284) almost word for word in Robert Giddings, Keith Selby and Chris Wensley (eds), *Screening the Novel: The Theory and Practice of Literary Dramatization* (New York and London, 1990), 50–1.
13 Christine Edzard, in an interview with Graham Fuller in *Film Comment*, 24/5 (October 1988), 30.
14 *Little Dorrit*, 34–5. (The programmatic statement in the film contained one significant change, reading 'The story must be seen through Little Dorrit's eyes.')
15 Phelps (1988), 109. At the same time, even this subjective use of the camera lens was attacked by unsympathetic critics since the predominance of the protagonist's – i.e. Little Dorrit's – viewpoint 'has

elevated Clennam from a narrative cipher into a romantic lead, and . . . the camera transforms him into an object of filmic desire' (Samuel (1989), 280).

5

'THE DEVIL IS BEAUTIFUL'

Dracula: Freudian novel and feminist drama

Jan McDonald

In the well-appointed drawing-room of a Victorian villa situated high above the Clyde Estuary sit seven women – the mother, the grandmother, the aunt, three great-aunts and the girl. The girl is stretched out on the window-seat, apart from the others, reading. She is oblivious to the much-praised view below and to the murmur of adult conversation behind. Suddenly, a sentence from one of the old women pierces the peaceful twilight: 'Ah, yes, the Devil is beautiful.'

Bram Stoker's novel, *Dracula* (1898) and Liz Lochhead's play of the same title (Royal Lyceum Theatre, Edinburgh, 1985)[1] are in themselves adaptations of an ancient and world-wide myth. The myth of the vampire, the Undead, who feasted on the blood of the living, was referred to on the stone tablets of the Assyrians. The ancient Greeks, who believed that offerings of blood could effect the return of the dead from the Underworld, called it 'sarcamenos' – 'flesh made by the moon'. Our noun, 'vampire', is cognate with the Siamese word, 'vampra', the term for a lunar Sabbath, a day particularly noted for its supernatural potency. In more modern times Jean-Jacques Rousseau was a believer:

> If ever there was in the world a warranted and proven history, it is that of vampires; nothing is lacking, official reports, testimonials of persons of standing – of surgeons, of clergymen, of judges.[2]

As late as 1928, the Revd Montague Summers asserted 'There can be no doubt that the vampire does act under satanic influence and by satanic direction.'[3] The *World Weekly News* reported a series of vampire killings in the United States in December 1980, which is evidence for the hold the topic still has on the popular imagination.

Today a plethora of good and bad horror- or chiller-movies may have reduced the myth and tamed the fear that it inspired. In these rational times, scholars have sought for, and found, a scientific explanation for the physical state of suspected vampires, disinterred to be rendered harmless with a stake through the heart. Paul Barber, for example,[4] explains how the tell-tale characteristics of vampirism – the ruddy complexion, the blood on the lips, the bloated appearance, even the emission of a 'groan' as the stake pierces the heart – can be accounted for rationally since the rate and quality of post-mortem decay is accounted for by the cause of death, and by the conditions of the burial, in terms of ground temperature, the chemical composition of the soil, and so on.

But the fascination, indeed the power, of the vampire myth cannot be totally undermined either by the extravaganzas of Hollywood or Hammer horror-films or by the rationalism of the modern scientist. It belongs to that class of phenomena, described by Freud as the 'Uncanny' – 'That class of the frightening which leads back to something that is known of old and long familiar . . . something old-established in the mind but alienated from it only through the process of repression.'[5] The myth of the vampire is part of our cultural heritage, and so it is worth while to compare the treatment of it by a late-nineteenth-century male novelist and a late-twentieth-century female dramatist.

The gender of the author is as significant as the literary forms that each adopted and as relevant as the cultural and social context in which each wrote, for the vampire story, certainly in a post-Freudian era, cannot be divorced from a sexual frame of reference. It is for this reason that I have chosen to concentrate primarily, although not exclusively, on the role of women in each version, before proceeding to an analysis of the formal and structural features of the theatrical adaptation.

BACKGROUND TO THE NOVEL

Bram Stoker, prior to the writing of *Dracula*, was best known as the manager of Sir Henry Irving's celebrated company at the Lyceum Theatre in London. Not unnaturally, perhaps, Irving was regarded by many contemporaries as the prototype of Stoker's diabolic Count, not simply in appearance, but also in personality, for Irving, in common with many other actor-managers of the period, exploited younger and less-celebrated performers in order to promote his own role within the company. According to George Bernard Shaw, the chief victim of Irving's 'vampirism' was his leading lady, Ellen Terry, who in Shaw's opinion sacrificed her individual talent, her intelligence, her artistic integrity and, not least, the opportunity to play leading Shavian roles to Irving's will and pleasure. In the novel, the children who imitate Lucy Westenra as a vampire, the 'Bloofer Lady' who leads them away, imagine themselves to be as 'winningly attractive as Ellen Terry'. Needless to say, Stoker strongly denied any resemblance whatsoever between Irving and Dracula, but physical similarities do exist, such as the height and the slenderness, the long hair, the high forehead and heavy brow, the aquiline features, the thin high-bridged nose and the arched nostrils, the intense fiery eyes and the expressive hands. It has to be said, however, that it is also possible to detect echoes of descriptions of Irving as the saintly Dr Primrose in *The Vicar of Wakefield* in Stoker's portrayal of Van Helsing.[6] Whether the parallels in Stoker's descriptions of Dracula and of Van Helsing prefigure Liz Lochhead's concept of the characters as being symbiotically linked as two opposite facets of the same cosmic force, a point to be developed later, remains questionable.

Although Stoker's rendering of the vampire myth was the most celebrated in nineteenth-century English literature, it was by no means the only one. From 1800 the theme of a living body being usurped or inhabited by a 'dead' creature was relatively common. In poetry there was Byron's *Gaiour* (1813) and Keats's *Lamia* (1819). Dr John Polidori's short story, *The Vampire* (1819), introduced the evil Lord Ruthven (alias Lord Byron), a character to be picked up in J. R. Planché's play of the same name a year later. This heralded a spate of Gothic melodramas on the subject, including George Stephens's *The Vampire* (1821), John Dorset's *The Vampire Bride* in the same year, and W. T. Moncrieff's *The Vampire* (1829). Stoker's Dracula has much in common with Lord Ruthven, a cultured scholarly man of wealth and reputation, a soldier who exerts a hypnotic charismatic power over his lovely and virtuous victims. Stoker, however, choosing the more leisurely canvas of the novel, investigates the characters and the myth in more depth, and, significantly, from more than one point of view.

The story in Stoker's novel is recounted largely by means of the journals and letters of the principal characters, who are not romanticized lords and ladies in a misty Highland Never-Never Land, but unexceptional members of late Victorian middle- and upper-middle-class society. Jonathan Harker is a West Country solicitor, Mina, his worthy and competent wife, Lucy, a young heiress of impeccable background, Quincey Morris, an all-American upright young man, Arthur Holmwood (later Lord Godalming), an upstanding pillar of the English aristocracy, and Dr Seward, a dedicated psychiatrist. The danger from the vampire, the battle for good against seductive 'evil', is brought into the most ordinary – the most respectable – of settings. Van Helsing is, it is true, summoned to oppose Dracula by a mixture of medicine, psychology, white magic and a dash of Christianity but, ultimately, it is the ordinary people who defeat the forces of the Undead. Nina Auerbach comments on these 'relentlessly up-to-date antagonists, who destroy [Dracula] with the modern weapons of committee meetings, shorthand minutes and the phonograph'.[7]

WOMEN IN THE NOVEL

If his contemporaries in general thought the novel to be little more than a fairly good horror-story, the late-twentieth-century interpretation of Stoker's *Dracula* is unashamedly post-Freudian. Victorian woman was denied sexuality by the very men who worshipped her. Cast into an angelic mould of purity, chastity, passivity and unassuming loveliness, she was not thought to have any physical desires. Since the bearing of children necessitated sexual intercourse, she had to endure it out of duty and wifely devotion. No decent woman 'enjoyed' it, or could admit to so doing. This repression of both desire and pleasure among respectable women meant that when such passions were experienced, in order to avoid in-built censorship, they had to be seen as emanating from a source other than the woman herself – Dracula, a Victorian construct. Normality is threatened by the monster. The figure of the monster dramatizes 'all that our civilization represses or oppresses, *ie* female sexuality, the proletariat, other cultures'.[8]

It is uncertain whether or not Stoker knew of Freud's case-studies.

He refers to the work of Charcot, Freud's teacher, in the novel, but it is more likely that, in parallel with the psychiatrist's scientific investigations, he was expressing in fictional terms a social fact of his time, the tendency towards neurasthenia in apparently healthy young women, such as S. Weir Mitchell describes in his book, appropriately entitled *Fat and Blood* (1877):

> The woman grows pale and thin, eats little, or if she eats does not profit by it. Everything wearies her, – to sew, to write, to read, to walk – and by and by, the sofa or the bed is her only comfort. Every effort is paid for dearly, and she describes herself as aching and sore, as sleeping ill, and as needing constant stimulus and endless tonics.[9]

Such maladies were assumed to be self-induced. Robert Carter in his *On the Pathology and Treatment of Hysteria* (1853), ascribes the cause to the woman's discovery 'that she can, at will, produce an apparently serious illness, and thus make herself an object of great attention to all around her, and possibly among others, to the individual who has been uppermost in her thoughts'.[10] As Auerbach has pointed out, even before Dracula's arrival on the scene, Lucy has demonstrated a predisposition to instability, 'her penchant for somnambulism, trance and strange physical and mental alterations would find her a place . . . in Freud and Breuer's garland of female hysterics'.[11]

For Dracula, Lucy is an easy prey. She is on the threshold of an imposed maturity, no longer the child of her father, no longer the pretty sweet virgin with gallant suitors, but the future wife of a nobleman. In a somnambulistic state, she encounters Dracula, who plunging his teeth into her neck (the euphemistic symbolism is obvious) awakens (or confirms) her sexuality – but a bestial predatory sexuality, a perversion of the shared physical experience of loving partnership. With her newly acquired carnal knowledge, she attempts to seduce her future husband, only to be thwarted by the intervention of Van Helsing, the Christian and the patriarch.

In the novel, Mina is first presented as an assistant schoolmistress, already affianced to Jonathan Harker. During his travels on the Continent she spends a holiday with her more affluent friend, Lucy, whom she takes care of with devoted attention, until she is called away to nurse her future husband back to life. She is clearly the stronger of the two friends, yet despite her ability to earn her own living and her literary and secretarial skills, she dismisses contemporary notions of the 'New Woman' lightly. Mina is no feminist pioneer. After Lucy's death and the involvement of Van Helsing, however, Mina's role changes. She becomes, first, a partner and fellow-worker with the 'committee' that includes Lucy's betrothed, Arthur Holmwood (now Lord Godalming), Quincey Morris and Dr Seward, Lucy's rejected suitors. Indeed, it is her assiduity in keeping a meticulous record of the events in Whitby and her shorthand skills in transcribing Dr Seward's phonographic records that form the basis of the campaign. Yet, it is not long before the men demand more of her. Arthur breaks down in grief for Lucy. She holds his hand and strokes his head 'like a baby' and promises to be like a sister to him. Quincey Morris, on the very same day, also begs for her friendship, kissing her hand. 'Impulsively', writes Mina, 'I bent over and kissed him.' Choked with grief, he calls her 'Little girl': ' "Little girl!" – the very words he had used to Lucy', muses Mina. Having won the devotion of two of Lucy's admirers in one afternoon, Mina gains the admiration of the third, Dr Seward, who, on the same day, expresses praise for 'Harker's wonderful wife', 'so appealing and so pretty'. Lucy had always thought that Seward and Mina would make a good match. Just as Lucy had received three proposals in one day in the innocent pre-Dracula spring, so Mina receives three overtures from the same three men in the post-Dracula autumn. That evening the men resolve that she should not have any more to do with the enterprise. Her heart or her nerves may fail her, 'And, besides, she is a young woman and not so long married.' So, banished from the comradeship and councils of the others, subtextually because she is a temptation to them, she becomes vulnerable to Dracula.

With the enlisting of Mina into *his* ranks, Stoker's Dracula is at his most powerful. She is no neurasthenic little heiress, but the perfect Victorian wife. The scar made by the sacred Host on her brow must be borne by every 'good' woman, until Dracula, along with the threat which he represents, is destroyed. Lucy may die – truly die – as her bridegroom drives the phallic stake through her heart. The orphan virgin is dispensable. But Mina, 'the angel in the house', must be cleansed and restored to her role as helpmeet and, even more significantly, as potential mother, a potential happily fulfilled in the novel's postscript.

WOMEN IN THE PLAY

Nina Auerbach, while admitting that 'It is fashionable to perceive and portray Dracula as an emanation of Victorian sexual repression', puts forward the alternative or complementary view that 'it seems more plausible to read the novel as a *fin-de-siècle* myth of newly-empowered womanhood, whose two heroines are violently transformed from victims to instigators of their story'.[12] While it may only be with hindsight that such a view can be applied to Stoker's novel, it provides a useful starting-point for an examination of Liz Lochhead's drama. In this work the nineteenth-century male view – that a fiendish vampire preyed on young women, awakening in them passions and desires that were best left dormant – is replaced by a twentieth-century female view, that Dracula liberated his victims from their sexual and psychological repressions, induced by male-dominated social mores and by the patriarchal authority of the dominant religion, Christianity.

One of the sources of Liz Lochhead's play was *The Wise Wound* by Penelope Shuttle and Peter Redgrove (1980). In the chapter entitled 'The Mirror of Dracula', the authors speculate on the 'benefits' bestowed by Dracula on his ladies.

> Before they were bitten, they were chlorotic weak creatures with vapours, dressed in stiff constricting corseted garments, who spoke in faint and genteel voices expressing deep frustration. After their blood had been shed for the vampire, though (and it is always from the *neck*; as we say neck or cervix of the womb), and they had suffered their first death into their new lives as vampires – why, what creatures they become! The corsets were replaced by practical white unhampering shrouds, very free and easy . . . . Their eyes shone, they spoke energy with every glance, and their smiles, full of bright teeth, with handsome canines, were flashing and free.[13]

Both Lucy and Mina are seen to find release after their encounters with Dracula. The audience first sees Lucy on a swing in her petticoats, apparently a young carefree girl, looking into a mirror, wondering who will be her husband. But within a few lines, Lucy has to be laced up in a corset. If she must be dressed up for public consumption, she says she wants to have 'the thinnest

thinnest waist', so she urges Mina 'Tighter, tighter, Mina . . . I want to feel it nip me in.' Likewise she wants 'the highest, highest hair', and Mina proceeds to tame her curls into an acceptable coiffure.

Lochhead's Lucy, however, more explicitly than Stoker's, is a hysteric – 'simple girlish hysteria. She'll soon grow out of it with exercise' is the medical verdict. She refuses to eat and disrupts the adult lunch-party in Scene 5:

> Oh yes, crazy Lucy, mad sleepwalking skinny Lucy with her migraines and her over-vivid imagination.

While Mina dismisses the outburst as an attention-seeking tantrum, in Lochhead's view 'Lucy is almost certainly anorexic, and, though she doesn't know it yet, is waiting for Dracula.' The dramatist later wrote a poem in the form of a dramatic monologue by Lucy which contains the lines:

> This gross flesh I will confine
> in the whalebone of my very own
> hunger[14]

Anorexia may be regarded as the twentieth-century equivalent of Victorian neurasthenia. An adolescent female refuses to eat in order to retain a boyish figure without breasts or rounded hips. It is often seen as a subconscious rejection of mature womanhood.

Lucy's first encounter with Dracula occurs off-stage, but the actress appears, little disguised, in Dracula's castle as the third vampire, the one who really tempts Jonathan Harker, who recognizes in her 'the lynx-eyed' Lucy. The ensuing stage-directions, describing the erotic foreplay of Vampire Lucy, interrupted by an angry Dracula, are Stoker's; but, presented on stage by a female performer, they had an additional eroticism,

> [*There is a deliberate voluptuousness which is both thrilling and repulsive and as she arches her neck she actually licks her lips like an animal till he can see in the moonlight the moisture shining on the red tongue as it laps the sharp white teeth. . . . He closes his eyes in languorous ecstasy and waits with a beating heart.*]

When the audience next sees her in her own person, she is being carried into her bedroom by Arthur, not as a lover but rather as a father, lifting a sick child. However, she is no longer a child. She questions the maid, Florrie, closely about her sexual experiences ('Is it absolutely the most sweetest delicious swoony magical marvellous thing you ever – ?'). She loosens her hair, drops her shawl and undoes her night-dress in preparation for Arthur's return to bid her goodnight. She begs him to stay – she (and the audience) is aware that he could save her if he stayed – but his 'sacred trust, in the absence of her sister', prevails.[15] He promises, however, (Dracula-like) to sneak back in and kiss her when she is asleep. He is pre-empted. Lucy's next invitation is not refused, 'Come to me, my love. Come in.' Dracula embraces her and 'red petals fall'.

By the second scene of Act II, Lucy's hair has been shaved off, for health reasons, by her fiancé. (He had Renfield, the madman, shaved too.) He is subconsciously trying to return her to the childlike creature who attracted him. Lucy, without her glorious hair, is rendered an asexual object by the man for whom she was trying so hard to be a woman. He has 'cut off bits of me', she complains, but more important he fails to recognize the woman she has become, or always was. 'I am six hundred years old. I am thousands of years old. I'm not just a little girl,' she whispered to Jonathan.

Lucy's apotheosis occurs when she appears to her fiancé and his friends as a vampire. She is 'lovely and terrifying and ethereal'. She is accompanied by two children, a boy and a girl, each holding her by the hand. She speaks: 'Come, Come with me, Arthur. Come to me, my arms are hungry for you. Leave those others, and come to me, my husband, come.' This is the image of a mature woman, children by her side, inviting sexual union with her chosen partner – this by courtesy of Dracula, the beautiful Devil. Stoker's Lucy at this point is likewise transformed, but transformed into evil:

> They were Lucy's eyes in form and colour; but Lucy's eyes unclean and full of hell-fire, instead of the pure gentle others we knew . . . the lips were crimson with fresh blood . . . the stream trickled over her chin and stained the purity of her lawn death-robe.

By instigating Lucy's sexual initiation, Stoker's Dracula is seen as committing her to spiritual damnation. No longer 'pure', 'gentle' and virginal, she has become unclean, as defiled as her white robe. Lochhead's Vampire makes Lucy powerful, even terrifying in her sexual fulfilment. The contrast is equally, or even more strongly, highlighted by an examination of the dramatist's approach to the character of Mina.

Mina in Lochhead's play becomes Lucy's elder sister rather than her impecunious friend, but they are as different as 'chalk and cheese' to Jonathan, and 'night and day' to Dracula. Mina is the heiress, but must wait until her twenty-fifth birthday to inherit and, therefore, to marry Jonathan. If Lucy's sexual fulfilment is stunted for psychological reasons, Mina's is delayed for socio-economic ones. She will not have intercourse prior to her marriage, despite Jonathan's imminent departure for Transylvania. She will give him a locket with her picture instead, 'and he'll keep you in his pocket', says young/old Lucy, no doubt along with his wallet and other masculine possessions.

Lochhead's Jonathan, like Stoker's, is consciously determined to distance his fiancée from the predatory women of the Castle of Dracula. Sexual fantasies are reprehensible enough when they involve one's future sister-in-law, but are taboo in the case of one's betrothed. In a composite setting, representing on stage Heartwood, the asylum and the Castle, Jonathan screams 'Those . . . women . . . my God. Help me, I . . . Mina! Mina has nothing in common with these women.' The ensuing stage direction contradicts him:

> [*But as we see Mina, in her underwear and barefoot and, in her indolence and impotence, wander round Heartwood, we might momentarily see her as a very recently powdered one of them.*]

All women are potentially Dracula's brides, given the appropriate circumstances.

Mina, however, escapes the traumas at Whitby, to join Jonathan on the continent. Returning as a married and apparently sexually fulfilled woman, she is heart-broken at Lucy's death, but appalled at Jonathan's revelations under hypnotism that he lusted after her sister, albeit when she was in the guise of a vampire. Mina and Arthur are drawn together in sexual jealousy. Stoker's picture of Mina's platonic friendship with the men is given a physical dimension. Desire for another man is planted in her. Worse is to come – Van Helsing's claim that Lucy 'invited' Dracula to come to her, albeit subconsciously:

> He takes her when she is all unconscious . . . . He sucks

> secretly at her: stealing from sources-she-does-not-even-know-that-she-possesses. *But you know.*

Mina knows well what inner passions bring Dracula. Within two scenes he is in her room where she has been left alone by her 'protectors', sucking her blood and making her drink his. He is to Mina incubus and succubus. This is a deeper and more profound pact than that made with Lucy. He promises his mate

> Oh, and you will be revenged on them. Not one of them but shall minister to your needs. You will love me for the love they all shall spill for you.

Mina's awakening by Dracula is not to sexual maturity like Lucy's but to power. The devoted helper and servant becomes the leader, conducting the men across sea and land. In Jung's *Symbols of Transformation*, the chapter on 'Symbols of the Mother and Rebirth' gives an account of 'the night sea-journey in the womb belly of a fish, or in an ark, chest, barrel, ship, each of which is an analogy of the womb'.[16] The night sea-journey is Dracula's, but also the blindfolded Mina's. Together they travel to death, and 'rebirth', both imprisoned by day but by night 'flying wild and free'. The brute force of the men cannot move the gates of Castle Dracula; one word from Mina and the gates fly open. The new powerful Mina is as remote from the young apprehensive woman in the garden as the glorious vampire Lucy is from the child on the swing.

> [*Mina, wrapped in furs and deathly pale, blindfolded, reaching out straight ahead of her.*]

Nemesis, Justice, Fate – Mina is an implacable source of energy. This is the gift of Dracula; it was what she wanted.

Arthur and Dracula are killed almost simultaneously. 'Oh, my love', sobs the kneeling Mina, '[*very ambiguously*]'. As the blindfold is removed from her eyes, and Dracula's (or Arthur's) death clears the mark from her brow, Mina's newly discovered strength re-expresses itself in mercy. Jonathan is forgiven, largely because he forgives Dracula, in whose place, as Van Helsing points out, Mina might well have been. If Stoker's Dracula, in attacking Mina, assaulted the myth of ideal womanhood, Lochhead's Dracula leads her to realize the hidden potential of her female gender.

WOMEN AND NATURE

In general feminists have eschewed the vampire tale, disliking the image it presented of women as either victims or predators. By expanding the mythology to include the idea of women being transformed by the influence of a subversive secret impulse, Lochhead has added a new dimension to the legend. Her 'key' to the myth as she sees it was the circumstance that Dracula cannot enter unless first invited and visitors to his castle must cross the threshold of their own free will. His victims desire his intrusion or come to him voluntarily, at least on the first occasion. Dracula is not a rapist: his sexual partners acquiesce to – even welcome – his approach. He is stimulating as well as frightening; he challenges the conventions that restrict them; he is the liberator of their unacknowledged bondage. Linked to the moon, whose phases control his potency, Dracula has within him a strong female element, one of his seductive and liberating qualities for the women he chooses as partners. The links between the vampire and the moon and between the moon and menstruation are explored in the play. Barbara Walker goes so far as to claim that 'The primal notion that all life depends on the magic of menstrual blood – or "the blood of the Moon", as some primitives say – evolved a corresponding notion that the dead crave blood in order to live again.'[17]

In the nineteenth century girls were encouraged to behave like invalids while they suffered from 'the curse', 'the flowers', or, as Queen Victoria called it, their 'poorly time'.[18] Despite the medical fact that dysmenorrhoea is a painful and distressing condition, it is now known that for the majority of women the period of menstruation is no impediment to their continuing a full working, social and even sexual life. But in Victorian times, when delicacy and fragility were the hallmarks of femininity, an excuse for recourse to the invalid couch or the sick-bed was not to be lightly dismissed, and, since men regarded the natural process of menstruation as unclean and repugnant, a withdrawal from male society was politic at these times.

Jules Michelet in *L'Amour* (1859) voices a standard, if somewhat romanticized, view:

> Woman is for ever suffering from the cicatrization of an interior wound . . . so that in reality for fifteen days [!]

out of twenty-eight . . . woman is not only invalided but wounded. She suffers incessantly from the wound of love.[19]

The wise wound, perhaps? For fertilization is least likely to occur at the period of menstruation and so sexual activity during that period will be solely for pleasure and not for the legitimate purposes of procreation.

> [The woman's] sexuality if satisfied at her period will give her her own self-energy, but on the other hand she will inevitably proceed on her cycle and change to her instincts at ovulation, a fortnight later, that will if she has intercourse very likely dedicate her to nine months of pregnancy and an unknown time of dedication to the child that is born as a result.[20]

In Lochhead's play Dr Seward's first question on hearing of Lucy's 'feverish' behaviour is 'Did she have a loss of normal female functions?' The anorexic girl rejects menstruation, and the Lucy of Lochhead's poem makes the rejection consciously:

> All term
> I would not bleed, not
> for Matron, Mama, Mademoiselle,
> nor my sister, Mina[21]

The arrival of Lucy's period is coincidental with the arrival of Dracula, as he leaps ashore in the 'black wind'. Lucy is pale on the morning of the next day, a 'morning so sweet you'd think it'd never get dark again', as she says. She dismisses the maid's solicitous enquiries on her pallor: 'I've got a visitor . . . . Must have come in the night . . . . My friend, my bloody friend'. 'The curse', says Mina. Florrie, the maid, holds the traditional view of the needs of women at such times. She offers 'herb tea and a hot-water bottle'. Mina dismisses such old-fashioned practices, and Lucy, with heavy irony, quotes her views: 'We've got to learn not to give in to such weaknesses! Exercise! Swedish callisthenics! And no whingeing or the gentlemen'll never treat us as equals.' 'No gentleman need ever know', responds Mina, drily. But Dracula will know, Lucy's 'visitor' and her 'bloody friend'.

According to Liz Lochhead, her linking of menstruation with the visit of Dracula was only part of a larger thematic strand in the play, namely, the cyclical nature of the earth and of human life upon it. Woman, by her physical nature, represents a microcosm of this process. If not put to any reproductive use, the womb, like the snake, sheds its lining and prepares for the next cycle. Woman is the symbol of eternal dying and eternal rebirth, as demonstrated in the myth of Persephone, who annually descends to the Underworld (or dies) only to rise again to the upper air to herald a new year, a new birth. For Lochhead, it was important that the play should open in the spring with the stage-picture of two young women in a garden. Dracula comes at the height of summer; the pilgrimage to his castle ends in winter with his true death. The next spring, a natural resurrection, is heralded not so much as a result of Dracula's demise as of the mutual forgiveness and reconciliation of Jonathan and Mina ('Dracula is dead, long live Mina and Jonathan'). Mina admits her desire for Dracula, her liberator, Jonathan, his lust for the three Vampire Brides, yet it is he who reverently crosses the arms of his dead rival in an act of mercy, and kisses his living wife as stakes are hammered through the hearts of his Undead temptresses. Jonathan must forgive Dracula for knowing Mina better than he ever could, and Mina must forgive Jonathan for his fear of her female potency which he is forced to acknowledge. A more self-conscious and comprehending marital union is forecast, while the falling snow changes to 'blush pink petals like apple blossom and confetti'. The petals darken in colour so that they are 'finally red, red petals as the curtain falls'.

The second act ends with the same visual image as the first[22] – a couple embracing under a shower of red petals. But Lucy and Dracula are replaced by Mina and Jonathan, and the white of Mina's wedding-dress in which the Count wraps his 'bride' turns to the black of the Vampire's discarded cloak on which Mina and Jonathan sink. The wheel of fortune goes round, as does the moon. The red petals, like menstrual blood, 'the flowers', signify the end of one cycle and the beginning of another.

DRACULA AND NATURE

Dracula's tragedy in the play is that he has become detached from the regenerating wheel, from the cyclical pattern of death and rebirth. Physically dead, he cannot cease to exist, therefore he cannot be reborn as part of the natural world. The director,

Hugh Hodgart, described him as being 'trapped in the prison of eternity'. In a youthful cast, Dracula too was a young actor of about 30; pressure to employ an older 'star' performer was resisted. The similarity in physical age between the Count and Harker paradoxically heightened the discrepancy in their 'real' ages. Jonathan, a bright young man, a product of his society, was contrasted with Dracula, who looked like a romantic *jeune premier*, but who had all the gravitas of an ancient, ageless creature of darkness.

Dracula, in common with all vampires, ghosts and disturbed manifestations of the supernatural, casts no reflection in a mirror. Stan Gooch poses a chilling question: 'Why is it that Dracula has no reflection? Because he *is* the reflection: *you are on the other side of the mirror.*'[23] On 'the other side of the mirror' is Jonathan, and Seward, who wants to kiss Lucy as she sleeps, and even Van Helsing, whom Lochhead sees more as Dracula's redeemer than as his destroyer. She believes that it is Dracula, himself, who calls up Van Helsing, his age-old antagonist to release him back into the regenerative natural order. Van Helsing almost seems to recognize the real source of the summons to England:

Arthur, dear friend, I come
And, old enemy, I come

Dracula waits for, even wills, the end of his sterile dislocated state.

Van Helsing's 'partnership' with Dracula is nowhere more evident than the occasion on which he is predisposed to laugh hysterically at Lucy's funeral. 'King Laugh', as he calls the inappropriate urge to mirth at a solemn occasion, is an expression of ultimate irony. Van Helsing, like Dracula, knows of life and death, of good and evil, of a cosmic system that far exceeds the comprehension of the 'ordinary' people with whom they are involved. 'King Laugh' is the 'laughter of the apocalypse' as described by Kristeva:

> So . . . laughter burst out, facing abjection, and always originating at the same source, of which Freud had caught a glimpse: the gushing force of the unconscious, the repressed, suppressed pleasure, be it sex or death. And yet, if there is a gushing forth, it is neither jovial nor trustful, nor sublime, nor enraptured by pre-existing harmony. It is bare, anguished, and as fascinated as it is frightened.[24]

Such is the shared awareness of Dracula and Van Helsing, in collusion as well as in conflict, each the mirror-image of the other. Dracula's tragedy, his 'exile from human happiness', was highlighted in the production: 'Dracula is no spoof vampire but a powerful man weary of his strange power.'[25]

ADAPTATIONS FOR THE STAGE

Liz Lochhead, an Art School graduate, had made a considerable reputation as a poet by the time she wrote her first full-length play, *Blood and Ice* (1982). The piece linked Mary Shelley's fictional story of Frankenstein and his Monster to her 'real' life with Shelley and his circle. It was on the strength of this that she was commissioned to write *Dracula* by Ian Wooldridge, Artistic Director of the Royal Lyceum Theatre, Edinburgh. Coincidentally the Edinburgh Lyceum was opened in 1883 with a performance of *Much Ado about Nothing* by the stars of Bram Stoker's London Lyceum, Henry Irving and Ellen Terry. Lochhead retained the late-nineteenth-century setting, and the production used costumes and properties appropriate to the period, while the ambience of the Victorian theatre's auditorium assisted in this recreation of Stoker's own time.

Lochhead succeeds in bridging the gap between what Patrice Pavis calls 'the source culture' and 'the target culture'.[26] The story is Stoker's (followed remarkably closely), the plot is her own, if we accept Tomashevsky's distinction between 'story' (the pretext for the plot) and 'plot' (the story organized by the artist to suit his or her own purposes).[27]

There is no doubt that Lochhead's *Dracula* is a 'new' work, an independent aesthetic achievement, and it is as such that it must be approached.

> The basic aesthetic imperative is to approach a work through the attributes of the work itself and not to assume it to be in any important sense derivative because it bears resemblance to a prior text . . . then it is not aesthetically realised, then its use of source material is of historical, not aesthetic, interest.[28]

Yet an examination of the structural alterations to the source necessary to create this new work may prove illuminating in interpreting the theme as well as assisting in a dramaturgical analysis. There are several factors to be considered. First, to render 450 pages of printed text as a script of a length acceptable to actors and audience demands rigorous selection and discarding. In addition, a theatre director commissioning a play for a subsidized company would expect the dramatist to keep within reasonable bounds in terms of requirements for setting and casting. Lucy's three suitors are compressed into one, Arthur Seward, an amalgam of Arthur Holmwood and John Seward, the psychiatrist, whose profession Lochhead's character follows. The American, Quincey Morris, is cut out. The Vampire Brides are played by the actresses who play Lucy, Florrie (the maid), and the performer who presents Mrs Manners (the housekeeper), the two Nurses and Dr Goldman. Mina is not one of them, although she could have been as far as the staging is concerned. Renfield's two nurses, Grice and Nisbett, are played by one performer. This double-casting was not only motivated by economy but was designed to disorientate the audience as much as it did Renfield, who never knows whether he will be confronted by the nasty Nurse Grice or the nice Nurse Nisbett: 'A vertiginous effect' was what the writer and director aimed for. The two parts of the whole are reconciled at Renfield's death. In sum, then, there are eleven actors required, a massive reduction of Stoker's densely populated novel.

In terms of locale, the novelist can move easily from Transylvania to Whitby, from Highgate Cemetery to the Harkers' home in Exeter. The dramatist has one stage-space and various constraints of time and expense on elaborate scene-changes. Lochhead used a composite setting, 'a huge grey set, that although dappled with sunlight for Lucy and Mina Westerman, becomes a prison for the lunatic, Renfield, and in fact, forms a screen before Dracula's castle'.[29] The Castle, a three-dimensional backdrop, was more or less visible throughout, a constant, if at times shadowy, presence, looming over the action. It was most dominant at moments when Dracula's power was at its strongest, for example, in the graveyard scene where Vampire Lucy approaches Arthur. As the characters are literally 'all in one place', so psychologically they are all in similar states. There is as much potential for madness in the garden as in Renfield's padded cell. The scene change between the first and second scenes demonstrates this felicitous economy:

[*The two girls run off laughing: swing goes up: maids pick up linen: noise of pump begins: lights change and suddenly it's grim nurses with soiled laundry in the asylum.*]

A further economy is effected by Lochhead's use of the composite settings, for example, Act I, Scene 10: Renfield in Bedlam: Jonathan in Dracula's Castle: Mina and Lucy in Heartwood. Renfield sings Poor Tom's Song from *King Lear* as he is chained and strait-jacketed; Mina worries about Jonathan as she is 'tape-measured and poked and pinned' at a fitting for her wedding-dress (a dress, incidentally, which she never wears but is used in the intercourse between Lucy and Dracula); and Jonathan, having given his key to freedom to the Vampire Bride (not waiting for his own, who is preparing for him), yells 'I will get free or die trying.' The scene ends with the sound and lighting effects of the storm that brings Dracula, and the chorus of the sleep-walking Lucy, 'Coming, coming, coming, coming, coming', and of the mad Renfield, 'Fasterfasterfasterfaster faster *Master!*' All the characters are shown to be prisoners, in geographically discrete, but psychologically similar, environments.

The specially composed, largely electronic music had the same dramaturgical function as music in melodrama, where a sense of unity in the episodic narrative is created by the score, rather than by continuity of action. The opening sounds of bird-song and distant piano-playing that established the atmosphere in the garden-scene changed to a bleak, rhythmic pumping sound for the asylum and to grand organ chords for Dracula's castle. The reiteration of musical motifs, associated with particular characters or locations, reinforces the wholeness of the play in performance.

Another dramatic unifier exists in Renfield's constant presence on stage, from his introduction in the second scene until the end of the first act. Renfield is, according to Liz Lochhead, a John the Baptist figure. His function is to prepare the way for the 'Master's' coming. With the cyclical changes in the power of Dracula, the vampire's control over him waxes and wanes like the moon. When 'free', he is a male Cassandra, prophesying doom, warning of disasters that will not be diverted because he is unheeded. At other times he is Dracula's creature. The stage direction reads:

[*Renfield falls to the ground at front of stage and we see him as an unacknowledged presence through most of the rest of the act as*

> *he gibbers sympathetically with a character elsewhere he's tuned in to, or fears, or loves with them, very restrained though, we forget him for ages at a stretch. He 'knows' everything, though . . .*]

This device worked well in performance.

> [Renfield] lurks on his chain at the front of the stage, a damaged, pitiful reminder that some kinds of horror begin in the mind. [He] becomes in the end a tragic choral figure, a commentator ultimately more sane than the forces around him.[30]

Crouched on the forestage, at a lower level than the locus of the main action, his behaviour and reactions were linked particularly to Lucy's. He became a kind of alter-ego, sympathetic, literally, to her plight.

Stoker tells his story largely through the journals, diaries and letters of the principal characters, interspersed with business documents and independent newspaper reports of escaped animals and abused children. There is no overall authorial voice, and the point of view shifts according to the perpetrator of the document. In the opening part of the novel, Harker tells of his trip to Transylvania, Mina narrates the events at Whitby until she leaves, Seward then takes over, and the last chapters are related by the three principal narrators, with an intervention by Van Helsing. The events take place between 1 May and 6 November – six months, if one omits Jonathan Harker's concluding note, written seven years after 'we all went through the flames'. The narrative structure employed, then, is one that allows a variety of characters a voice. Each character not only relates the events but includes in the telling his or her gloss on them in terms of emotional and rational reactions. One might imagine, then, that the novel's characters must emerge as more complex, more rounded, despite all that the actor can add in a live performance. This certainly would be the view of Pfister, who believed that a drama could never be as complex as a narrative text:

> Whilst this process [the adaptation of a long narrative text for the stage] may achieve gains in concrete realism, the original is usually simplified in terms of its psychological and sociological complexity.[31]

Rather than simplify either 'the psychological or the sociological complexity' of Stoker's novel, however, Liz Lochhead contributes an additional profundity. This she achieves principally by her use of language, referential language, imagery, word-play, punning and inarticulate sound, in order to penetrate the disturbed psychology of the dramatis personae. This is nowhere more apparent than in the first words of the choric Renfield:

> I once knew a woman who swallowed a fly. Perhaps she'll die. Perhaps she won't die. To die or not to die, that is the question. BED-LAM BED-LAM BED-LAM. Bats in the belfry, bats, set of screw-looses . . . screw Lucy's Lucy's screw Lucy's . . . Doctor Seward! Sewer, Lord Muck-mind. Mr Pissriver shit floats! Doctor Seward, you bastard.

Beginning with a nursery rhyme, Renfield picks up on the word 'die' and makes an oblique reference to Hamlet's soliloquy on the nature of human existence. 'Die' then comes to equal 'be'. Death equals existence to the vampire. 'Die' has also sexual connotations – to reach a climax, an orgasm. 'Bed' is linked to sex and 'lam(b)' to 'blood' as in the blood of the Lamb, perverting a Christian allusion. The colloquial descriptions of being insane, being 'bats' or 'having a screw loose', link us to Dracula in the first instance and to Lucy ('screw Lucy's') in the second. To 'screw' is, of course, a crude expression for 'have intercourse with'. The word-play on Seward's name associates him, not with a sterilized profession, but with human excrement. Much of Renfield's speech is similarly layered, strengthening the choric quality of his interventions, the word-play of the wise fool.

Two sets of images recurring throughout the play are those associated with food and those associated with flowers. The vampire, like the infant, sucks sustenance from another. When the child grows up he or she probably at some time eats the flesh of another creature. To eat is obviously to destroy what is eaten, that is, to destroy something one likes (or someone one loves). So, according to Liz Lochhead, Dracula and Renfield, who love life, destroy it by devouring living things. Lochhead's Mina first enters, eating a peach. Lucy compliments her on 'looking good enough to eat'. Miss Bell, Jonathan's secretary, is also described as a peach, 'delicious', presumably also ripe for devouring. Opening the next scene is Renfield, the zoophagous lunatic, whose story Lucy likes to hear repeated. ('Lucy-Lucid-Lucy'd-she would', rambles Renfield.) He moves on from flies to birds. 'Fuckin' fevvers in his teeth. Eatin' sparrers', complains Nurse Grice. It is cold chicken for luncheon at Heartwood when the young ladies entertain their beaux. Jonathan, who has just been fondling Mina's bosom, is offered 'a breast or a leg'. He chooses both. 'Saucy' Florrie flirts with him by offering him more food. He praises the 'sauce'. Lucy refuses to eat the dead cold meat. Renfield in Bedlam similarly expostulates:

Something inanimate
Something on a plate
Is something I hate
. . . Now something blood heat . . . that's what I call sweet

Next, Jonathan enjoys hot *paprika hendl* at Dracula's Castle, but the Count whose 'appetites have grown capricious in old age', like Lucy and Renfield, refrains from consuming 'something on a plate'. He has 'already supped'. As Jonathan and Mina return home, he asks her to guess what he is most looking forward to. It begins with 'L': 'Loving-Mina-to-bits-on-Mina's-big-fat-goosefeather-bed', his 'insatiable' wife jokingly suggests; but no, it is English Sunday lunch – roast beef, with no garlic. Laughingly, she calls him a 'monster'. Lochhead constructs an intricate web of references, sparked off perhaps by the assiduous documentation of foreign recipes by Stoker's Jonathan to be cooked by Mina in the marital home.

The flower images in the play may likewise have developed from Stoker's description of the countryside on Jonathan's journey to the Castle. 'There was everywhere a bewildering mass of fruit blossom – apple, plum, pear, cherry; and as we drove by I could see the green grass under the trees spangled with the fallen petals.' The poet uses this simple description as the basis for a series of references to flowers which enrich the texture of the dialogue; Mina, 'the perfect English rose'; the choice of red or white roses for the wedding; the funereal lilies in the drawing-room at Heartwood; the roses Arthur brings to the dying Lucy:

> Roses, roses, oh, I do love roses. So sad when all the pretty petals fall . . . . Mina and I used to gather up all the petals in the garden when we were little, and put them into a jar with rainwater and try to make perfume . . . . But after we

> left it a week it always festered. So then we'd turn it into poison.

By the end of the scene, the red petals fall (to be changed into perfume or poison?) as Dracula claims his bride. Lucy's next flowers are Van Helsing's garlands of garlic, fatally discarded in favour of lavender-water. The play's final image, described above, is the transformation of the snow to May blossom, to pink and, finally, to red petals.

The interweaving systems of imagery serve not only to deepen the emotional subtext of the characters but also to assist the dramatist in practising the economy forced on her by the genre itself. Like the use of music, the verbal texture works for overall unity in the epic structure.

The final noteworthy stylistic feature of the play is Lochhead's deployment within the drama of the irony that inspires Van Helsing's 'King Laugh'. A great deal of the play is very funny, quite self-consciously so, as Stoker's novel is certainly not. There are good jokes, particularly from the sardonic Dracula: for example, his remarks to Jonathan 'And the day you deliver yourself to me, that is a feast day' and, on his learning colloquial English, 'A good slanging! The lifeblood of the language . . . I drink in your every word.' Renfield, like Dracula, has the power of objectivity in his 'saner' moments. This is how he expresses his determination to escape Dracula's power:

> Dr Seward, excuse me, but it's time for me to love you and leave you, time to say toodlepip, *au revoir* or should I say adieu-arrivederci-if-you'll-just-arrange-for-the-old-trousers-and-topcoat-to-be-returned-to-me-forthwith-I'll-be-off-good-and-sharpish. He wants me to be an instrument of evil, but I've changed my tune.

Significantly, as Renfield breaks his chains he gives 'a shortened inarticulate parody of Van Helsing's "King Laugh" ' ('Sobbing and laughing' he escapes).

The dramatist's use of irony (particularly in relation to these two characters, who with Van Helsing are closest to the audience in terms of awareness) serves to undercut any tendency towards misplaced mirth from the spectator who has, after all, come to the theatre with a competence that may or may not include Stoker's novel, but almost certainly will include the Hammer horror-film and the various spoofs thereon. According to the director of the Lyceum production, the jokes worked as points of release for the audience which, forced repeatedly into an objective, cerebral response, was allowed temporary respite from the profound emotional implications of the main theme.

At the first performance, the text worked less well towards the end, when Lochhead adhered more closely to the letter, rather than to the spirit, of Stoker's novel. The production descended into 'a flurry of boo-hooing melodrama', said one reviewer; the dramatist was 'shoving the plot into place almost brutally like the stake being hammered in', complained another; 'she has in the end to scrabble madly to be faithful to the book and tell the story', bemoaned a third.[32] The reasons for the 'falling-off' are to be found both in the dramaturgy and the *mise-en-scène*. The director felt that as the figure of Dracula became more concrete, he lost his fascination, becoming diminished by familiarity. He personally found the mundane realities of the chase less stimulating as raw material than the exploration of the psychology of the myth. Technical demands and problems dominated the latter part, lengthening the performance to the limits of audience toleration. The humour and the wealth of imagery diminished as narrative took over. In fairness to the author, the printed version differs substantially from the original playing text, and many of the difficulties in presentation would seem to be resolved.

Stoker's adaptation of the myth of the vampire was an excellent horror-story. It may be that, operating in a socio-political culture that was concerned with the profound changes that threatened the hitherto 'sacred' role of women, he chose a myth particularly appropriate to his time. Written almost ninety years later, Liz Lochhead's drama had to adopt a different attitude to the original myth and to the social reality presented in Stoker's novel. Some adaptations necessarily arise from the change in form, but, in this instance the translation to another semiotic system in the main enhanced, rather than impeded, the new revised interpretation. Pavis wrote 'The theatre translation is a hermeneutic act – in order to find out what the source text means, I have to bombard it with questions from the target language's point of view.'[33] Lochhead's questioning of her source has produced a novel image of a myth, and a theatrical text pointedly targeted in its language.

The critic Owen Dudley Edwards in a radio review of Lochhead's drama called it 'the most remarkable intellectual contribution which has yet been made to the direct story of Dracula'. He saw it as 'a very important play too in the relationship of women to the vampire legend and what this means in terms of women's relationships to man in general'.[34] Joyce Macmillan acknowledged it to be 'an astonishingly brave and ambitious piece of work' delving 'deep beneath the psycho-sexual surface of Stoker's story in an attempt to marry his imagery with modern ideas about women's sexuality'.[35]

'Hush', said the mother to the old woman, 'You'll be giving that girl nightmares.'

NOTES

1 The texts used are Bram Stoker, *Dracula* (London: Puffin Books, 1986) and Liz Lochhead, *Mary Queen of Scots Got Her Head Chopped Off and Dracula* (Harmondsworth: Penguin Books, 1989). I am very grateful to Liz Lochhead for talking to me so articulately about her script, to Hugh Hodgart, the director of the first production for his views on the staging of his piece, and to my former research students, Barbara Bell and Audrey Keith, for their assistance.
2 Barbara Walker (ed.), *The Women's Encyclopedia of Myths and Secrets* (San Francisco: Harper and Row, 1983), 1042.
3 ibid., 1041.
4 Paul Barber, *Vampires, Burial and Death: Folklore and Reality* (New Haven and London: Yale University Press, 1988).
5 Quoted in James Donald, 'The Fantastic, the Sublime and the Popular', in J. Donald (ed.), *Fantasy and the Cinema* (London: British Film Institute, 1989), 23.
6 The physical resemblance between Henry Irving, Dracula and Van Helsing is explored in Audrey Keith, 'Bram Stoker: A Nineteenth-Century Theatre Administrator' (unpublished M. Litt. Thesis, University of Glasgow, 1991).
7 Nina Auerbach, *Women and the Demon: The Life of a Victorian Myth* (Cambridge, Mass.: Harvard University Press, 1982), 16.
8 Donald, *Fantasy and the Cinema*, 236.
9 Quoted in Ronald Pearsall, *The Worm in the Bud* (Harmondsworth: Penguin Books, 1971), 521.
10 ibid., 519.
11 Auerbach, *Woman and the Demon*, 22.
12 ibid., 24.
13 Penelope Shuttle and Peter Redgrove, *The Wise Wound* (Harmondsworth: Penguin Books, 1980), 267.
14 Liz Lochhead, 'Lucy's Diary: Six Entries' in *Bagpipe Muzak* (Harmondsworth: Penguin Books, 1991), 60–2.
15 The actor playing Seward thought that this part of the script was

under-written from the point of view of his character. He could not believe that a medical man would have hesitated to spend the night at a patient's bedside, even if he were her fiancé. The director disagreed, bearing in mind the historical context of the script.

16 Quoted in Shuttle and Redgrove, *The Wise Wound*, 109.
17 Walker, *Women's Encyclopedia of Myths and Secrets*, 1039.
18 Fraser Harrison, *The Dark Angel* (London: Sheldon, 1977), 59.
19 Quoted ibid.
20 Shuttle and Redgrove, *The Wise Wound*, 262.
21 'Lucy's Diary', 62.
22 The scene described here is from the printed text. In the first production, Jonathan went off with Van Helsing to see to the Vampire Brides, leaving Mina on stage cradling the body of Dracula, as the petals and the curtain fell.
23 Stan Gooch, *Total Man* (1972), quoted in Shuttle and Redgrove, *The Wise Wound*, 273.
24 Julia Kristeva, *Powers of Horror* (New York: Columbia University Press, 1982), 206.
25 Joyce McMillan, *Guardian* (16 March 1985); *Stage and Television Today* (11 April 1985).
26 Patrice Pavis, 'Problems of translation for the Stage' in Hanna Scolnicov and Peter Holland (eds), *The Play out of Context* (Cambridge: Cambridge University Press, 1989), 26.
27 Robert Giddings, Keith Selby and Chris Wensley (eds), *Screening the Novel: The Theory and Practice of Literary Dramatization* (New York and London: Macmillan, 1990), 2.
28 William Lukr and Peter Lehman, *Authorship and Narrative* (London: Putnam, 1977), 192.
29 Quintin Cooper, *The Times* (4 April 1985).
30 Melanie Reid, *Scotsman* (16 March 1985).
31 Manfred Pfister, *The Theory and Analysis of Drama* (Cambridge: Cambridge University Press, 1988), 202.
32 Mary Brennan, *Glasgow Herald* (18 March 1985); transcript of a review of Lochhead's *Dracula*, at the Royal Lyceum Theatre, BBC Radio Scotland, 17 and 18 March 1985 (participants were Douglas Gifford and Owen Dudley Edwards); *Scotsman* (16 March 1985).
33 Pavis (1989), 26.
34 Transcript of a review, BBC Radio Scotland.
35 *Guardian* (16 March 1985).

6

A WOMAN'S LOVE

D. H. Lawrence on film

Neil Taylor

> The car ploughed uphill through the long squalid straggle of Tevershall . . . . The stacks of soap in the grocers' shops, the rhubarb and lemons in the greengrocers! the awful hats in the milliners! all went by ugly, ugly, ugly, followed by the plaster-and-gilt horror of the cinema with its wet picture announcements, 'A Woman's Love!'
>
> *Lady Chatterley's Lover* (Penguin edition, 1961, p. 158)

D. H. Lawrence occupies an ambiguous position in British culture, simultaneously associated as he is in the public consciousness with the realms of high art, popular romantic fiction and soft porn. The ambiguity is a product of the history of the publication of his books and journalism. It is reproduced each time one of his novels or stories is translated into a stage play, a radio play, a television play, an audio tape, a film or a video. At the same time, it is that ambiguity which makes the play, tape, film or video commercially viable.

In this chapter I consider just one of these acts of translation, the making of Lawrence texts into films – of which there are at least twelve examples.[1] I am not going to provide either a comprehensive survey of these films or an analysis of their relationships to the texts upon which they are based. My intention is to consider Lawrence as a cinematic commodity. For this reason, I shall restrict myself to those films that, at the time of writing, are readily available on video or appear regularly on television. This means I shall be discussing just four films, as if they were a small sub-genre, 'Lawrence on film':

Women in Love (UK, 1969), directed by Ken Russell, screenplay by Larry Kramer, starring Alan Bates (Birkin), Oliver Reed

(Gerald), Glenda Jackson (Gudrun), Jennie Linden (Ursula), Vladek Sheybal (Loerke), Richard Heffer (Leitner), Christopher Gable (Tibby), Rachel Gurney (Laura) and Eleanor Bron (Hermione) [United Artists] [video 1990].

The Virgin and the Gipsy (UK, 1970), directed by Christopher Miles, screenplay by Alan Plater, starring Joanna Shimkus (Yvette), Franco Nero (the gipsy), Maurice Denham (Yvette's father), Honor Blackman (Mrs Fawcett) and Mark Burns (Major Eastwood) [London Screenplays].

Lady Chatterley's Lover (UK/Fr, 1981), directed by Just Jaeckin, screenplay by Just Jaeckin and Christopher Wicking based on an adaptation of the novel by Marc Behm, starring Sylvia Kristel (Connie), Nicholas Clay (Mellors), Shane Briant (Clifford) and Ann Mitchell (Mrs Bolton) [Columbia Pictures] [video 1991].

The Rainbow (UK, 1988), directed by Ken Russell, screenplay by Ken Russell and Vivian Russell, starring Sammi Davis (Ursula), Paul McGann (Skrebensky), Amanda Donohoe (Winifred), Christopher Gable (Will), David Hemmings (Uncle Henry), Dudley Sutton (MacAllister), Jim Carter (Head teacher) and Glenda Jackson (Anna) [Vestron Pictures] [video 1990].

ADAPTATIONS IN THE FILMS

Homogenization

The film of a novel is a new text. Part of what makes it new is its departure from the original; part of what makes it new is its conformity to the conventions of the new form, the film. If one compares the length of a Lawrence novel with the length of a film made out of that novel it becomes immediately apparent that the act of translation is not just an act of compression, but an act of homogenization too.

While an absorbed reader might finish a short story or novella at one sitting, a novel takes days, if not weeks, to read. Turning the 535 pages of *Women in Love* into a film of 129 minutes, or the 490 pages of *The Rainbow* into a film of 104 minutes, or the 313 pages of *Lady Chatterley's Lover* into a film of 100 minutes, clearly involves a radical reconception of the scope of the text. *The Virgin and the Gipsy* is only 86 pages and became the shortest of the films (92 minutes); but while *Women in Love* the novel is more than six times longer than *The Virgin and the Gipsy* the novella, the film of *Women in Love* is only 33 minutes longer than the film of *The Virgin and the Gipsy*. Because of the conventions of the medium and the institutions in which it operates, whatever goes into the adapter's brain comes out in packages of a similar size.

How is this achieved? How is the narrative adapted to make a film of an hour and a half or two hours? First, of course, there is cutting. For example, Just Jaeckin's *Lady Chatterley's Lover* simplifies the story by eliminating those early sections devoted to Connie Chatterley's first lover, Michaelis.[2] However, any form of cutting alters the shape, the proportions, the rhythms of the narrative, giving a new prominence to what remains. The adapter then begins to realize that rearrangements or even additions may be needed in order to establish coherence in what is left. That search for coherence is an invitation to the adapter to create a new text, a filmic text.

In *Women in Love* Ken Russell (or rather Larry Kramer) pruned the original narrative without having to omit any major characters or incidents. The resulting rewriting is not, in terms of the broad outlines of the story, radically different from the original.[3] But in *The Rainbow* Russell dispensed with all but a few paragraphs of the first 210 pages of the novel and restricted the film to the remaining 286 pages. This enabled him not only to reduce the amount of text to be translated into the new medium (57 per cent of the original), but to provide the film with an entirely new structure.

Where the novel is simultaneously the story of a family (the Brangwens), the representation of a process of socio-historical change (cultural change in nineteenth-century England determined by economic and educational pressures), and also an argument about the nature of sexual relationships at a deep psychic level, the film restricts itself to one innocent girl's adventures as she begins to break away from home.

As well as cutting, Russell adds. Unity of characterization is provided by Ursula's persistent display of a spirited courage, but that courage is tested and developed through encounters with characters largely of Russell's making. He invents a perverted artist called Mack, and a charming, benevolent, albeit ideologically challenging, uncle called Henry (a curious alteration of Lawrence's very minor character, the industrialist Uncle Tom).

The biggest addition, though, is the enhancement in importance of another character from the novel, Ursula's schoolteacher Winifred Inger. Winifred becomes the second most important character in the film, appearing in 40 per cent of the shots (408 out of 974). Although she is a mildly threatening and disturbing character in respect of her bisexuality and the power she exerts over Ursula, she represents independent thinking and, through her own beauty and her association with beautiful places, she is rendered ambiguous as an element in the film's meaning. In a development that seems quite arbitrary and is handled with almost no irony, Winifred marries Uncle Henry while retaining her lesbian interest in Ursula. Russell thereby manages to arrange that *The Rainbow* repeats the formula of *Women in Love*: two women, two men, and a homosexual as well as a heterosexual relationship.

Conventions

In his introduction to the Penguin edition of *Three Plays by D. H. Lawrence*, Raymond Williams quoted Lawrence: 'To me even Synge, whom I admire very much indeed, is a bit too rounded off . . . I can't bear art you can walk round and admire.'[4] Williams went on to argue that Lawrence's emphasis on

> flow, incompleteness, unfinished rhythms because the lives were unfinished, would not easily be accepted as 'dramatic' at all . . . Lawrence was stuck with a theatrical pressure to unify, within a fixed place, a fixed room, on the stage, and with the conventional need for a single overall crisis.
>
> Stuck in a room, as the only modern drama he knew then was, he had to check the flow of action and of feeling at door and window, with that shaping social landscape of mine and railway and farm left outside, for description or report: a dramatic limitation that with the mobility of the film or television camera he could now surpass.[5]

What was true of the play was equally true of the short story, the novel, the essay and the poem. Lawrence's work represents a continual straining against the conventions of each generic form he adopted. He always wanted them to do something more. In his handling each form infiltrated the others, and in each his own voice insistently pushed itself into prominence. Williams may be right that Lawrence would have welcomed as a liberation from the stage play the conventional form of the film.[6] But he would no doubt have found himself as frustrated by film as he was by every other form.

In the cases of the four films under discussion, once the novel or novella has become film, it has also become subject to the conventions of film. These conventions include the expectations of a film audience. Inevitably, Lawrence's interest in subverting and challenging literary conventions, including the literary conventions of his own period, are rendered invisible. The novel of *Lady Chatterley's Lover* deliberately breaks the rules of literary good taste by including such passages as ' "What is cunt?" she said . . . . "Cunt! It's like fuck then" ' (p. 185). However, the film's one use of 'fucker' and two uses of 'fucking' now seem quaint, rather than shocking. The novel also breaks the conventions of fictional narration by allowing into its narrative line seemingly authorial idiomatic comment on the English reader's society ('Ours is essentially a tragic age', p. 5; 'England my England! But which is *my* England?', p. 162) and, above all, some blatant theorizing about the nature of the novel form itself ('the novel, properly handled, can reveal the most secret places of life', p. 104). Within the film, however, there is no directorial self-referentiality to break the sealed world of its fiction.

Similarly, the novel of *Women in Love* is generally recognized to be formally at odds with the conventions of the novel. But to some extent its modernist, fragmented, decentred structure is actually derivative of filmic cutting and juxtapositions, and therefore defused by its translation into the medium of film. Ken Russell's occasional inventive camera-angles and bursts of theatricality, and his large-scale use of close-up, zoom, and the hand-held camera, still retain some of their original refreshingness, but hardly amount to any equivalent of the novel's challenge to literary conventions. Where the novel refuses realist individualist characterization, disappointing the reader who wants to build up and sustain a vividly distinctive image of Gerald as opposed to Birkin, and Birkin's ideas rather than Hermione's ideas, the realization of these characters in the bodies of actors – particularly in the bodies of well-known actors like Oliver Reed and Alan Bates and Eleanor Bron – provides the film or video spectator with the means of identifying those characters as credibly distinctive individuals.

In *The Rainbow*, of course, Lawrence is reputedly challenging the very concept of

> the old stable *ego* – of the character. There is another *ego*, according to whose action the individual is unrecognisable, and passes through, as it were, allotropic states . . . . The ordinary novel would trace the history of the diamond – but I say, 'Diamond, what! This is carbon'.
>
> (Letter to Edward Garnett, from Lerici, 5 June 1914)

In neither of his films does Russell attempt to represent this level of his characters' lives. Being a photographic medium, film fosters the conventions of naturalism before all else, and automatically records the state of diamond at the expense of carbon.

It can be argued that by 'carbon' Lawrence is actually alluding to the operations of the unconscious. His own technique for representing it is poetic. Through sustained use of metaphor he proposes a language beyond language, a language at the level of carbon rather than diamond. Film is an established medium for surrealism, but the only technique that Russell or Jaeckin employ to invoke the unconscious is the dream sequence. These are always incorporated perfectly into the realist mode (we know who is dreaming and why). Only in Miles's *The Virgin and the Gipsy* is there any attempt to explore the carbon in his characters. When Yvette first encounters the gipsy, he opens the door of the car in which she is a passenger and she willingly steps out to accompany him to his caravan. This short sequence, and another in which he helps her take off her coat, are re-run a number of times to suggest her memory, her fantasy and her profound (carbonate) engagement with the gipsy. When, near the end of the film, the Rectory is flooded and the wet and shivering Yvette shelters naked in the arms of the equally naked gipsy, this special sequence is run once again but is no longer exclusively assimilable as *her* memory or fantasy: it is almost superfluous to her characterization and has begun to act, instead, as a poetic authorial commentary upon the quality of her experience and *our* engagement with it.

Social context

It is one of the conventions of realist films – and all these films fall broadly within that tradition, the dominant cinematic mode – that the characters must belong to a precise historical period, articulated in their dress, their speech, the houses they inhabit and the countryside through which they travel (hence the greatest directorial sin is to allow an anachronistic detail of modern life to stray into shot). H. M. Daleski argues that *Women in Love* is set 'in the same pre-war England as that in which Ursula of *The Rainbow* reaches maturity'[7] but Graham Holderness points out that,

> Criticism has generally taken the hint . . . and recognized the war as some kind of context for the novel. But Lawrence's suggestions are contradictory, and in an illuminating way. The novel 'does not concern the war': war does not constitute its subject, and is not the object of its discourse. But 'the bitterness of war' is to be 'taken for granted' in the characters – so the war, though neither subject nor object, is still somehow inside the novel.[8]

In his film of *Women in Love*, Ken Russell decided to provide the story with an historical context. Where Lawrence deliberately fails to locate the novel precisely in time, alluding to the Boer War but avoiding all explicit reference to the Great War, Russell deliberately portrays an England of the 1920s, with references to the Great War (unveiling a statue of the Unknown Soldier at shot 234) and newspaper headlines about miners' riots (shot 70). However, the contextualization is largely ineffectual, as indeed it is in all the films except *The Virgin and the Gipsy*. *Lady Chatterley's Lover* is a pretty costume-drama, in which everyone is kitted out in brand-new period outfits and Wragby Hall has been converted from the novel's long, low house of brown stone with dismal rooms into an elegant Palladian stately home. Similarly, Ursula's time in school in *The Rainbow* receives lengthy treatment, but the experience is focused on staff relations rather than the material conditions determining the staff and children's daily lives, and on Ursula's developing perceptions and state of feeling. Winifred deplores the way that industrialization is ravaging the countryside, Skrebensky alerts us to the Boer War and Ursula is clearly representative of newly liberated young women of her time; but it is all on the surface, traces of elements within the text. Russell's interests are with the psychosexual capacities of free individuals.

By contrast, Christopher Miles's carefully planned and implemented *mise-en-scène* (he uses fewer shots per minute, fewer close-ups, less music than the other directors) reflects a more thoughtful, more intelligent and, ultimately, more penetrating reading of his text. Part of his reading is the establishment of a social context for the action. There are credible servants earning their livings in the Rectory where Yvette lives, and social realities are thereby suggested. The house and the household make sense. There is a kitchen with pots in which the horrible food is made and there are chamber-pots in which it is eventually deposited and which a maid has to empty. Even the social anomalies, Mrs Fawcett and Major Eastwood, and the gipsy and his family, have an intelligible social relationship to the Rectory and to Yvette.

Endings

One convention of all realist texts is the commitment to closure. Lawrence's fictions are characteristically open-ended, unresolved. The novel of *Women in Love* closes with dialogue between Birkin and Ursula. They are in disagreement: he is arguing that for his life to be complete he needs eternal union with a man as well as with a woman.

> 'You can't have it, because it's false, impossible,' she said.
> 'I don't believe that,' he answered.
>
> (Penguin edition, p. 541)

The last word is the man's, asserting his refusal to accept closure. Birkin's final words are the film's final words too; but the film closes with a reaction-shot – a close-up of Ursula's face, responding to Birkin's words. The image is frozen and the credits are superimposed upon it. In so far as she looks alarmed, sceptical, envious, taken aback, and in so far as she is reacting to Birkin's assertion of the incompleteness of her view of things, the ending (rendered stylishly arresting by an accompanying burst of dramatic music) is just as open as the novel's, if not more so; but the need to provide the reaction-shot could be regarded as symptomatic of a dissatisfaction with Lawrence's lack of closure, and the decision to end with a close-up of the woman's face coincides with the decision of each of these films to focus ultimately on the woman's love.

Jaeckin's *Lady Chatterley's Lover* follows the novel in foregrounding Connie's actions and experience, but he attempts to provide the film with a complete statement of closure. It had begun with a slow zoom into Wragby Hall and it ends with a slow zoom out. Rather than Connie, it is Mrs Bolton who is at the window now, and (ironically enough) closing the window, shutting in her invalid Sir Clifford, and shutting out her rival Connie. The novel is far more indefinite. It ends with a long letter from Mellors on a farm near Heanor to Connie in Scotland, a letter which expresses hope that they will be able to live together but which nevertheless records his fear for the future, 'There's a bad time coming!'

Both the novel and the film of *The Rainbow* end with a woman and a rainbow. But whereas the novel ends with the woman's view of the rainbow, the film ends with the woman in the distance beneath the rainbow, running away as if in a cinematic cliché into the sunset.

The Virgin and the Gipsy expands the role played by Mrs Fawcett and Major Eastwood, transforming the ending of the film by writing them into it. After the flood the Yvette of the novella, rendered passive and acquiescent by the experience of spending a night with the gipsy, is reunited with her immediate family, her father and sister; the film, however, ends, like the film of *The Rainbow*, with the woman leaving – Yvette rejects her family and is driven off with the Eastwoods, seemingly for ever.

The Laurentian

What none of these films achieves is any adequate objective correlative for Lawrence's own voice, for his deepest interests, for the emphases he manufactures through his distinctive use of language. The only attempt to be true to his language is their use of the language for which Penguin Books were prosecuted in 1959: however, whereas Lawrence only introduced the infamous four-letter words in *Lady Chatterley's Lover*, Russell's reconstructed Winifred in *The Rainbow* talks casually to Ursula about 'fucking'.

In each of the four films something equally recognizably 'Laurentian' emerges, reflecting the strength of his literary personality, but it is very different from what is 'Laurentian' about his own texts. This is because each text has been subjected to two further sets of conventions – the conventions of film itself, and the conventions of films based on Lawrence texts.

All four films work within the conventions of the realist text, being unified, coherent narratives, usually centred on a woman, ending in closure. In the process of transformation from book to film, the discourse of high art is drowned out by the discourses of popular fiction and, above all, of soft porn.

For example, characters are discovered in the nude (above all in *Women in Love*, with 14 per cent of its shots featuring nudity), usually outdoors in pastoral settings such as woods, mountain tops, lakesides or country cottages, with accompanying music (either lyrical or orgasmic). When the nudity is outdoors there is often water to be seen. When it is indoors it takes place often on a rug in front of a wood fire. The nudists may be washing or purifying themselves (Mellors, entirely nude in the film, where he was only stripped to the waist in the novel; Birkin recovering from Hermione's assault with a paperweight; Connie in the rain), swimming (Gerald on his own; Ursula with Winifred; Ursula with Gudrun; Laura with Tibby; Mrs Fawcett with Major Eastwood), copulating outdoors (Connie and Mellors; Birkin and Ursula; Ursula and Skrebensky), copulating indoors (Connie and Mellors; the gipsy and Yvette's maid; Gerald and Gudrun; Ursula and Skrebensky), masturbating (Connie), at some athletic pastime (Gerald and Birkin wrestling; Winifred, Skrebensky and Ursula running up a mountain in Ursula's dream), inspecting themselves in their bedroom mirror (Connie), being an artist's model (Ursula), or having had a ducking (Yvette and the gipsy).

Characters are often to be found half-dressed or with a noticeable amount of bare flesh (Sir Clifford going to bed, being massaged or doing his exercises; the gipsy in his working-gear; Yvette undressing, being undressed, or in bed; Connie copulating with Mellors; Connie being kissed by Mellors).

There is a variety of sexual activity – heterosexuality (many examples), implied homosexuality (Loerke and Leitner; Gerald and Birkin), explicit lesbianism (Winifred and Ursula), masturbation (Connie), anal intercourse (Connie and Mellors), beating (Mack), sadistic violence (Mellors with the poachers; Gerald with Gudrun; Gerald with the mare; Hermione with Birkin; Winifred with schoolgirls; Ursula with Jim), voyeurism/child abuse (Ursula's Head teacher), and, in the cases of Ursula, Connie and Yvette, a woman's sexual fantasy.

MARKETING

The book is the parent of the film of the book; but once the birth has taken place, the book may well become commercially dependent upon the film. When, in 1950, Penguin Books first published *The Virgin and the Gipsy* they put it in one volume with *St Mawr*. Twenty years later they decided to market it separately. Why? Because of Christopher Miles's film. The front cover carried the following legend:

> THE VIRGIN AND THE GIPSY/ Now a major film starring Joanna Shimkus and Franco Nero/ D. H. LAWRENCE [over still from film of Nero and Shimkus]

On the back cover, the blurb reads:

> *The Virgin and the Gipsy* affirms the powers of instinct and intuition in their struggle against the constraints of civilization and anticipates *Lady Chatterley's Lover* in its theme. In it Lawrence tells the reverent tale of a young girl's emotional awakening in the elemental presence of a gipsy.

The language is designed for a sophisticated academic readership (what, even so, can they have meant by 'reverent'?); but this is a book and, above all, a Penguin Book. In 1970 Penguin were still targeting a highly educated market and D. H. Lawrence was still academically respectable; F. R. Leavis was still the dominant voice in literary criticism and Marxist and feminist critics had not begun to drive Lawrence off student reading-lists. Furthermore, Penguin Books were still famous for publishing *Lady Chatterley's Lover*. Ten years earlier, after all, they had been prosecuted under the Obscene Publications Acts, and they were still keen to market minor Lawrence on the back of the novel's notoriety. In 1961 they had exploited that fame by publishing the transcript of *The Trial of 'Lady Chatterley'*, edited by C. H. Rolph, and even in 1972 they were bringing out the early drafts of Lawrence's novel, *The First Lady Chatterley* and *John Thomas and Lady Jane*.

By 1989, however, things had changed. That year Penguin marketed *The Rainbow* in a very different way. The front cover read:

> *The Rainbow*/ Now an unforgettable film from Ken Russell, director of *Women in Love*/ D. H. LAWRENCE [over still of Davis and McGann]

Lawrence is still foregrounded, but for all his capital letters, his name makes the least impact on the cover, which is more than anything else a visual image. Now the book is riding on the back, not of another book, but of a film. The film is identified not with an author, but with an *auteur*.

On the back cover of the 1989 Penguin *Rainbow*, the appeal is to a less intellectual readership than that of *The Virgin*, a slightly down-market middle-brow readership impressed by fame, in love with good reads and interested in sagas (that is, the staple diet of television drama) and characters who make daring individualistic moves:

> One of Lawrence's most famous and best-loved novels, *The Rainbow* follows the lives and passions of three generations of the Brangwen family./ The Brangwens have been established at Marsh Farm, near Lawrence's native Nottinghamshire, for many years. They are a strong-willed family whose son Tom marries a Polish widow and adopts her daughter, Anna. But it is Ursula, Anna's own daughter, who dominates the family. Sensitive and rebellious, Ursula breaks away from the confines of her family traditions and, in a daring move, makes a new life for herself.

Less intellectual the appeal may be, but the readership is still interested in Lawrence the writer.

However, a new market was being created by the introduction of video. The video of *Women in Love* has as its cover 'KEN RUSSELL'S/ "WOMEN IN LOVE" ', framing a close-up still of Ursula and Gudrun dancing cheek to cheek in Hermione's ballet. The message is ambiguous. If we don't know the novel or the film we might take them to be lesbian lovers. On the back there is just one photograph, this time even more challenging of heterosexuality – a still of a naked Gerald and a naked Birkin wrestling on an oriental carpet in front of an open fire in a stately home. The text goes:

> The sexual awakening of two young girls in the Midlands during the 20s. Ken Russell's explicit and sensational work caused so much controversy that Hollywood branded it

> 'Women in Heat'. Powerful performances by Glenda Jackson, Oliver Reed and Alan Bates and excellent period detail make for addictive entertainment . . . . Suitable only for persons of 18 years and over.

The front cover of the 1991 video of *Lady Chatterley's Lover* superimposes one still from the film (in silhouette long-shot a clothed Lady Chatterley receives the key to his hut from Mellors, who is accompanied by his dog) upon another (in close-up the naked Lady Chatterley and Mellors lie in post-coital bliss on a straw-strewn floor). The text is brief and does not mention Lawrence: '*Lady Chatterley's Lover*/ SYLVIA KRISTEL NICHOLAS CLAY'. On the back there are three further stills. In the biggest, a full-length, full-frontal nude Connie lies on Mellors's bed, decorated with wild flowers, and adorns his head with still more while he, also naked, holds a bunch of hyacinths in his hand. In another, he fondles her semi-naked breast while she swoons in ecstasy backwards against his clothed chest. In the third, she stands over and behind the seated Sir Clifford Chatterley, massaging his aching temples (the cuckold's horns?). The text reads:

> D. H. Lawrence's erotic novel, banned for many years, has been transformed into a sensual masterpiece of erotic cinema, starring Sylvia Kristel (Emmanuelle)./ A rich, titled and beautiful young woman becomes bored and frustrated by a sexless marriage. She seeks emotional satisfaction in an affair with her husband's gamekeeper, oblivious of the social scandal she is creating./ From the creators of 'Emmanuelle' comes another high calibre classic with the emphasis on eroticism.

Not only has the novel succumbed to the conventions of cinema (Connie Chatterley's beauty is no topic for the novel but a requirement in Hollywood-style casting), the film has succumbed to the imagination of the blurb-writer (Jaeckin's story-line has little, if any, interest in a social scandal). But it is the blurb-writer's language that is more interesting. Are we to understand that *Emmanuelle* was a 'classic'? Is this just another way of saying it was 'a sensual masterpiece'? Or is it that the makers of *Emmanuelle* have also made 'classics'? And are they 'classic films' or films of literary classics (such as Lawrence novels)? As for 'erotic' and 'eroticism', one recalls what John Ellis wrote:

> the campaign for Just Jaeckin's *Emmanuelle* (1974) in Britain featured respectable, homely Katie Boyle's radio commercial offering it as 'The film that makes you feel good without feeling bad.' The spectator was specified by the formula Pornography minus Shame equals Eroticism.[9]

The stills used on the front covers of Penguin's *The Rainbow* and *The Virgin and the Gipsy* are medium close-up shots of a man and woman, each sexually aware of and desirous of the other; but they are clothed, modest, restrained. The video of *The Rainbow*, produced in 1990, has a medium close-up of Davis and McGann again on its front cover, but this time naked, in a sexual embrace, against a waterfall. The still has been augmented by the addition of a rainbow. Where Lawrence's rainbow is a personal symbol of the union of elemental forces (sun and rain, earth and sky, man and woman, past and future), a promise of Truth and, as in his famous sketch in a letter to Viola Meynell on 2 March 1915, arises always above an industrialized landscape, Russell's rainbow is a decorative device to open and close the film symmetrically, closer to Wordsworth than the Bible, and closer to *Finian's Rainbow* than to Wordsworth. If it has a significance, it is as a symbol of Ursula's undaunted spirit, her love of life.

The text on the front cover of the video reads 'Ken Russell's/ film of D. H. Lawrence's/ *The Rainbow*'. But Russell's name is bigger and bolder than Lawrence's. Despite the reference to Lawrence, the video is sold on the director's name, on the names of other films already successfully marketed, and on the names of the film's stars.

John Ellis describes stars in classic Hollywood cinema as 'marketing devices'.[10] They are clearly still operating as marketing devices in these Lawrence films. Sylvia Kristel sells Jaeckin's *Lady Chatterley's Lover* because of her immense fame in the *Emmanuelle* movies. Ken Russell knew he had to have a star if he wanted to persuade anyone to back *The Rainbow*. In an attempt to recreate some of the team which made *Women in Love*, Russell rehired two of his earlier actors, Christopher Gable to play Will and Glenda Jackson to play Anna.[11] But Jackson was not enough of a name. In his autobiography Russell quotes the attitude of Vestron, his backers: 'No name, no movie.'[12] So he hired David Hemmings, casting him in the minor role of Uncle Henry. Hemmings had been a name in the 1960s. It was doubtful whether he was still one at the close of the 1980s. The film's credits treat Hemmings as a star, but the video cover is unconvinced and ignores him. Hemmings was the last throw. Russell had already tried other, bigger names, and failed to secure them. He had gone back to the old *Women in Love* team: he had approached Alan Bates; Bates was not willing, so Russell had asked Oliver Reed; Reed was not available; that was when he turned to Hemmings. Before even Bates, though, he had managed to secure a really big name. That name had agreed to play Uncle Henry and only pulled out at the last minute. That name *was* a star – a pop star: Elton John.

On the back cover of the *Rainbow* video, there are six further stills from the film: the central one features Winifred and Uncle Henry at their wedding; the others are Winifred and Mack, both in male attire, a naked Ursula and Skrebensky in bed, Anna bathing a baby, Ursula and Skrebensky walking clothed through a cornfield, and Ursula dashing through the cobbled streets of London in the rain. The text reads:

> In the game of love she played by her passion and not by the rules./ Ken Russell's sensuous film version of DH Lawrence's THE RAINBOW follows his Academy Award winning adaptation of WOMEN IN LOVE and stars Sammi Davis (HOPE AND GLORY, A PRAYER FOR THE DYING), Paul McGann (EMPIRE OF THE SUN), Amanda Donohoe (LAIR OF THE WHITE WORM) and Glenda Jackson (WOMEN IN LOVE)./ Set in the Midlands of Victorian England, THE RAINBOW tells the story of a rebellious young woman (DAVIS) who, after defying her parents and society's morality, engages in an unbridled and passionate affair first with her beautiful schoolteacher (DONOHOE), then with a fascinating young soldier (MCGANN), before setting out on her own to capture the fuller sensuality of life itself./ '. . . the film is a triumph . . . . Don't miss it' (FILM MONTHLY). Suitable only for persons of 15 years and over.

Penguin Books had employed the discourse of social relationships – 'sensitivity', 'strong will', 'rebellion' and 'daring'. The video describes Ursula as 'rebellious' but makes more use of the discourse of asocial sensation – recalling the film as 'sensuous' and concerned with beauty, fascination, unbridled passion and 'sensuality'.

One could argue that Lawrence's novels and stories are built around the dialectical relationships of forces each of which is 'the other' to the other. In *The Rainbow* Lawrence pits English against Poles, working farmers against educated aristocrats, nature against industrialization. In *Lady Chatterley's Lover* the individuals of the title represent a meeting of two different classes and of two different linguistic registers as much as of two different sexes. In the novella the virgin and the gipsy of the title similarly represent opposed worlds. Yet, in the hands of the film-maker, these dualities are ignored. The pressure is always to make of Lawrence's text a linear narrative about an individual. In *Women in Love* Kramer's relative fidelity to the novel's structure resisted this pressure, and the dynamics of acting skills and star-identities within the central quartet of Bates, Reed, Jackson and Linden made Ursula the least significant of the major characters – until the closing shot, when suddenly Russell declared his wish to foreground an individual. That individual was a woman, Ursula. In the film of *The Rainbow*, Ursula is explicitly defined by the narrative structure to be its subject. Each of the stills from the film printed on the cover of the video features a woman – Anna, Winifred or Ursula – and the blurb encourages its readers to imagine the chief heroine, Ursula, to be playing 'the game of love'. The relationships represented by the titles of *The Virgin and the Gipsy* and *Lady Chatterley's Lover* are read narrowly by the film-makers as the heart of Laurentian matter. The title of *Women in Love*, like its closing shot, seems to reinforce the formula. As the blurb-writer on the cover of the *Women in Love* video puts it, Hollywood branded it 'Women in Heat'.

Such is Lawrence on film. It is not so far from 'A Woman's Love!'

NOTES

1 Excluding the four films discussed, they are: *The Rocking Horse Winner* (UK, 1949), directed and written by Anthony Pelissier, starring John Mills and Valerie Hobson (Two Cities Films); *L'Amant de Lady Chatterley* (Fr, 1956), directed by Marc Allegret, based on a stage play by Gaston Bonheur and Philippe de Rothchild, starring Danielle Darrieux, Leo Genn and Erno Crisa (Columbia); *Sons and Lovers* (UK, 1960), directed by Jack Cardiff, screenplay by Gavin Lambert and T. E. B. Clarke, starring Dean Stockwell, Heather Sears, Mary Ure, William Lucas, Donald Pleasance and Ernest Theriger (Twentieth

Century Fox); *The Fox* (USA, 1967), directed by Mark Rydell, screenplay by Lewis John Carlino and Howard Koch, starring Anne Heywood, Sandy Dennis and Keir Dullea (Claridge Pictures); *The Trespasser* (UK, 1980), directed by Colin Gregg, starring Alan Bates and Pauline Moran; *The Captain's Doll* (UK, 1981), directed by Charles Whatham, starring Jeremy Irons; *The Rocking Horse Winner* (UK, 1982), directed by Robert Bierman; *Kangaroo* (Aust., 1986), directed by Tim Burstall, starring Colin Friels and Judy Davis.

2 This makes the film closer to that early version of the novel now known as *The First Lady Chatterley*. Indeed, there are at least two places where the film uses incidents from this text – Connie's dream of a suddenly disturbed horse (Penguin edition, p. 24) and the later scene when she covers her face with a veil and contemplates her naked body in a mirror (p. 30).

3 Note, however, that F. R. Leavis refused an invitation from Larry Kramer to attend a screening of *Women in Love*, replying 'It's an obscene undertaking to "write again" for the screen . . .' *Films and Filming* (September 1970), 30.

4 *Three Plays by D. H. Lawrence* (Harmondsworth: Penguin Books, 1969), 12.

5 ibid., 13, 14.

6 Lawrence's attitude to the cinema, as reflected in his novel *The Lost Girl* (1920) and in his poems 'When I Went to the Film' and 'Film Passion' (from *Pansies*, 1929), was disparaging.

7 H. M. Daleski, *The Forked Flame* (London: Faber & Faber, 1965), 127.

8 Graham Holderness, *D. H. Lawrence: History, Ideology and Fiction* (London: Gill and Macmillan, 1982), 200.

9 John Ellis, *Visible Fictions: Cinema, Television, Video* (London: Routledge & Kegan Paul, 1982), 79.

10 ibid., 108.

11 Russell also rehired his key technical team: Billy Williams as director of photography, Lucina Arrighi as costume designer, and Ian Whittaker as art director.

12 Ken Russell, *A British Picture* (London: Heinemann, 1989), 277.

7

SHARED DREAMS

Reproducing *Gone with the Wind*

Harriett Hawkins

It is no more than a dream remembered.

Film 'Foreword' to *Gone with the Wind* (USA, 1939)

'Laura Palmer and I had the same dream!'
'But that's impossible!'
Agent Cooper to Sheriff Truman (and the TV audience that, in fact, shared the identical dream with him) in *Twin Peaks* (1990)

Dreams hung in fragments at the far end of the room, suffered analysis, passed, to be dreamed in crowds or else discarded . . . [There was a meeting] on the subject of *Manon* with a happy ending, and Stahr had his say on that as he had before – it had been making money without a happy ending for a century and a half. He was obdurate.
F. Scott Fitzgerald, Hollywood studio scenes in *The Last Tycoon* (1941)

DREAMING IN CROWDS: THE QUESTION OF FIDELITY

Margaret Mitchell's *Gone with the Wind* has 'been making money without a happy ending' for a half century. So has David O. Selznick's film adaptation. As opposed to the alteration suggested by the film's distributor Louis B. Mayer, where Rhett turns back to embrace Scarlett in the end, the audience at the sneak preview in 1939 unequivocally preferred the ambiguously 'open' ending in the movie as in the novel.[1] And this response confirmed the theory of fidelity so obdurately held by the film's producer.

David O. Selznick himself believed that film versions of successful novels and plays were likely to succeed *because* they provided the public with a welcome change from the hackneyed plots and stock characters that film audiences knew 'even better' than did the makers of the formulaic movies that (then as now) were being ground out with 'machinelike efficiency and standardization'.[2] He thus produced a true-to-text adaptation of *Gone with the Wind* in opposition to conventional wisdom concerning the need for 'sympathetic' heroines, macho heroes and happy endings. By contrast, the experiences portrayed in *Gone with the Wind* are a succession of defeats countered only by sheer determination to surmount them on the part of an unsympathetic heroine and unrequited lover whose final fate is left in doubt.

Primarily because of, rather than in spite of, Margaret Mitchell's glamorous but unconventional and unsympathetic heroine, and her other departures from the conventions of romance, the film and novel alike share the magical capacity to transform their admirers into emotionally and imaginatively active participants in the experiences portrayed. 'Scarlett O'Hara was not beautiful but men seldom realized it when caught by her charm as the Tarleton Twins were . . .'[3] Likewise, once caught in the spell of the film or the novel, many of us cease to be critics even of obvious flaws and become just what we are nowadays repeatedly told that informed adult readers and enlightened film-goers ought *not* to be: starry-eyed, enraptured fans. 'For sheer readability', the novel's *New York Times* review proclaimed, *Gone with the Wind* was 'unsurpassed in American fiction'.[4] And it still is. In a reader's poll sponsored by the American Library Association[5] Mitchell's novel was the overwhelming choice for the 'best book read'. Newspaper columnist Ann Landers, who was among the respondents, spoke for thousands of American women when she cited 'GWTW' as 'both her personal favourite and the book having the greatest influence on her life': 'I immediately identified with Scarlett O'Hara's determination not to let customs, proprieties, people or events dictate the terms and quality of her life.' Likewise, since its release in 1939, the film version has been seen (often again and again) by more people than the entire population of the United States: 110 million people watched the first television showing;[6] and from the première of Selznick's film adaptation in 1939 to the present time the success of the movie and the success of the novel have boosted each other to achieve an unrivalled popularity.

From *Gone with the Wind* and *Rebecca* to *The Godfather, The Bonfire of the Vanities* and *The Silence of the Lambs*, best-selling novels have offered their film adapters two major commercial advantages: proven appeal and a 'pre-sold' audience. And critical acclaim often follows. The number of Oscars won by successful adaptations of popular novels is extremely impressive. On the other hand, if a film adaptation fails to satisfy readers who 'couldn't put the book down', 'didn't want it to end', and 'thought it would make a *great* film', it will inevitably fail. 'Fans of the novel will despise the film' announced the *Washington Post* review of Brian De Palma's damp version of *The Bonfire of the Vanities* (USA, 1990). As Richard Corliss observed,[7] novel readers 'are a possessive lot' because they have 'already made their own imaginary film version of the book – cast it, dressed the sets, directed the camera'. In many cases, so have the novelists themselves: De Palma's film flopped because 'Tom Wolfe had already created a great movie in the minds of his readers'. Thus Corliss concludes that the trick involved in successful adaptations is to convince 'the people who like what they read' that they 'like what they see' on the screen. And in no adaptation of a best-selling novel has this been more triumphantly accomplished than in David O. Selznick's production of *Gone with the Wind*.

Produced at his own studio, after the era of silent films when directors reigned supreme, and prior to the age of the independent director as *auteur*, Selznick's film is remarkable on both theoretical and historical grounds because of the producer's fidelity to a female author's text. Based on the success of previous adaptations such as *David Copperfield* (USA, 1935), *A Tale of Two Cities* (USA, 1935) and *Dinner at Eight* (USA, 1933), Selznick's governing theory was that the same elements that drew people to a classic or a Broadway hit or a best-selling novel would attract them to the film. Audiences, he felt, understood the conventions of the cinema and were prepared to forgive necessary cuts and omissions, but they did not like gratuitous alterations to familiar scenes and characters. In his productions of *Gone with the Wind* and *Rebecca* (USA, 1940) alike he adamantly vetoed changes to the original characterization and construction on the grounds that no one, not even the author, could be certain why a play or novel had caught the fancy of the public: 'If there are faults in construction', he told the journalist Bosley Crowther,

> it is better to keep them than to try to change them around because no one can certainly pick out the chemicals which contribute to the making of a classic. And there is always the danger that by tampering you may destroy the essential chemical.[8]

From his first reading of *Gone with the Wind*, Selznick realized that, in visual details, dialogue, costuming and characterization, Margaret Mitchell had imagined a great movie. He therefore wanted the film to seem like an exact photographic reproduction of the book, including 'every well-remembered scene' either in 'faithful transcription of the original or in keeping with the exact spirit of Miss Mitchell's book'.[9] Before the film went into production, Walter Plunkett designed the major costumes described in the novel, such as the white dress sprigged with green flowers that Scarlett wears to the barbecue and the green velvet dress she wears to visit Rhett in the jail at Atlanta. At the same time, Selznick's production designer, William Cameron Menzies, illustrated all the major scenes and settings directly from the novel and, used as models by successive directors, these pictorial recreations of Mitchell's scenes and situations gave *Gone with the Wind* its extraordinary visual continuity. The search for Scarlett was a major problem because no known actress seemed true-to-text in the way Clark Gable seemed right for Rhett. Another actor, Selznick observed, might have 'read a different dimension' into the character. But Gable 'brought to life precisely what Mitchell wrote and what millions of readers wanted'. So did Selznick's film as a whole. As the original *New York Times* review prophesied, 'Mr. Gallup's palpitantly waiting audience of 56,500,000 persons will not be disappointed in Vivien Leigh's Scarlett O'Hara, Clark Gable's Rhett Butler, or for that matter in Mr. Selznick's Miss Mitchell.'[10] And this prediction proved true not only for a host of people who had already screened private versions of the novel in their own imaginations; it also held true for innumerable women who had imaginatively cast themselves in the central role.

Ordinary readers, unknown actresses and major stars alike identified with Scarlett, sometimes because they felt they were like her and sometimes because they wished they could be like her.

The cover of *Scarlett's Women*, Helen Taylor's book about *Gone with the Wind* and its female readers, shows a dowdy, middle-aged housewife being swept off her feet by Clark Gable as Rhett Butler, but innumerable young girls (like Ann Landers) also identified with Scarlett's spirited and courageous rebellion against a restrictive society. In New York, Hollywood and London, actresses of entirely different types and backgrounds felt that they were destined to play the part. Tallulah Bankhead thought that, as a Southerner, only she could play Scarlett; the Yankee Katherine Hepburn and the British Vivien Leigh likewise believed themselves perfect for the role, even as countless women since then have vicariously enacted the part while reading the novel. This phenomenon may explain why the female readers polled by fan magazines did not strongly support any particular star for the part. They saw Scarlett in the mind's eye as described by Margaret Mitchell – green-eyed, dark-haired, with a tiny waist – and otherwise imaginatively and emotionally projected themselves into the role. By contrast, Clark Gable was the public's overwhelming favourite for Rhett. Even so, Gable himself feared that Mitchell had so indelibly etched the way her hero 'looked and acted' into the minds of millions of individuals that he would 'be lucky to satisfy even the majority'.[11] From the outset, to admirers of the novel, the film version of *Gone with the Wind* seemed like a highly personal as well as a collective 'dream remembered'.

As *Scarlett*, Alexandra Ripley's risibly feeble attempt to replicate Mitchell's characters demonstrates, the original problems of adapting and casting *Gone with the Wind* have compounded exponentially for any author or *auteur* or actor or actress who would dare to write or film or star in a sequel (to say nothing of attempting a re-make of the 1939 production). For over the years since the film was first released, *Gone with the Wind* has been 'dreamed in crowds' by successive generations of moviegoers, all of whom have grown up, and many of whom have grown old knowing that Rhett Butler looked and acted exactly like Clark Gable looked and acted when he played the part. And if countless admirers of the original novel agreed that green-eyed Vivien Leigh acted just like Scarlett as described by Margaret Mitchell ('She is my Scarlett!' Mitchell is often quoted as saying at the première), innumerable later readers have seen Scarlett O'Hara as looking, dressing and acting just like Leigh did in the film.

Given this unprecedented imaginative interface, practically

everyone who admires the novel will enjoy the film – and vice versa – even as people who dislike either one almost invariably dislike both. The film's visual reproductions of the novel's central images have so fused in the imagination and memory of readers and audiences as to be virtually identical. Although the film's running-time mandated cutting its host of memorable minor characters, Selznick scrupulously maintained the novel's essential chemistry. And that is why his film remains so successful. For what accounts for the world-wide, enduring success of both the film and the novel is the way in which Margaret Mitchell's original novel broke new ground. *Gone with the Wind* is *the* woman's war novel – that is, the woman's anti-war novel. And that, arguably, is why macho men do not like it.

WOMEN AND WAR

In his definitive distinction between the two genres, Georg Lukács observed that, in contrast to the historical drama where the protagonists are makers and movers of history, such as Antony and Cleopatra or Tamburlaine, the central characters in the 'bourgeois' historical novel are comparatively ordinary people who are caught up in historical circumstances over which they have little, if any control.[12] *War and Peace*, for instance, is not 'about' Napoleon; *Dr Zhivago* is not about Lenin. *Gone with the Wind* differs from other major historical novels by focusing so forcefully and consistently on the way war, social upheaval, hard times, worlds turned upside-down, historical bonfires of the vanities, affect women of all ages and classes who survive unaided to till the fields, bear and raise the children, bury the dead, pick up the pieces after the battles are over. Margaret Mitchell once considered 'Tote the weary load' – a refrain from the song 'My Old Kentucky Home' that is sung by Prissy in the film – as a title for her book. 'Ain' nuthin lef' now but mizry an' trouble' says Mammy when Scarlett returns to Tara to find her mother dead and her father mentally and physically broken: 'Jes' weery loads, honey, jes' weery loads'. 'Those were the same two words that had hummed in Scarlett's brain so monotonously that they had sickened her' and now she remembered the rest of the song with a sinking heart,

> Would her load never be light? . . . Through the window, in the faint light of the rising moon, Tara stretched before

> her, negroes gone, acres desolate, barns ruined . . . . This was the end of the road, quivering old age, sickness, hungry mouths, helpless hands plucking at her skirts.

And no one to shoulder the burden for her: 'Tomorrow she would fit the yoke around her neck' (pp. 416–20).

People who dismiss *Gone with the Wind* as romantic slush generally add that they are proud to say that they have never read it. But adults of both sexes who read or reread the novel before or after seeing the movie tend to be surprised, sometimes astonished at how good it is, how well it stands up, at its irony, its wit, its bite. Back in the 1930s historical novels were not sneered at, since they were (as in Russia they still are) primarily associated with traditional classics such as *A Tale of Two Cities* and *War and Peace*, and not exclusively associated with women authors and consequently denigrated, as they have been in Anglo-American literary circles ever since the success of Mitchell's Pulitzer Prize winning blockbuster (and of Kathleen Winsor's *Forever Amber*). At the time it came out, men were not ashamed to read or admire *Gone with the Wind*. Selznick's friend and colleague Merian C. Cooper, the creator of *King Kong*, was likewise enthralled by Mitchell's novel and, in a letter urging the distinguished playwright Sidney Howard to write the screenplay, accurately described *Gone with the Wind* as 'the story of a bitch' that is also 'the most supreme book written on courage in the English language'.[13] Both these components – the bitch and the courage – contribute to its enormous popularity with women and with men who have no illusions about their own invulnerability.

As 'a bitch', Scarlett can think and say radical things that many women have thought but no 'good' woman would dare to say out loud: ' "Why, why," Scarlett's mind stuttered, "I believe women could manage everything in the world without a man's help – except having babies, and God knows, no women in her right mind would have babies if she could help it" ' (p. 620). Compare Alexandra Ripley's conventional 'Scarlett' who rejoices in being such a good mother to a cardboard cut-out of a child (as well she might, since there is nothing to it): 'The baby never fussed, she had an infinite capacity to amuse herself.'[14] Then contrast the original Scarlett's problems of coping, as a matter of dire necessity, with unwanted pregnancies, frightened children, whining children, helpless parents and relatives likewise dependent on her for their survival. However much women may deplore her behaviour, hardly any woman can fail to sympathize with Scarlett's situation. For that matter, it is in the teeth of the historical evidence supplied by classical and popular literature alike – from Richard III to J. R. Ewing and from Becky Sharp to Alexis Carrington – that past and present moneymen and directors assume that audiences do not like to see or read about unsympathetic characters.[15]

Merian Cooper's point about the courage displayed by the characters in *Gone with the Wind* is also valid. But significantly (and, by the way, in marked contrast to the quintessentially passive Fay Wray in his own classic adventure fantasy) the more than simply physical courage and gallantry portrayed in *Gone with the Wind* is most conspicuously and consistently displayed by women *and* men who suffer the loss of children, parents, power, status, security, wealth and love. It is completely different from most 'romantic' novels and films in this regard. No wonder both the book and the film have served as forms of communal inspiration and consolation to so many people of differing nationalities and ideologies who, over the past fifty years, have likewise experienced and survived loss, war, deprivation, depression, famine, occupation, devastation, defeat. *Gone with the Wind* has recently proved as popular in the former Soviet Union as it was in post-war Europe (Hitler would not let it be shown in occupied Europe because he thought Scarlett a dangerous symbol of resistance) and, of course, it also proved tremendously popular in post-war Japan.

Nowadays the film and novel tend to be characterized as deplorably romantic glorifications of a patriarchal slave-state. There is no disputing the racism; the defence of the Ku Klux Klan is the worst feature of the book. But is *Gone with the Wind* all that romantic? No romantic love ever achieves emotional consummation or is ever completely reciprocated within it, while throughout the central section of the novel dealing with hard times at Tara both male love-interests are absent. And does it extol patriarchy as well as slavery?

Arguably, one of the most interesting aspects of the novel (which provides a kind of subtext that resonates throughout the film) is its warts-and-all depiction of a caste system involving comparable class distinctions within as well as between races. The black elite look down on 'poor white trash' and black 'field hands' alike. Mammy initially scorns Rhett, along with Scarlett, as a 'mule' decked out in 'horse-harness' that does not fool anyone, and she is one of the few people whose respect he sincerely seeks. Gerald O'Hara's Yankee overseer, Jonas Wilkerson, has no social standing whatsoever, and turns for companionship to 'no-count' Tom Slattery's daughter, Emmie. And in the hospital sequences and the scenes where veterans beg food at Tara, there are intangible caste-distinctions as well. Soldiers who look equally tired and dirty speak with accents that mark them as 'quality folk' or 'Cracker'. All this gives the film and novel an extraordinary sense of social interaction. In our age of economic ghettos and cultural apartheid – in some places in the United States as in the United Kingdom people rarely have any significant personal relationships (including personal enmities) outside their own social group – *Gone with the Wind* is historically interesting in its portrayal of intimate bondings and enmities as well as wartime levellings and interactions between members of differing castes. Moreover, throughout the novel you get a behind-the-scenes insight into the way women in a patriarchal society commonly talk about the gullibility, conceit and inconsistency of their masters.

When the 16-year-old Scarlett says she is tired of flattering 'fool men who haven't got one-half the sense I've got' and asks Mammy why a girl has to 'be so silly to catch a husband', Mammy replies,

> 'I specs its case gempmums doan know what dey wants. Dey jes' know what dey thinks dey wants. An' givin' dem what dey thinks dey wants saves a pile of mizry an' bein' an ole maid. It doan make a gempmum feel lak mahyin' a lady if he suspicions she got mo' sense dan he has.'
>
> (p. 79)

Mammy therefore advises the clever and wilful Scarlett to adopt the docile and childlike demeanour of a slave:

> 'Young misses what frowns an' pushes out dey chins an' says "Ah will" an' "Ah woan" mos' gener'ly doan ketch husbands' prophesied Mammy gloomily. 'Young misses should cas' down dey eyes an' say, "Well, suh, Ah mout" an' "Jes' as you say, suh." '
>
> (p. 59)

'Don't you suppose men get surprised after they're married to find that their wives do have sense?' asks Scarlett. 'Well it's too late den. Dey's already mahied. 'Sides, gempmums specs dey wives ter have sense' (p. 79).

But not too much sense. Later on, when Scarlett makes a success of her mill, she appals her husband when, to demonstrate to a contractor that her lumber was cheaper and better than her competitors', 'she ran up a long column of figures in her head and gave him an estimate then and there'. 'It was bad enough', Frank thought, 'that she had intruded herself among strange rough workmen', but 'it was worse still for a woman to show publically that she could do mathematics like that' (p. 638). Throughout the novel there are comparably vivid and wryly ironic portrayals of categorical bigotry: 'Now if there's one thing I hates worse than a nigger or a woman, it's a Yankee', announces the fierce old mountain-man, Archie. 'Why?' asks Scarlett, 'Did you ever know any Yankees?' 'No'm. But I'd hearn tell of them. I'd hearn tell they couldn't never mind their own bizness. I hates folks who can't mind their own bizness' (p. 754).

Socially speaking, in its portrayal of a world turned upside-down, *Gone with the Wind* documents a major historical alteration in American assumptions about what wealth can and cannot buy. 'Ah!' thought Scarlett angrily, 'Even though they're poor they still feel like ladies and I don't. The silly fools don't seem to realize that you can't be a lady without money' (p. 609). At this point, Scarlett (here as elsewhere associated with the New South in general and Atlanta in particular) decides that the Yankees were right when they equated status with wealth, not with birth or breeding, so she goes after the Yankee dollar at whatever cost to the values cherished by her mother. Deciding to become Rhett's mistress if that is the only way she can get the money to pay the taxes on Tara, Scarlett compares herself with Belle Watling, whom she had previously despised, and wishes she had new clothes with which to catch Rhett's eye, like the bright 'red plaid dress, the red-topped boots with tassels and the pancake hat' worn by upwardly mobile Emmie Slattery, the white-trash girl (now Mrs Jonas Wilkerson) who aspires to live at Tara (p. 544).

STRONG WOMEN, SCARLET WOMEN, STARRING WOMEN

At its worst, the novel's taken-for-granted racism (like the film's) is, at its best, accompanied by a taken-for-granted feminism that might well seem historically surprising to younger audiences nowadays. For ironically, in our so-called post-feminist era, *Gone with the Wind* stands alone in that no other comparably popular film or novel produced before or since so dramatically portrays bonding, solidarity and parity between women of various types, classes and races. One reason a lot of men do not like it is that it portrays such a powerful matriarchy even as it portrays women, from Ellen O'Hara (whose was the one voice instantly obeyed at Tara, where her husband's blustering and roarings were quietly disregarded) and Mammy to Melanie Wilkes and Belle Watling as its strongest and bravest characters. Great ladies, old ladies (Grandma Fontaine in the book), prostitutes, black women (the stalwart Dilcey, in the book, is also part-Indian), self-effacing Melanie and selfish Scarlett alike behave with conspicuous gallantry and often encourage and comfort each other as well as their menfolk. Belle provides the alibi that saves Ashley's life – for Melanie's sake; sword in hand, shy, gentle Melanie rushes to help Scarlett kill the Yankee soldier; a 'realist more uncompromising then herself', Mammy helps Scarlett 'pleasure' Frank Kennedy into marrying her and saving Tara. Women also bond together to shield their men. The dying Melanie thus asks Scarlett to 'look after' her husband: 'Ashley isn't – practical.' ('Only death could have forced that disloyalty from Melanie.') 'Look after him, Scarlett' but 'don't ever let him know.' 'Their glance sealed the bargain that the protection of Ashley Wilkes from a too harsh world was passing from one woman to another and that Ashley's masculine pride should never be humbled by the knowledge' (p. 1011). Subsequently, Scarlett comforts Ashley, left desolate by the death of Melanie, just as she had comforted her father, whose mainspring was broken by the death of Ellen. Yet throughout the novel, strong and vulnerable men and women likewise gain sympathy and respect rather than losing it when they confront defeat, display love, weep at the loss of their loved ones. Clark Gable feared it would wreck his manly image as a romantic hero if Rhett wept in the scene where he thought Scarlett would die of a miscarriage. But the scene enhanced Gable's image as much as Rhett's.

Ideologically speaking, things have changed for the better in American film circles since the film was produced, in that nobody today would reproduce the novel's patronizingly and infuriatingly racist subtext: 'You must be firm but gentle with inferiors, Scarlett, especially darkies.' Conversely, one could argue that in its production of feature films, Hollywood has become more sexist than it was in 1939 in so far as it is almost impossible to imagine a comparably (unselfconsciously) feminist version of *Gone with the Wind* being produced today. For, as it were in spite of the feminist movement, in top media circles as well as in down-market video shops it is generally taken for granted that 'cinema is produced entirely by men for men' while film criticism – both popular and theoretical – is generally written and read 'mostly by men' who perpetuate the same fraternal concensus.[16] For instance, in a poll seeking views of 'professionals' as to 'Who or what they most want to see in films',[17] 'Michael Winner wanted to see Dustin Hoffman and David Ankin chose Jack Nicolson.' 'Longed for directors included Martin Scorsese for Deak Rossell and Krzysztof Kieslowski for Thaddeus O'Sullivan . . .' Not a single woman's name was inscribed among the stars. Nowadays, women do not even appear as equals in matched pairs (of lovers, spouses, singers, dancers, and so on). Think of Scarlett and Rhett – and Garbo and Gilbert, McDonald and Eddy, Astaire and Rogers, Hepburn and Tracy, Loy and Powell, Bogart and Bacall. Today's co-starring counterparts are all same-sex, mainly male buddies.

Back in the studio days, when Selznick made *Gone with the Wind* big-budget features were entitled *Jezebel, Anna Karenina, Ninotchka, Camille, The Little Princess, Dancing Lady, Blonde Venus, She Done Him Wrong*. Their counterparts today are entitled: *Robocop II, Mad Max III, Lethal Weapon III, Predator II, Three Men and a Little Lady, Turner and Hooch, Oscar*, and so on. 'No doubt,' as Julie Burchill has perceptively observed, if *Gone with the Wind* were remade today, 'it would be retitled *Rhett and Ashley*, or perhaps *Raging Rhett II*' even as its *auteur* would no doubt soften the characterization of the female lead so as not to cast the live-in mother of his children as 'a true blue bitch'. All this, Burchill ironically concedes, might be well and good, 'were it not for the fact that, especially in the cinema, an interesting, strong woman is, by her very nature, a bitch and a ballbreaker'; 'Go on', she adds, 'you think of a "nice" female role as famous as Scarlett O'Hara.'[18]

It is, certainly, impossible to name a female role, sympathetic or unsympathetic, that has been so sought after by strong, interesting actresses. Warner Brothers gave Bette Davis her

Oscar-winning part in *Jezebel* as a consolation for not getting Scarlett; Katherine Hepburn implored RKO to buy the rights to Mitchell's novel as a vehicle for her. In those days, studios competed for properties that would show off the highly distinctive personalities and abilities of their leading ladies (Davis, Hepburn, Dietrich) to best effect, even as MGM would advertise its forthcoming attractions to distributors simply by naming its female superstar – 'one Garbo, two Shearers, three Crawfords' and so on. By contrast, as Julie Burchill has demonstrated, in the post-studio era the canonization of *auteurs* such as Alfred Hitchcock has coincided with the cinematic suppression of women who have, if they are 'good' girls (like Barbara Bel Geddes in *Vertigo*), been generally relegated to supporting roles and, if they are in any way 'bad' girls, stripped and slashed in the shower (like Janet Leigh in *Psycho*). Looked at historically, since the end of World War II, there has, Burchill concludes, been 'a gradual *breeding out*, like a mongrel strain', of starring female personalities on screen, and 'the result has been steady artistic and financial bankruptcy': 'In the Thirties, Mae West saved Paramount single-handed' (compare Shirley Temple at Fox and Deanna Durbin at Universal) while 'in the Eighties, Michael Cimino broke United Artists the same way with *Heaven's Gate*, which lost a striking forty-two million dollars'.[19]

For that matter, the number of powerful women actually involved in the production of *Gone with the Wind* seems almost inconceivable today. From Margaret Mitchell, the author, to Annie Laurie Williams, the agent who spotted it as an ideal film-source, to Kay Brown, Selznick's East Coast story editor whose impassioned recommendations ('I beg, urge, coax and plead with you to read it at once') persuaded the producer to buy it (against the advice of the male West Coast story editor who dismissed it as 'ponderous trash') to the star, Vivien Leigh, who carried a copy around with her on the set, women were professionally and emotionally – they took it personally – involved from the outset in every stage of the production. Indeed, the whole production testifies to the success of a collaborative, creative interation between men and women as effective as the chemistry between Leigh's Scarlett and Gable's Rhett. For if, as Bruce Jay Friedman observes, people now refer to 'Coppola's and not Puzo's *Godfather*',[20] there still is no way other than the première announcement accurately to describe '*David O. Selznick's* screen version of

MARGARET MITCHELL'S '*GONE WITH THE WIND*'. 'To have treated so long a book with such astonishing fidelity', the *New York Times* reviewer concluded, 'required courage – the courage of a producer's convictions and of his pocketbook and yet, so great a hold has Miss Mitchell on her public, it might have taken more courage still to have changed a line or scene of it.'[21]

'Striving to better, oft we mar what's well.' When Hitchcock wanted to change the shy narrator-heroine of *Rebecca* into a savvier, more 'attractive and amusing' type in the film, Selznick adamantly refused permission on the grounds that, as producer, he did not think that he, personally, could create anything better with the characters and situations than Daphne du Maurier had, and frankly, he did not think Hitchcock could either. Hitchcock forthwith submitted a new treatment following the 'exact line of the novel'. Without question, as Thomas Schatz has observed, *Rebecca* was a project where the 'master of suspense adjusted his own style to the story, rather than adjusting the tale to suit his own interests' – as he subsequently did in films which, as Burchill and others have noted, became more and more perversely misogynistic and sadistic. For that matter, when Hitchcock could write his own ticket the quality of his work fell sharply and he ended his career with a succession of what were decidedly second-rate pictures.[22] Selznick's production of *Rebecca* was, by the way, the only film directed by Hitchcock ever to win the Oscar for best picture.

Selznick's old-fashioned and comparatively humble theory that a faithful film adaptation will succeed with the public in the same way the original succeeded is not without commercial and critical support. Steven Spielberg's faithful adaptation of Alice Walker's *The Color Purple* (USA, 1985) proved far more popular – not only with admirers of the original novel, but with film-goers generally – than Brian De Palma's free 'interpretation of the material' in *The Bonfire of the Vanities*. Discussing screen adaptations ('how to retain the spirit if not the letter of the text')[23] scriptwriter William Goldman echoed Selznick's argument that no director can say for certain what will or will not succeed with the public. When today's egotistical *auteurs* confidently say what the audience wants 'It's all bullshit . . . . *They don't know* . . . . NOBODY KNOWS ANYTHING.'

In effect, Selznick's fidelity 'in spirit and in mood' to works that the public had already taken to its heart has assured that his adaptations of *Gone with the Wind* and *Rebecca* have survived unchallenged as classic cinematic versions of the two most popular novels of their time and, simultaneously, has assured their continuing commercial success as a result of successive reissues in cinemas, on television and on video where people can play them again – and again.[24]

Like Woody Allen watching *Casablanca* in *Play It Again, Sam*, or like Shakespeare's Caliban who, on awakening, 'cried to dream again', many people, when they close a compulsively readable novel such as *Gone with the Wind* (as when an enthralling film ends and the lights go up) feel rudely awakened by the recognition that, after all, it was 'only a book, only a movie', only a dream of passion that had so engaged them imaginatively and emotionally. These readers and film-goers constitute an audience that returns to relive the experience again and again over a lifetime. Thus the narrator's opening line in *Rebecca*, 'Last night I dreamt I went to Manderley again' could also be spoken by anyone seeing Selznick's film or reading Daphne du Maurier's novel again. And, of course, it is, likewise, sad to outgrow the original sense of enchantment, because that means we have outlived our former selves. 'I would not tell my dream.' 'For Manderley was no more'; or 'no more than a dream remembered'. What therefore remains most satisfying about re-experiencing a dearly loved film such as *Gone with the Wind*, or *Casablanca* or *Rebecca*, is that our most cherished images (like Tara) remain intact, still there, unchanged on the screen, as time goes by. There is, moreover, a recapturing of past selves and past times when the film was first seen, or the book was first read. This is exactly the process enacted when the ageing Ashley recalls the way the young Scarlett looked at the barbecue, wearing a 'white dress covered with tiny green flowers' and an 'enormous leghorn hat' (p. 921). And she in turn remembers her past self and her old friends and long-dead relatives, like familiar characters in a fiction; that is, exactly like the characters and scenes and selves that we return to when we see the film or read the book again.

NOTES

1 For detailed discussion of the production and reception of the film see Ronald Haver, *David O. Selznick's Hollywood* (New York: Bon-

anza Books, 1985) 236–301. 'Not one preview card mentioned that they would prefer to see Scarlett and Rhett together again' (p. 293).

2 See Thomas Schatz, *The Genius of the System: Hollywood Filmmaking in the Studio Era* (London: Simon & Schuster, 1989), 168.

3 Margaret Mitchell, *Gone with the Wind* (London: Macmillan, 1936), 1. Subsequent page references are inserted parenthetically in my text.

4 On *Gone with the Wind* as an enrapturing 'read', see Catherine Belsey, *The Metaphysics of Desire* (forthcoming). Unlike most romantic novels whose readers 'hate to put it down', but then enjoy the next one just as much, *Gone with the Wind* is read again and again. The process whereby the spectator or reader is repeatedly carried away by, or transported into, the film or novel and subsequently brings its characters back into his or her own experience is perfectly depicted by Woody Allen in *The Purple Rose of Cairo* (USA, 1985) and 'The Kugelmass Episode', a short story wherein a magician transports a reader into the world of Madame Bovary, where he becomes her lover, and subsequently brings her back with him to New York.

5 *Atlanta Journal* (6 September 1987), 14ff.

6 See Helen Taylor, *Scarlett's Women: Gone with the Wind and its Female Fans* (London: Virago, 1989), 7.

7 *Time* (1 April 1991), 72.

8 Selznick's *New York Times* interview with Crowther is quoted by Roland Flamini in *Scarlett, Rhett and a Cast of Thousands: The Filming of 'Gone With the Wind'* (London: Macmillan, 1978), 199.

9 See the producer's statement in the souvenir programme issued at the première of the film.

10 See Haver, *David O. Selznick's Hollywood*, 305.

11 Gable makes these points in the souvenir programme.

12 Georg Lukács, *The Historical Novel* (London: Merlin, 1969), 148–9.

13 Haver, *David O. Selznick's Hollywood*, 238.

14 Alexandra Ripley, *Scarlett* (London and New York: Macmillan, 1991), 552.

15 *Gone with the Wind* was rejected by RKO because the heroine was such an unsympathetic character and *The Bonfire of the Vanities* was likewise considered too unsympathetic in the treatment of all its most memorable characters to make a popular film. In an interview broadcast on the television programme The South Bank Show (3 February 1991) De Palma and his scriptwriter explained that they therefore changed Wolfe's slimy English journalist into an American narrator the audience could 'feel chummy with'. They also made the central character younger and much less aristocratic and snobbish than he was in the novel because they thought their audience would not 'sympathize' with a character to the manor born, with pride of birth as well as wealth. But Scarlett too was a child of pride. In both cases that is what makes their loss of status and pride (not only wealth) so dramatic. For further discussion see Harriett Hawkins, *Classics and Trash: Traditions and Taboos in 'High' Literature and Popular Modern Genres* (Brighton: Harvester, and Toronto: Toronto University Press, 1990), 167–82.

16 See Pam Cook, 'Missing Persons in the Movies', *Observer* (21 April 1991), 44.
17 *Observer* Magazine (28 April 1991), 28.
18 Julie Burchill, 'In Praise of the Casting Couch', *The Face* (December 1990), 87–9.
19 Julie Burchill, *Girls on Film* (London: Virgin Books, 1986), 174–80.
20 See Friedman's Foreword to David Wheeler's *No, But I Saw the Movie* (New York: Penguin, 1989), p. v.
21 Haver, *David O. Selznick's Hollywood*, 305.
22 Schatz, *The Genius of the System*, 280.
23 *The Independent* (26 April 1991), 19.
24 As a matter of historical interest, back when Selznick made *Gone with the Wind* and *Rebecca* the idea of the autonomous genius-director-as-*auteur* (which seemed avant-garde in the 1960s and 1970s) seemed outmoded. See Fitzgerald's notes to *The Last Tycoon* describing an old-fashioned silent-film director: 'He doesn't see that a director isn't everything in pictures now' as he was in the early days of movie-making when films were shot 'of the cuff'. Back then, 'the director was supposed to have the plot on his cuff'. 'There wasn't any script. Writers were all called gag-men. . . . They stood behind the director and made suggestions, and if he liked it and it fitted with what was on his cuff, he staged it and took his footage' (Harmondsworth: Penguin, 1960), 191.

8

SPIES IN THE HOUSE OF QUALITY

The American reception of *Brideshead Revisited*

Spencer Golub

THE FANTASY OF ENGLISH CULTURE

Oscar Wilde's lecture tour of North America, from 9 January to 13 October 1882, was a pre-electronic prototype for the 'Great Performances'/'Masterpiece Theatre' import. It was, as *The New York Times* television critic John J. O'Connor said of the later series, 'a uniquely American creation, a [cultural] package'.[1] With his advance publicity criss-crossing the country faster than he could, Wilde was, given the limitations of the day, simulcast to the nation – or at least to thirty-one states and the district of Columbia, along with five Canadian provinces. On tour, swathed in a seal- or otter-trimmed aesthete's coat, a shirt with a Lord Byron collar and small patent-leather shoes, the former Oxonian and Anglicized Irishman disparaged the English and railed against 'that calendar of infamy, English history'.[2] Even so, he embodied for shocked and titillated North Americans the romanticized essence of an ephebic culture within a traditional civilization, which they coveted. Wilde represented the best of both worlds for American audiences: a tradition of quality and a history of decline, cohabiting in the form of residual eccentrism. Homosexual aesthete and involuntary wanderer, Wilde ended his days in France under the pseudonym 'Sebastian Melmoth', a forerunner of, although not a named model for, 'Sebastian Flyte', the outsider/insider anti-hero of Evelyn Waugh's novel *Brideshead Revisited.*

'Cultured' Americans (especially those imbued with foreign

culture) still long to feel the mother tongue in their ear, to be seduced in a romance with a country we deem to be our national inferior but cultural superior. On Monday evening, 18 January 1982, at 8 p.m. Eastern Standard Time, the romance was rekindled. On that night *Brideshead Revisited*, an eleven-part dramatization of Evelyn Waugh's 1945 novel, premièred on 250 of America's Public Broadcasting stations, our 'missionary' channels, beaming culture from the Motherland. In *Brideshead* Wilde's standard tour lecture, 'The House Beautiful', a verbal tour of a grand home, was translated into electronic sound and image; but, unlike Wilde's house, Waugh's home housed an Edenic parable of family and class tragedy with climactic redemption achieved through the reclamation of Christian faith. Waugh's nostalgia for manor-house architecture and life, amid the aesthetic and moral confusion of modern history, reawakened a ghost-limb Englishness not only in England but in the world.

The packaging of English culture for an American audience has been so effective that it is routinely used to explain and, on occasion, to stand in for the history it describes and represents. Thus, when in his book *An American Looks at Britain* Richard Critchfield discusses the loss of empire, in order to elucidate contemporary Britain for an American audience, he does so in reference to the making of the 'Masterpiece Theatre' series *The Jewel in the Crown*.[3] Seamlessly, not only English culture but Wilde's maligned English history has become a quality product to be judged according to aesthetic criteria. At the same time, the cultural package fuses to history an enlightened post-historical critique, which exonerates a modern audience and especially a modern American audience from historical guilt. It permits an American audience to indulge its own racist and classist fantasies, along with its liberal conscience, defined in its break-up with the offending empire. We may gorge on the high tea of English culture, served up by television, but it is the English who must pick up the tab in the form of polite and decorous contrition, in which the 'Masterpiece Theatre' form of export plays its part. In *Brideshead* Lord Sebastian Flyte pays for his defilement of Charles Ryder's Oxford quarters on a drunken night with the morning delivery of a veritable riot of flowers, which provide new colour and scent. Politically liberal Americans believe that we have our own historical vomit to cleanse. Fittingly, *Brideshead* was imported to American shores by Exxon, in a gesture of corporate *noblesse oblige.* The sponsor's twice-displayed corporate logo, at the beginning and end of each transmission, was an indication of the decision of the 'patron' to spare the sensitive viewer tasteless and disorientating commercial interruptions. Whatever public good faith Exxon may have stockpiled from its cultural sponsorships, however, spilled out with the oil from the tanker *Valdez* on Alaska's distant shores.

The appellations 'Masterpiece Theatre' and 'Great Performances', under which such productions as *Brideshead* are presented, appeal to the cultural snobbism of Americans, robbed of the birthright of class consciousness. The majority of Americans indulge in television as habit and encounter the theatre infrequently (if at all) as occasion. Still, television remains, culturally speaking, a guilty pleasure, while theatre denotes cultural legitimacy and tradition. While relatively few Americans worry about the state of the American theatre and the lack of government support that theatres receive, they require theatre's imprint to feel culturally cleansed; a 'Masterpiece Television' or 'Great Television Performances' series simply will not suffice.

The fabled 'American public' is perhaps overly fond of clay-footed celebrity and constructs its idols to conform to a design for failure. In this it seems to replay a scenario of status deprivation, which configures America's own sense of lost Eden and empire. Both American intellectuals and 'Middle Americans' (our nation's geographical and mythic core constituency) embrace disempowered royalty, in whom historical eminence persists, and dissolute aristocrats, in whom tawdriness seems to enhance breeding. Finally, cultured Americans embrace the liminality of English geography and class structure, which seem to have foreshortened interior distance and bred in its citizenry a talent for doubleness and deception. We are especially fond of the Cambridge spies, who were turned against their class on the very playing-fields where class was paraded. These modern-day 'University Wits', double operatives against class and country, served also as referents for other outsider groups trapped inside Britain. Guy Burgess and Anthony Blunt were homosexuals, and Kim Philby was (erroneously) believed to be a Catholic, based upon Graham Greene's introduction to Philby's memoirs, *My Silent War*. Cambridge historian and intelligence-expert Christopher Andrew expressed surprise that the upper-crust, homosexual Cambridge 'mole', representative of 'the traditional British caste system and the end of Empire', holds an even greater fascination for audiences abroad than at home.[4]

In discussing Guy Burgess, playwright Alan Bennett wrote that betrayal of one's country is 'irony activated'. Patriotic America, especially during the Reagan (and Thatcher) years when *Brideshead* was broadcast, is and was anti-irony and anti-doubleness. Yet cultured Americans are continually fascinated by the wit and sexual ambiguity that English personae model for us, so long as we can clearly identify the performativeness and the foreignness of the pose. English 'feyness' is accepted by the American public as the cultural tic of an imperial and imperious civilization now decadently frayed at the edges. English rituals and performances of betrayal of class, sex and station satisfy the secret desires of closeted elitist Americans whose nominal freedoms subvert transgression and whose fabled openness condemns 'façadism'. As outsiders ourselves, we are gratified by insider discomfort and are moved by the insider who feels himself to be an outsider. Unsurprisingly, we made a hero of Sebastian Flyte, who, more spied upon than spying, fed his loneliness with alcohol, and yet shared an essential trait with Guy Burgess. Alan Bennett wrote of the latter that 'he wanted a place where he was alone, and . . . having a secret supplies this'.[5]

Brideshead's American viewers openly embraced Sebastian Flyte as they would a character in a Tennessee Williams play, that is, as part of the mythic 'tradition' of 'the tragic homosexual', who struggles to forget his 'malady' by drinking to excess. Sebastian's beauty is simultaneously marred and enhanced by his 'condition', as though he were dragging around Byron's club-foot. The Charles Ryder–Sebastian Flyte relationship was acceptable to largely homophobic American culture on the terms offered in the novel and the film by Lord Marchmain's Italian mistress, Cara, who describes it as 'a kind of love that comes to children before they know its meaning'[6] (p. 102). By the time of *Brideshead*'s transmission, the American film-going public had already grown accustomed to the 'lost boys' innocence in the on-screen male bonding of such macho Hollywood stars as Paul Newman and Robert Redford. The 'buddy movie' (an update of the Huck Finn–Tom Sawyer too-rough-for-women 'romance of the open road' adventure) implicitly suggested that two men together are more powerful and resourceful (and thus more attractive) than a man and a woman. The cinematic expression of this sentiment represented, in part, the American male's unease with the developing women's liberation movement in the 1960s and 1970s. The violence that often accompanied these fables and not infrequently targeted women was dismissed as 'boys being boys', showing off and acting out their aggressions in play form. *Brideshead*'s effete 'buddyism' imploded violence in the form of satire and irony and presented sexuality as a fluid, indivisible union of pleasure and pain, power and powerlessness, which somewhat lessened the responsibilities thought to be inherent in gender roles.

Evelyn Waugh said that he could not imagine 'more than about eight Americans' enjoying his novel *Brideshead Revisited*. To his surprise and feigned consternation, *Brideshead* was extremely popular in America, where it sold nearly three-quarters of a million copies.[7] As a self-made snob, Waugh viewed American popular acceptance as a cheapening of his literary achievement. His own half-hearted efforts at selling *Brideshead* to MGM Studios in Hollywood in 1947 ended when he realized that the film version of the novel would have little to do with spiritual rebirth and would probably be packaged as an English *Gone with the Wind*.[8]

The task of bringing Waugh's gourmet feast, written in a time 'of soy beans and Basic English',[9] to America's gourmand consumer culture finally fell to John Mortimer, who did the television adaptation. Like Waugh, an Oxonian and child of the English middle class, Mortimer had already given American television audiences the populist hero Horace Rumpole (in *Rumpole of the Bailey*), whose solid sense of self-worth and class pride routinely bests the supercilious scorn of the QCs and MPs who rule over him.

Unsurprisingly, from among the *Brideshead* characters, Mortimer particularly liked Rex Mottram, the Canadian businessman and surrogate American, who is engaged to the aristocratic Julia Flyte and disdained by the novel's protagonist, Charles Ryder. Citing a scene in which Ryder subtly abuses Mottram at a Paris restaurant, Mortimer writes:

> Charles feels such vulgar superiority to the ambitious Rex, who is, after all, paying for the meal, and congratulates himself so warmly on knowing that caviar shouldn't be eaten with onion or that brandy should not be taken in large

balloon glasses, that I was tempted to write in a swift hack on the shins from Rex under the table.[10]

Like Ralph Nickleby, Rex Mottram prides himself on knowing the world and on the world knowing him. Polite society, however, condemns him for this bluntness and for attempting to expand his free-enterprise energy into the area of social improvement without sincere regard for the significance of social tradition (as seen in his facile conversion to Catholicism in order to marry Julia). Not being a part of this tradition, *Brideshead*'s American enthusiasts can appreciate Rex for what he has achieved and seeks to achieve in spite of who he is, rather than scoffing at his dogged determination to attain what by reason of class and social circumstance he cannot become. The 'ugly American', says Rex Mottram, '*c'est moi*'. Mottram is preferable to the 'ugly Englishman', the despised academic spy, Mr Samgrass, who plays the patronizing 'Victorian tourist' reviewing the 'foreign things' from inferior cultures, which parade before him for his amusement and approval (p. 110).

Like Rex, whose kingly name is undercut by his common manner, 'the average American viewer' feels both inferior and superior to the house of quality into which he or she has been invited. That corporate America has, in a sense, paid for the feast seems at least as important to him or her as being able to appreciate its quality. Television, the portal through which we enter *Brideshead*, has essentially sat its viewers at the head of the table by privileging the democratic eye over the refined cultural palate. It offers connoisseurship to the rank and file. The serial form allows us 'to live through a literary work' (Mortimer's stated goal in adapting *Brideshead*) with an aristocrat's disregard for economy of time (the production was leisurely paced) and a bourgeois's innate adherence to schedule (the show appeared weekly at a regular viewing-hour).[11]

Aside from minor dialogue transpositions and some telescoping of lines and scenes, Mortimer's adaptation is faithful to Waugh's novel. Mortimer does add several purely cinematic passages, such as the Christmas fox-hunt at Brideshead. The major differences in the televised *Brideshead* are in the translation of literary descriptions into visual imagery, conveying the book's chronological detail instantaneously and simultaneously. The languor of lived-in, durative time is arguably better communicated via slow camera-pans and in Ryder's somnambulant, distanced voice-over narrative than long literary descriptions. The visual shorthand of the actor's characterization distils without dissipating Waugh's sensitivity to characters' vocal tics and behavioural mannerisms. Beyond this, camera placement and movement insinuate the viewer into the continually shifting space between a character's subjective consciousness and the world's (non-) response.

On film, the aforementioned Ryder–Mottram dining-scene is effectively introduced by a sepia-toned image of the diners at table. The photographic quality of this moment anticipates a statement that Rex will make during the ensuing scene. Social-climbing Rex speaks of having 'royalty and the Prime Minister photographed going in' to the church to view his wedding with Julia (p. 177). Later, the memory of Rex's statement and of the 'photographic' image of two social lions dining out in the public eye will serve as an ironic riposte to the 'hole-in-corner' wedding (p. 177), devoid of publicity and of church and family approval, that Rex and Julia endure. Our memory of the sepia-toned photograph at the end of the dining-scene also subconsciously helps us segue, along with Ryder's voice-over line, 'It is time to speak of Julia', into his next memory of 'that high summer of 1923' when Julia was a social lioness in the public eye and 'there seemed time for everything' (p. 179).

The film accomplishes lyrical spatio-temporal transitions of high contrast. Thus sun-drenched Morocco, where Ryder leaves the bed-ridden Sebastian on the morning of his mother's death, fades into Brideshead's green, rolling hills, where Lady Marchmain's funeral procession passes in long shot, as her mortal remains are carried to their final resting-place. Later, a potted visual history of Ryder's Gauguinesque sojourn in the rain forests of Mexico and Latin America yields to the bright lights and dark silhouettes of the New York City skyline, marking Ryder's re-entry into 'civilization'. Here, Ryder suffers through a reunion with his wife Celia (whose world represents the self-conscious 'Art and Fashion' counterpoint to Rex's 'Politics and Money', p. 276), following his two-year absence. The camera studies Ryder's face as he listens without interest to his wife's nervous chatter, measuring the distance that still separates them.

The camera documents the Julia–Ryder relationship some two years hence at a virtually unpopulated Brideshead, which is photographed to resemble a vast, empty stage-set. As the story draws to a close, cars make long, mournful approaches to and departures from Brideshead, and autumnal hues mirror the characters' moods. Time itself seems to lengthen, casting dark shadows, before 'irising in' with the camera to capture the death of romance in what Waugh called 'the shadow, in the corner of the stair', where Ryder and Julia part forever (p. 340). The film, like the novel, then shocks us back into Brideshead's future as temporary military quarters in the desolate wartime 'age of Hooper' (Ryder's subaltern, p. 351), where Ryder takes leave of memory and finally accepts the Catholic faith as his destiny.

The full-page advertisement in *The New York Times* announcing the American première of *Brideshead Revisited* proudly quoted a British critic as saying (the series premièred two years earlier in Britain): 'The settings were superb and so they should be, since they're the genuine thing.'[12] This remark previewed America's fetishizing of the living artefacts of 'Brideshead culture' as monuments of authentic history. The world of Brideshead, the phenomenology of memory rising above the geography of yearning, became for Americans the real England, owing in large part to its 'genuine' settings.

Actually, just the façade of Castle Howard, which impersonated Waugh's fictional ancestral seat, remained after fire destroyed its interior in 1940. At that time, 'the house was doing war service as a school', and it had to be rebuilt. The Brideshead company spent some five months filming in 17 of the house's 130–40 rooms. John Vanbrugh, the designer of the original Castle Howard and later of Blenheim Palace, brought his theatrical flair to the building's central cupola and lantern dome, which rises 70 feet above the great central hall. Evelyn Waugh, who visited Castle Howard only once, was nevertheless greatly impressed by this central feature, as well as by the magnificent fountain which faces its south front.

Castle Howard was built and altered in stages, between 1700 and 1737, and so acquired its present 'rumbustious character' and 'fatal lack of harmony'. Perched majestically above a 10,000-acre estate, it is neither a real castle nor a splendid county seat but rather a dramatic façade before an interior jumble of small rooms arrived at via an 'immaculately straight' 5-mile approach road which in itself constitutes 'great theatre'. 'The view of the house', wrote one contemporary observer, 'unfolds much as it did to Ryder on his return to Brideshead at the start of the serial.'[13]

The mystery and centrality of the Brideshead/Castle Howard image in the serial accounted in part for its celebrity among American viewers. Charles Sturridge, the serial's co-director (along with Michael Lindsay-Hogg) revealed that 'at first the house is meant to seem awesome, then more like a house and finally, as a dominating presence'.[14] The looming, stationary image awaits and absorbs the recurrence of time, fate, memory and visitation. Beginning with his first visit to Brideshead and his instantaneous conversion to the baroque, each new visit reveals to Charles Ryder new rooms in the massive building and, figuratively speaking, new rooms in himself. Finally, Ryder only truly sees Brideshead whole when he stops painting it and begins remembering it. Our own viewing eye seeks to penetrate the building's stolid image, as memory penetrates history to imbue it with (added) radiance. We conspire with our senses to make the building appear satisfyingly impenetrable. This 'sensory address', in which we conspire with the story's narrator/the picture's maker, affects us only through the phenomenological world of objects and things and the 'realm within which these elements have fictional meaning', that is, the artificial and fictional world of performance.[15]

The conflation of the real and the reel, between Castle Howard and Brideshead, is captured in this description of the Castle by a travel journalist in *The New York Times*:

> So little has been altered in the house and on the grounds that as you walk, your ears need to close just a little to the modern sounds and your eyes must only drop below the industrial horizon for you to see Charles and Sebastian playing in the fountain after a drunken spree or cavorting in the entrance hall, as real to you as it was to Waugh.[16]

The experience of the televised *Brideshead* is not unlike this. Its somnambulant narrative flow encourages in the viewer a half-shaded visual and mental perspective rendering fictional characters real by virtue of the real surroundings that they inhabit. The edited reality of *Brideshead*, however, describes the continuity of story, not history. Still, Castle Howard's resemblance to the fictional amalgam Waugh dubbed 'Brideshead' reinforced the American fantasy of England as a storied place of living history, a locus of pronouncedly yet not entirely definable aristocratic and aesthetic tradition and style. The reported fact that real people live at Castle Howard and receive paying guests by the tens of thousands annually underscored for the average American the eccentric continuity of English country life and, in this, of 'Englishness' as a quality that we outsiders can continue to revisit.[17]

RECEPTION

The impact of *Brideshead Revisited* in America was sudden, pervasive and on the level of celebrity. *The New York Times* devoted space in seven separate sections to the 'culture of Brideshead', over an eight-month period, from 14 January 1982 to 30 September 1982. The sections represented included: Fashion/Design; Travel; Arts and Leisure; (Television) Notes on People; Op-Ed; Style; and *The Sunday Book Review*.

The strangest indicator of *Brideshead*'s popularity was the celebrity status accorded to Sebastian's teddy bear 'Aloysius'. *New York Times* readers were treated to a background-piece on the 'real' bear who 'played' Aloysius. The 91-year-old actor-bear was the prized possession of the aptly named English actor Peter Bull, the author of *The Teddy Bear Book*. Bull's bear, we are told, originally hailed from Saco, Maine, where he spent the first seventy-four years of his life in a delicatessen. This background-piece parodied the American romance with 'log cabin to White House' and 'Horatio Alger' success-stories. At an interview session for the *Times* piece, Anthony Andrews, who played Sebastian Flyte, in an act of 'English whimsy', ordered his actor-bear 'friend' a jar of honey for dessert, which the uncomprehending bear left untouched.[18]

Barbara L. Isenberg, an American designer who had earlier made such celebrity merchandise as 'Running Bear' ('made of sweatsuit fabric'), 'William Shakesbear', 'Bjorn Bearg', :'Zsa Zsa Gabear' and 'Bear Mitzvah', received permission from the Waugh estate to create a mass-market 'Aloysius'. Isenberg's 'worn-looking, comfortable' faux-antique Aloysius, with its 'pointed, old-fashioned face' (contemporary teddy bears have rounded faces) and a hand-embroidered nose, demonstrated American industry's talent for manufacturing authenticity by faking age and the American public's capacity to accept such fakery as real experience and genuine tradition.[19]

While *Brideshead*'s characters engaged their passions over precisely selected and designed objects, the American audience engaged their passions for these objects. In most cases, the publicity of acquisition was thought to be the better part of possession. In its 'Catalog for Fans and Friends of Public Television', *Signals*, Public Broadcasting flagship station WGBH (Boston) sells bits and pieces of its manufactured and appropriated empire of taste: these include everything from Sherlock Holmes and *Blackadder* videos to Edward Gorey coffee-mugs (Gorey designed the opening credits sequence for the popular 'Mystery' series) and Russian 'Monopoly' board-games – a possible John le Carré tie-in.[20] Certainly, Rex Mottram would have appreciated the industry applied to the manufacture and home-delivery of pre-screened and selected good taste for a mass-market audience seeking cultural validation. As a 'colonial', he would also be gratified at the culturally disenfranchised making capital out of Englishness and besting quality with their quality control.

Brideshead also satisfied the American audience's 'Broadway' attitude, which wants to see the full extent of a lavish production budget on ostentatious display in performance to justify their own personal expenditure of time and money. The sumptuousness of *Brideshead*, with its official budget of $9.5 million (rumoured to have been closer to $15 million) and with its immoderate devouring of 13 hours of viewing-time, spread over eleven episodes, filled the bill and conflated artistic and production values.[21]

To understand why America was so taken with *Brideshead*, beyond a love of things English, consider that the Reagan presidency was one year old when the series was first transmitted in America. In the same week that *Brideshead* premièred, a major television network aired a week-long retrospective of Reagan's first year in office. In a newspaper advertisement for this series, which was published alongside an article on *Brideshead*, the iconic Ronald Reagan, the movie cowboy who pioneered style over substance as the media president of the monied peoples, smiled out at the constituents whom his charm and charisma had transformed into fans. Reagan disproved Anthony Blanche's belief, expressed in *Brideshead*, that fatal charm is the exclusive possession of the British upper classes. Quite pointedly, the televised Reagan retrospective, which weighed in with episodes devoted to such serious matters as the Economy, Defence, Foreign Policy and Politics, concluded with a segment entitled 'The Reagan Style'.[22]

During Reagan's administration, the ambition to live well was (mis)represented as being every American's inalienable right and amassing capital as a patriotic duty. The Reagan Republicans' 'Let them eat Americana' campaign created a perfect smoke-screen for insider traders, corporate raiders, junk-bond kings, savings-and-loan operators and a legion of urban cowboys. While middle-class America, which largely paid for this acquisition spree, sought in *Brideshead* a fantasy past it had never known, corporate America glimpsed a fantasy future of impenetrable privilege it hoped to achieve. That money and politics could purchase class was embodied by the person whom Public Broadcasting chose to introduce the *Brideshead* series in America – William F. Buckley. An outspoken Conservative Republican editor and columnist, spy-novelist and patrician author of the faux-Oxonian undergraduate memoir, *God and Man at Yale*, Buckley's overwrought vocabulary and plummy tones at once invoked, parodied and even outdid British and Oxbridge upper-crustness. As an American to whose level of taste and sophistication we can all aspire and yet somehow can never hope to achieve, he was the perfect points-man in the battle for the hearts and minds of the American middle class, waged by an upper class that was rapidly seeking to distance itself from them.

As it had during the Great Depression of the 1930s, the American fashion world of the 1980s conspired with Hollywood (and under Reagan, with Washington, DC) to create the illusion that 'everyone was rich'. Although 'fashion was a subject that clearly interested Waugh a good deal less than architecture', American viewers of the *Brideshead* series and their clothiers were greatly interested in what Waugh's characters wore. The details of clothing, like those of architecture, not only brought this foreign world closer to American viewers; they helped the citizens of a nominally classless society define a class reality for themselves. Clothing not only signified to Americans who in the series was wealthy but whom they, the viewers, had to look like in order to be perceived by others as being wealthy. Before long, as one observer of the fashion scene noted, 'the make-believe elegance' of not only *Brideshead* but of the English period-films *Chariots of Fire* (UK, 1981) and *The French Lieutenant's Woman* (UK, 1981) was 'beginning to penetrate the real world both here and abroad'. While celebrated designers of American ready-to-wear Perry Ellis and Ralph Lauren 'featured Fair-Isle sweaters and baggy English tweeds' in their new lines (the first major movie-inspired fashion-trend since Woody Allen's *Annie Hall*, USA, 1977), Blooming-dale's employed *Chariots of Fire* co-star Ben Cross to model its spring menswear fashions, which the film inspired.[23] As with the 'genuine settings' used in the *Brideshead* series, Cross's participation in the advertising campaign lent it an air of authenticity.

Actor Jeremy Irons (Charles Ryder) emerged from the *Brideshead* cast and from the ensuing film-roles to become the exemplar of 'effortless style' for the American public. *Brideshead*'s co-director Michael Lindsay-Hogg is quoted as saying that fashion merely describes what you are wearing and perhaps why you are wearing it (because trend-setters tell you to do so); style is *how* you wear it, your expressed individuality.[24] The problem for the American public was that in cultivating the *Brideshead–Chariots* look', without an inborn or inbred sense of style – that is, in affecting the 'what' and 'why' without the 'how' – it was left only with a fashion which one pundit described as resembling 'a bandwagon parked and ready for everybody to climb aboard'.[25]

'Fashion', wrote Franco Moretti in reference to Leopardi's *Dialogue between Fashion and Death*, 'is *nothing but* time'. A 'man of fashion' must refurbish his wardrobe incessantly, always 'keeping up with the times', while at the same time struggling to divorce timeliness from mortality.[26] Whatever their specific themes, film and the novel are concerned with and reproduce the texture of time. The centrality of this truth to Waugh's novel of paradise lost is reflected in the title of its first book, 'Et in Arcadia Ego,' which translates as 'Even in Paradise there am I'. The first-person voice is that of Death, Time and Fashion's alter-ego.

THE TELEVISED VERSION

The aesthetics of the televised *Brideshead* extended far beyond fashion. The serial negotiated between the viewer's eye and the narrator's voice, which told the eye that it must not be seduced by what it sees, because what it sees is inauthentic. We only seem to enter into space, when in fact we enter time, which edits these spatial images together. What we covet is not the images which we only think we have lost but the time that we have lost and have yet to lose. Before his narration of the story begins, Charles Ryder has come to realize that the beauty of Brideshead and, by extension, the entire material world is 'delusive', and that his own paintings, his life's work, are only a 'mirage'.[27]

The flatness and numbness of Ryder's narrative voice seems to be telling his ear and ours to refrain from enthusiastically embracing or even passively accepting the beauty that the eye sees. While the eye luxuriates in the specificity of detail, his voice remains stubbornly and purposely generic. It is prudent, he implies, to remain uncommitted and unmoved. In this he recalls a character in E. M. Forster's novel *Maurice* (written 1914; published 1971), who remarks that 'the atheist is nearer the Kingdom of Heaven than the hellenist'.[28] Yet, Ryder's suggested conversion to Catholicism at the story's end says that being 'nearer' is not near enough. Prior to this moment and for the duration of the story, Ryder casts us as his fellow spies and artists. He tunes our ears to a higher frequency, screening out reality and rendering faith and authenticity problematical. His vocal neutrality instructs us to distance ourselves from the visual images it evokes and describes. But what should be our attitude toward the narrative voice itself?

We first 'glimpse' Brideshead as an aural image summoned up in conversation. 'It was', says Ryder at its first mention, 'as though someone had switched off the wireless . . .' (p. 15). Like Brigadoon, Brideshead bodies forth in visual memory as a mystical silence, interrupting the endless, unnuanced drone of modern life during wartime. The camera's strategies, overpopulating the (scenic) frame with architectural façades at Oxford and Brideshead, flooding it with light to remove mass and expand space, first in Venice (where Ryder describes himself as 'drowning in honey, stingless', p. 101) and later in Algiers, translate into visual terms the mechanics of literary narrative. In the serial, both sound and image describe not only forms of spectatorship but spectatorial modes of being. We become like spies whose duplicitous identity shifts in relation to the backgrounds with which they merge. In this sense, we resemble the figures in a work by the architectural and landscape painter Charles Ryder, as well as the figure of the artist himself, as created by the author.

The sound that the educated Briton makes denotes class. Ryder is born into the English upper-middle class (like Waugh) and speaks 'proper' Oxonian English. Ultimately, his voice serves as his means of entry (along with Sebastian's sponsorship) into the social whirl at Brideshead and into that world's self-delusion, which its language armours and defends against encroachment by the real, plainly spoken world. In one sense, what we hear in the narrator's voice is the sound of what Ryder describes in the novel as 'the mind sequestered and self-regarding' (p. 79). Ryder's is a 'spectatorial' voice, a recording eye lodged within a voice that conspires with his vision to paint everything of a piece and at a safe middle distance. This distance frames Ryder's painting with quiet good taste and polite charm, qualities that the inveterate truth-teller Anthony Blanche views with a disdain born, however strangely, out of caring and friendship for the artist. *Ryder's Country Seats, Ryder's English Homes, Ryder's Village and Provincial Architecture* and *Ryder's Latin America*, as their generic serial titles suggest, document a numbing history of counterfeit(ed) feelings, of art dissociated from its subjects and from the artist himself as subject. As co-conspirators in the *Brideshead* reconstruction/revisitation project, we help to authenticate Ryder as a real presence, if not as a real artist.

Spying and memory entail the monitoring of vision and hearing, as well as the shaping of perspective, the opening-up of distance between subject and object. But as often they frame the turning of distance back upon itself. The novel's perspective is encoded in the physical action and attitude of turning out of the scenic frame and/or turning back to gaze over one's shoulder to catch a final glimpse of a retreating image as one turns a corner. The camera continually re-frames this action in the television serial. The road to and from Brideshead turns out of the frame as Ryder turns his head to catch its image over his shoulder. A sudden ten-year jump ahead in the narration catches Charles and Julia promenading and sharing shipboard confidences as they turn out of the camera frame. In the serial's final image, the jeep bearing the newly (religiously) converted Ryder travels down the muddy road away from Brideshead, and, splashing water from a mud puddle, turns and passes out of the frame. This repeated turning action negotiates between the two possibilities of perspective in time and space – the image/stimulus that recedes from the figure and the image/stimulus that outruns and overtakes the figure. As the memory of permanence, temporal and spatial continuity, history and architecture, recedes around one corner (in the past), the shadow of permanence, spiritual continuity and the pattern of faith, disappears around another corner up ahead (in the future).[29]

'Sometimes', Julia tells Charles, 'I feel the past and the future pressing so hard on either side that there's no room for the present at all' (p. 279). Artistically speaking, the ground closes in upon the figure and subsumes it, much as certain images and impressions eclipse others and dominate in memory and so become memory. 'Landscape is the only safe subject', states a character in Forster's *Maurice*, '– or perhaps something geometric, rhythmical, inhuman absolutely' (p. 93). For Ryder, the architectural and landscape painter, people are defined by the backgrounds before which they stand. 'Julia', he relates at one point in the novel, 'seemed to reflect the crimson and gold of the walls and [to] lose some of her wanness' (p. 208). Later he will restate this perspective as a firm belief: 'I regarded men as something much less than the buildings they made and inhabited' (p. 226). Waugh believed 'that men take their identity from the physical and spiritual structures they inhabit'[30]. Destruction of architecture puts human as well as cultural identity at risk. Ryder's self is vested in objects and in his framing of them as artist and spy. His 'taxonomy of the past' constitutes 'a gentleman's agreement without the support of transcendental authority'.[31] Yet, as one critic suggests, this 'aesthetic education' leads Ryder to 'a clear understanding of the division between subject and object', of the relationship between the self and the world, from which 'the individual can achieve a proportionate sense of his worth and limits'.[32]

'Science', says Ryder's father, 'annihilates distance' (p. 69); so does television. The world that television brings into focus, like the one that Ryder leaves Brideshead to find, is only conventionally real, a *trompe-l'œil* reality at best. By 'annihilating distance', television does not so much bring the world closer as destroy the reality of distance. In making history come alive, it renders it spectral and inauthentic by destroying its spatio-temporal difference from the present. Our fetishizing of period-style and image fattens us with nostalgia for an unlived-in past. In this regard, Ryder's distancing voice-over narrative, while it cannot properly retrieve the past, historicizes a past that allows us at least to experience the sensation of history.

Television extols 'textural' reality, a perception of the world from which a repentant Waugh retreated when he revised *Brideshead* in 1959, after the colourless, economically straitened days of the 1940s were safely past. *Brideshead Revisited* is television's equivalent of a perfect coffee-table book. Not only does it offer countless variations on good conversation and fine cuisine, it stages quality as *mise en scène*. The series reinforces the truism that memory makes the world into a more beautiful and better place. In these times of reduced and confused economic and aesthetic values, this message may in itself appear to be uplifting. And even if the serial's sensuous approach does not quite match the novelist's super-sensuous (that is, spiritual) intentions, one may realistically question whether Waugh would presently deny us or himself the comforts of a paradise on earth.

NOTES

1 John J. O'Connor, quoted in the 'Masterpiece Theatre' Twentieth Anniversary Show, Public Broadcasting Stations, January 1991.

2 Richard Ellmann, *Oscar Wilde* (New York: Alfred Knopf, 1987), 158.

3 Beginning with *The First Churchills* (originally telecast in the United States, January 1971), 'Masterpiece Theatre' was beamed into American homes from WGBH, Public Broadcasting's flagship station in Boston. See Richard Critchfield, *An American Looks at Britain* (New York: Doubleday 1991), in particular the two chapters, 'Shattered Illusions' and 'To Make A Jewel', which comprise the section of Critchfield's book entitled 'Loss of Empire'.

4 Critchfield, *An American Looks at Britain*, 261.

5 Alan Bennett, Introduction to *An Englishman Abroad*, in *Single Spies: Two Plays about Guy Burgess and Anthony Blunt*; and *Talking Heads: Six Monologues* (New York: Summit Books, 1990), 12.

6 All quotations are from Evelyn Waugh, *Brideshead Revisited. The Sacred and Profane Memories of Captain Charles Ryder* (Boston: Little, Brown, 1945).

7 John Mortimer, 'Adapting Waugh's "Brideshead" – Nostalgia Revisited', *The New York Times* (17 January 1982), II, 27; David Lodge, *Evelyn Waugh* (New York: Columbia University Press, 1971), 29.

8 Robert R. Garnett, *From Grimes to Brideshead. The Early Novels of Evelyn Waugh* (Lewisburg, PA: Bucknell University Press, 1990), 153.

9 Evelyn Waugh, in his preface to the revised edition of *Brideshead Revisited* (London: Chapman and Hall, 1960).

10 Mortimer, 'Adapting Waugh's "Brideshead" – Nostalgia Revisited', 30.

11 ibid., 1.

12 Bill Grundy, *Evening Standard*, quoted in *The New York Times* (18 January 1982), III, 20.

13 D. J. R. Bruckner, 'Rumbustious Glory', *The New York Times Book Review* (6 January 1991), 19; Steven Rattner, 'A Visit to the Real "Brideshead" ', *The New York Times* (24 January 1982), X, 39.

14 Rattner, 'A Visit to the Real "Brideshead" ', 39.

15 Stanton B. Garner, Jr, *The Absent Voice. Narrative Comprehension in*

the Theater (Urbana and Chicago: University of Illinois Press, 1989), 7.

16 Rattner, 'A Visit to the Real "Brideshead" ', 39.

17 ibid.

18 Albin Krebs and Robert McG. Thomas, Jr, 'Teddy Bear Makes It (Notes on People)', *The New York Times* (12 February 1982), 23.

19 Ron Alexander, 'New Bear Fact', *The New York Times* (13 June 1982), 73.

20 My examples are drawn from *Signals. A Catalog for Fans and Friends of Public Television* (St Paul, MN: WGBH Educational Foundation, Spring 1991).

21 John J. O'Connor. 'Why This "Brideshead" Is Memorable', *The New York Times* (31 January 1982), II, 33.

22 The print advertisement for the television series on Reagan's presidency was placed in the centre of an article by John J. O'Connor entitled 'TV: First Part of "Brideshead Revisited" ', *The New York Times* (18 January 1982), III, 17.

23 Marilyn Bethany, 'When the Mood Strikes', *The New York Times* magazine (4 April 1982), 92–6.

24 Ruth La Ferla, 'Effortless Style', in 'Men's Fashions of the Times', *The New York Times* magazine, II, (17 March 1991), 47–50, 72.

25 Bethany, 'When the Mood Strikes', 90.

26 Franco Moretti, 'Homo palpitans. Balzac's Novels and Urban Personality', in *Signs Taken for Wonders. Essays in the Sociology of Literary Forms* (London and New York: Verso, 1988), 114.

27 Jeffrey Heath, *The Picturesque Prison. Evelyn Waugh and His Writing* (Kingston and Montreal: McGill Queen's University Press, 1982), 167 and 170.

28 E. M. Forster, *Maurice* (New York: W. W. Norton, 1987), 186.

29 A. A. DeVitis, *Roman Holiday. The Catholic Novels of Evelyn Waugh* (London: Vision, 1958), 51.

30 Forster, *Maurice*, 93; George McCartney, *Confused Roaring. Evelyn Waugh and the Modernist Tradition* (Bloomington and Indianapolis: Indiana University Press, 1987), 73.

31 McCartney, *Confused Roaring*, 96–7.

32 ibid., 171.

9

FROM WALKER TO SPIELBERG

Transformations of *The Color Purple*

Joan Digby

The idea of filming Alice Walker's 1983 Pulitzer Prize winning novel, *The Color Purple*, first occurred to Quincy Jones, who enlisted Steven Spielberg to co-produce it for Warner Brothers. When the project was presented to him, Spielberg had some reservations, according to David Breskin,[1] about making a film that was clearly not 'populist' and that would push him 'over a high voltage line into a kind of film he couldn't handle'; but after reading the novel and meeting just once with Alice Walker he felt compelled to co-produce and direct it. The intensity of both experiences had a transforming effect on him that would carry over into his direction. Stylistically identified with special effects, he would use none of them in this film. Nor would he work from his characteristically detailed storyboards. Instead, he pruned down to a blueprint, blocked for stage (rather than film) and pushed his actors to experience their characters dramatically emerging from a script that was rationed out daily. Indeed, as *The Color Purple* evolved, almost organically, into a Steven Spielberg film, transformation – the process of becoming – became the film's controlling idea.

THE NOVEL

Transformation was an idea central to Alice Walker. At the end of the novel, signed 'A. W., author and medium', she thanked 'everybody in this book for coming'; and in a descriptive essay, 'Writing *The Color Purple*', she commented at length on the early visitations paid to her by her characters as they were 'trying to form', then the later ones in which 'Celie and Shug and Albert were getting to know each other'.[2]

Clearly, she thought of these three characters as the emotional centre of her novel, although they are enmeshed in complex, multiple subplots. The total pattern of the novel is important to understand as the background of filmscript alterations that abandoned, simplified and subordinated subplots as well as altering the ultimate relationship of Celie, Shug and Albert.

Celie is the book's heroine. At the opening she is 14, terrified and confused by her Pa's sexual use of her as a replacement for her sick mother. 'You better not never tell nobody but God. It'll kill your mammy,' he threatens. And so she writes letters to God to relieve the agony of rape, childbirth and her mother's death, which follows despite her silence. Written as she would have spoken, the letters tell her life-story with an ingenuous simplicity that the reader responds to as the poetic voice of betrayed innocence. Pa sells the two children she has by him, then passes her off, 'spoiled' as she is, to a widower she only knows as Mr ___ who has actually come to court her pretty sister, Nettie. Mr ___ and his vicious children continue to enslave and abuse her. Having run away from Pa's threatening advances, Nettie comes to Celie for protection. She intends to become a teacher and tries to teach Celie a way out of her lamentable marriage, but she does not get too far because Mr ___ turns her out of the house when she refuses his sexual overtures. Their parting establishes Nettie as the author of a second set of letters:

> I say, Write.
> She say, Nothing but death can keep me from it.
> She never write.

Half-way through the novel it becomes clear that Nettie has been replying for nearly thirty years, but Mr ___ has hidden Nettie's mail from Celie. These letters are written in schooled English, by contrast with Celie's dialect, and contain several of the book's important subplots. They tell how she came to live with Corinne and Samuel, missionaries who took her to Africa to work among the Olinka. By coincidence, Corinne and Samuel are the childless couple who bought Celie's two children, and so Aunt Nettie, their protector, also becomes the biographer of Olivia and Adam. She recounts their growing-up and how Adam falls in love with and marries Olivia's African friend, Tashi. Her expository comparison of African with African–American lives contains many digressions into theories of education, traditional rites of passage, and the destruction of African tribal life by colonial greed. Nettie's work in Africa comes to an end when the Olinka village is sacrificed to build a commercial road. By then Corinne has died in an epidemic, but not before revealing that she has been jealous of Nettie, believing her to be Samuel's mistress and the mother of Adam and Olivia. This provokes Samuel to unravel his own guilt-ridden history (eliminated from the film), which coincidentally proves that Nettie's real father was lynched and the man the sisters called 'Pa' was actually their stepfather. In the light of this truth – which would absolve Celie from the most profound curse of incest if she only knew about it – Nettie marries Samuel, who is the model of a loving husband. The children, having learned of their true mother, are anxious to go to America.

What brings these two halves of the novel together is the character of Shug Avery. She is the jazz singer who has been Mr ____'s passion for years. As Phillipa Kafka has recently pointed out, she is the Fairy Godmother and Prince Charming fused into a single transforming catalyst who turns Cinderella/Celie's ashes into gold.[3] The physical contrast between the two women is summarized by Shug's unforgettable greeting: 'You sure *is* ugly.' Celie, who shares this self-image which has taunted her from childhood, has already fallen in love with Shug's beauty from a photograph. When Mr ____ (called 'Albert' by Shug) brings his ailing mistress home, Celie cares for her. In the process she grows to love Shug's sensuous femininity in a way that opens her to sexual exploration and self-discovery. The women become intimate, not only as lovers, but also as conspirators in protecting Celie from Mr ____'s beating and bringing to light the hidden letters that give Celie the power to become her beautiful self.

Shug invests Celie with power. She teaches her figuratively how to wear the pants and literally how to make them. Sewing pants with Shug as they read Nettie's letters, Celie gains control of her rage and begins on the road to her economic freedom.

In their developing female friendship, Shug acts the role of the confidante, a stock character of the epistolary novel who links the traditional marriage-plot to the etiquette-book tradition. From the confidante the wife traditionally learns the conduct of marriage and management of the household. In this role, Shug teaches Celie by 'didactic example', a method Tamar Katz traces back to the eighteenth-century epistolary novels of Samuel Richardson which teach the rewards of virtue.[4] By contrast, Walker's confidante teaches the rewards of feminine strength and the cultural bonding that makes women powerful allies in subverting male control. Shug's examples validate Walker's 'Womanist' philosophy and coax Celie to find her voice. She teaches Celie that washing her body feels like praying, that blues is 'something you help scratch out my head', and that sewing is a form of thought. Shug's particular examples of women's work demonstrate, as Mae G. Henderson has shown in a very fine essay, how Walker appropriated the epistolary novel invented by European men to educate women and grafted it to an oral, Afro-American folk expression of women who were otherwise denied voice.[5]

Walker's favorite icon of folk expression is the quilt, with its repeat-pattern symmetries and patchwork of old fabric that makes something for the future out of scraps of the past. To use this metaphor, the subplots told in Celie's letters are a patchwork of love and marriage in Mr ——'s extended family. Like quilting, these plots carry the didactic messages 'Work together' and 'Learn from each other'.

As Sofia puts it, 'Everybody learn something in life.' She is Celie's daughter-in-law, married to Harpo, who is a wife-beater like his father. But Sofia is Celie's opposite and fights back at Harpo, teaching Celie in the process not to side with the abuser. After a fist-fight with the white mayor in defence of her right not to become his wife's maid, she is beaten, jailed and separated from her children, although her tribulations never save her from becoming the maid. Since Sofia's story makes a critical connection between gender and racial dignity, all but her relationship with the white child she raises is developed as the most important subplot in the film. Despite her affliction, she is a comic character, and with Shug she is a model of a woman who can hold her own. Sofia's marriage is much tempered by her suffering, and in the end Harpo becomes a doting husband who bows to her authority.

This marriage, like Celie's, is a triangle that includes a jazz-singer mistress. Henderson has pointed out that Walker's vision of marriage conduct 'not only redefines male and female roles', but suggests a new paradigm, 'the eternal triangle in which women complement rather than compete with each other'.[6] The third in this triangle, the singer, Squeak, appears after Sofia leaves Harpo and he turns their house into a juke-joint. In one of the novel's several comic scenes, Harpo's wife and mistress have a bar-room brawl. But their rivalry ends when Sofia is jailed and needs help.

Squeak, in a scene cut from the film, submits to rape by her white uncle, the jail warden, in order to secure Sofia's freedom. Shug becomes involved in this subplot by teaching Squeak how to use her singing voice and grow into her real name, Mary Agnes. The film preserves Squeak's role as Shug's double but eliminates the elaborate plot in which she becomes paired with Shug's husband Grady, goes to Panama to farm reefer and eventually leaves him to raise her children. Generally, the film simplifies sexual involvements and reduces triangles back to conventional pairs.

THE FILM

The film's most extensive subplot revision concerns Shug's marriages and reunion with Celie and Mr ____. Her life in the novel has been coloured by unsatisfactory relationships with her parents and farmed-out children, who disapprove of her, and two husbands who fail to satisfy her. The film only mentions her children, develops the character of a minister-father to account for disapproval, and gives her only one marriage. After Grady, in the novel, she marries a teenage flute-player, Germaine, which hurts Celie and Mr ____ so profoundly that it brings them to emotional understanding for the first time. Shug returns from her failed marriage to find that Celie has inherited her real father's property and has turned it into the Folkspants factory where Mr ____ helps her sew. In an ending very different from the film adaptation, Shug and Albert become Celie's plural other half – 'my peoples'. This is how she introduces them to Nettie, Samuel and 'our children' when they at last come home from Africa.

The complexity of the female kinship bonding that ties all these threads together is represented in the book by a quilt called 'Sister's Choice', which in the film Quincy Jones converted into a song, 'Miss Celie's Blues', also called 'Sister', with lyrics by Lionel Richie keyed to the film's imagery and sentiment. Darryl Pinckney said of Spielberg's film (though not intended as a compliment) that he used the novel as a libretto.[7] This is certainly one valid method of adaptation and quite true. Given the dense plotting of Walker's barely 250-page novel, Jones's thematic *leitmotifs* did much to assist the director and screenwriter in constructing a libretto that transmitted the characters' emotional convictions while telescoping narrative and softening Walker's approach to sex and religion in order to produce a mass-audience Hollywood film.

In fact, the film grossed over $94 million on its first run, which boosted paperback sales. It was so popular that Warner Brothers gave it a full re-release in 1986 and with unprecedented rapidity brought it out as a home video. Alice Walker's sister Ruth dedicated a Color Purple Scholarship Fund (which she now runs) when the film had a ceremonial première at the once-segregated Rex Theatre in their home town, Eatonton, Georgia. The author's concern, expressed to Susan Dworkin, was that a film made by whites might 'embarrass us'.[8] In her own mind this fear was put to rest by the film Spielberg made with her involvement and approval.

The script

Originally it was hoped that Alice Walker would write the screenplay. But after an unsuccessful attempt, Dutch-born screenwriter Menno Meyjes took over. However, Walker stayed close to the project, assisting in the revisions of dialogue necessitated by Spielberg's direction of the piece as evolving drama. What Walker instinctively liked about Spielberg's style, as she told Dworkin – his ability to 'think with his heart' – made him a compatible interpreter of the novel, particularly as Meyjes adapted it, focused on and controlled by Celie's intuitive point of view.

Voice presents a special problem in filming an epistolary novel since sustained voice-over to indicate writing or reading letters would easily wear on the viewer. Nettie's letters, moreover, are too dangerously close to polemic for drama. The solution was to reshape them dramatically to show the impact they made on Celie (Desreta Jackson / Whoopi Goldberg). Meyjes cut out most of the digressive African subplots and Spielberg converted Nettie's descriptions of Africa into tableaux that intersect Celie's landscape physically as she reads: an elephant appears over the railing of her porch; her footpath becomes the African road under construction; and the bulldozer that razes the Olinka mission seems to crash through the church where Celie sits reading in the pew. At one critical point, the African scarification ritual flashes across her mind as a subliminal justification for slitting the throat of Mr ____ (Danny Glover). This internalizing of language is an idea prepared for by two earlier scenes, original to the film, which are faithful to Walker's theme of didactic instruction by example. In one, Nettie (Akosua Busia) teaches Celie to read by pinning words to objects and acting out their meaning. In the other, Celie is shown reading *Oliver Twist*, a story presented as an implied parallel to her own. This is different from the novel in which both sisters go to school and read until Pa (Leonard Jackson) tries to hide Celie's pregnancy by preventing her going. 'The effect of language on the imagination', as Bernard Dick points out, is 'one of the novel's main points.'[9] The film concentrates more on the power of language to shape life.

Celie's exterior life is shaped by the words 'spoiled' and 'ugly'. They make Desreta Jackson speak in the quiver of an abducted child. They motivate the flat timbre of toneless expression that Whoopi Goldberg uses in her public voice to suggest the retreat of a subjugated woman. This is reinforced by the body-language of cowering and covering her mouth, which Shug (Margaret Avery) coaxes her to overcome. Shug's emancipating language is 'Miss Celie's Blues', a gift of self-expression that enables Celie to put on a red dress, look at herself in the mirror, have a lover and smile. Although the film eliminated all but gestural references to lesbian sexuality, it preserved, through dialogue taken directly from the novel, the sense that Shug's love undid Celie's spoiling. It brought her from virginity to womanly sexuality, uplifting her from the infantile toilet-language and experience of Mr ____ doing 'his business'.

In the love-scene with Shug Celie tests the consequences of saying what she feels. The film builds to an ultimate test, saying what she feels about Mr ____ directly to him. The viewer knows her feelings all along through the mischievous lilting tone that Whoopi Goldberg uses to convey the private and often subversive language of Celie's inner thoughts. The literary folk-idiom that Walker created for Celie's voice in the novel is full of aphorisms that reveal an energetic wit repressed by abuse. For as long as she accepts abuse, her sententious perceptions are presented as voice-over, as in the scene in which she spits in her father-in-law's (Adolph Caesar) water-glass and promises to give him Shug's urine next time. When she takes control of her life she delivers her one-liners out loud. This comes to a climax when she erupts into a dramatic monologue, announcing her intention to leave with Shug and Grady (Bennet Evillory). Meyjes invented Easter dinner as a symbolic family-gathering at which all the principal characters might witness the awesome power of Celie's spoken truth. In the novel the confrontation is more private and Celie herself is overwhelmed by the transformational magic of her words: 'Look like when I open my mouth the air rush in and shape words.' Meyjes's film monologue is faithful to key lines of Walker's text:

> Any more letters from Nettie come? . . . I curse you . . . Until you do right by me, everything you touch will crumble. . . . Anything you do to me, already done to you . . . I'm pore, I'm black, I may be ugly . . . But I'm here

adding, 'Just trying to be loved'.

This is probably the decisive moment that prevented the screenwriter from allowing Celie to be reconciled with Mr —— in the film as she is in the novel. His abuse of her is so painfully detailed and her wrenching-free so verbally and visually triumphant in this scene, that the film had not sufficient time to create the illusion of regeneration complete enough to bring her back. Instead, Meyjes focused the idea of reconciliation on other characters already transformed by their suffering. Rather than using the novel's plotting in which Sofia becomes Celie's shop-attendant, Sofia (Oprah Winfrey) and Harpo (Willard Pugh) are shown reunited and sharing the juke-joint business. For Shug, Meyjes invents the minister-father (John Patton, Jr) who finally throws his arms around her and accepts her appeal to understand that 'sinners have soul too'. Throughout the film the preacher is seen driving his horse past her and shutting doors against her, but when, like the Pied Piper, she leads her audience out of the juke-joint and into the church he confers an embrace of implied absolution. Since music is the essential language through which Shug speaks, the scene gave Quincy Jones an opportunity to illustrate a father–child relationship between gospel and blues and jazz. In the context of the film's ending the scene defuses Shug's restless quest for love and releases her from the spell of her own sexual self-image. In Shug's final appearance in the film she seems almost matronly, standing alone and overseeing the reunion of Celie and Nettie.

In the novel Walker makes Shug the active agent in locating Nettie after it is thought that her boat went down at sea. The filmscript's alteration satisfied Spielberg's desire to see a moral change in Mr ——. After Celie leaves, he becomes dissolute and the house falls to ruin. Whereas in the novel Harpo intervenes to save him, Meyjes portrays him saving himself. He casts out his own father as a punishment for his false instruction in marriage conduct. Then, in a redemptive mimetic sequence underscored by the gospel music of the church-scene, he is shown going to the Immigration office and arranging Nettie's homecoming which he can only witness at a distance from the field. Mr —— never speaks again in the film. In a long shot he is seen as a figure emotionally isolated, yet satisfied, straining to hear but utterly powerless to say a word. The film cuts from a diminutive Mr ——, dwarfed by an expansive panorama, to a close-up of Shug, the implied viewer of Mr ——'s moral act. Then he turns and leaves as Celie, in a scene that best illustrates Spielberg's theatrical blocking, runs through the whole cast gathered on her lawn to Nettie and the children standing in a field of purple cosmos. The film comes full circle to its metaphoric opening, with the sisters clapping hands among symbolic flowers in affirmation of the bond that ties them together and to the permanent joy of nature from which the book takes its title.

Visual imagery

In the novel, Shug's arresting observation 'I think it pisses God off if you walk by the color purple in a field somewhere and don't notice it' is part of a long philosophical argument on the nature of God that leads to an embracing (and, some critics believe, embarrassing) pantheism. The argument is replaced in the film by the visual symbol of the purple flowers. All the prominent symbols in the film show Spielberg to think not only with his heart but also with his eye. His imagery evolves directly from symbols in the novel: hands, eyes, colours, animals, road and house. Many are among Spielberg's own personal repertory, and his use of them sometimes alludes to his other films, particularly through the photographic direction of Allen Daviau, who also worked with him on *E. T.: The Extra-Terrestrial* (USA, 1982).

This is perhaps clearest in the gestural use of hands. As girls, Celie and Nettie use their hands in expressions of love. They clap, caress and clasp each other for protection against the brutal hands of Pa, shown snatching Celie's baby. Another brutal hand, that of Mr ——'s son Harpo, flings a rock at Celie when she arrives, and the close-up of her bloody handprint prefigures the beatings she will get for not being Shug. When Mr —— later tears Celie from Nettie, in a wrenching scene shot as a single long take to make the cast experience the horror of separation, they clutch at the porch rails and Celie is dragged along by her hand through the dust. After Mr ____ drives Nettie off with clenched fist, Celie recoils into herself, using her hands as a mask to hide her face until the love-scene with Shug when Celie's hand is shown gingerly responding. Through Shug she learns to touch again. Through Sofia she learns that women cannot win when they fight with masculine instruments. Twice Celie comes close to murdering Mr ____ with his razor. At the dinner-table speech when Celie pulls a knife on Mr ____ Sofia literally 'forces her hand' to language. This culminates in the curse, delivered with a conjuring gesture reminiscent of E. T., full of magical power that makes her untouchable by evil.

E. T. is referred to again in circle imagery, as Mona Gable noticed,[10] when Sofia is surrounded in the beating scene. Later the Mayor's wife becomes hysterical when she assumes she is being surrounded in a parallel sequence. What breaks the circle of entrapment is the nurturing family circle. Sophia is allowed to enter this space, shot from a high camera-angle, only briefly at the Christmas homecoming from which she is torn. The seasonal circle, which symbolizes the times of year when Nettie writes, is complete when Celie makes her departure speech around the Easter table, invalidating the extended family governed by Mr ____.

As Shug says in the novel, 'You have to git man off your eyeball, before you can see anything a'tall.' The eyes are intimate circles of truth. Spielberg's lighting emphasizes the emotional significance of eye-contact, from the flashing whites of Pa's evil eyes to Celie's innocent eyes, riveted to Shug's beauty. The romantic convention of beauty in the eye of the beholder is what dispels the myth of Celie's ugliness and allows her to look into the mirror. While the film received much criticism for its omission of the book's explicit scene in which Shug teaches Celie to observe the beauty of her sexual anatomy by looking in a mirror, the mirror remains a prevalent symbol of self in the film. It is the opposite of looking through a window, which is used many times figuratively, along with glasses of water and of lemonade, to convey the essence of Celie as a transparent female vessel who nevertheless has the power to see through deceptions to truth.

Here, as in Spielberg's other films, ideas of transparency and reflection are conveyed by the poetic handling of light. Since the colour purple stands for wholeness, its division into red and blue has the power to suggest component moods in a divided life. An aura of pink light suffuses the scenes associated with female strength and love. It has particular associations with Shug from the moment her photograph and then her fluttering pink letter arouse in Celie the idea of romance. Pink is Shug's colour in the novel too since she is 'the rose'. In her love-scene with Celie the warmth of pink light is transferred to Celie's face and informs her presence in all her moments of strength. When she reads Nettie's letters the film cuts to an intense African sun that bathes the savannah in pink light. In the absence of Nettie's letters – in the absence of Nettie or of love – blue light prevails. This begins with Pa snatching the baby after the birth-scene and carries through in all ominous contexts: Shug's arrival in a twister, the darkened blue sky rolling above the crooked mailbox; African road-builders chanting in monotone, covered in blue-grey mud; every room or circumstance in which a character feels 'blue'. Spielberg's characteristic lighting style (that is, slightly diffused and heavily backlit) conveys a dream-like quality to life filtered through moods. Celie's reunion with Nettie is shot in a clear, white daylight of recognition, emphasized by the luminous purple cosmos that resolves the red/blue division. Nettie and the children, with African robes billowing in the wind, repeat the colour theme of red and blue unified in purple.

In fact, the film's colour-consciousness comes from Celie's perceptions in the novel. She is always sensitive to colour and especially when she designs her trousers she describes in detail their patterns of colour, which are almost always red, blue and purple. Yellow also is significant; she embroiders yellow stars on Olivia's diapers and later uses yellow scraps from Shug's old dress in quilting 'Sister's Choice'. At the end of the book, yellow, red and purple are the colours she uses to decorate her own room. The film translates this association of yellow with hope into yellow sunflowers, Grady's get-away car and Shug's dress worn in the father-reunion scene. In Aggie Guerard Rogers's costumes and Virginia Randolph's set designs, the symbolic use of colour is so detailed that down to the stripes on men's ties, and the flowers on the wallpaper the red/blue division of purple is felt as a constant theme. Though she innocently wears pink and red as a girl, Celie under Mr ——'s rule is typically dressed in blue, with only a red apron or bandana. Her shift into Shug's red dress signals an emotional coming-out that is later modulated into a pink nightgown. This happens in the scene of Shug's homecoming when she marries Grady and announces that 'We both married ladies now'.

Significantly Shug is wearing Celie's blue. Throughout the film the two women are referenced by their costume colours. And very near the end of the film, as the truth becomes clear to them, each one shows her clarity by being dressed in black and white – Celie overlooking Shug's reconciliation with her father, Shug overlooking Celie's family reunion.

Across the field from where Shug stands is Mr ——, leaning on his horse. This resolves another symbol-pattern broadly adapted from the novel to the film, the use of animals to signify gender power. Mr —— comes for Celie on a horse and towers over her as she walks her cow behind. Shug also is represented as bovine when her opening performance at Harpo's juke-joint is advertised on a sign carried by a cow. The cow is used as passive women are by men, who are studs until, this final scene suggests, they are put out to pasture. Thus Mr ——, who first approached Celie sexually in a room hung with harnesses and threatened Nettie by chasing her on horseback is last seen leading his animal away.

Coming and going through the journey of life is conveyed by the pervasive image of the winding 'lonesome' road, frequently elongated by extreme wide-angle lenses. The road has symbolic meaning for all the principal women who are led along and driven over. It also stands for time as the mailman comes and goes but Celie gets no letters. In Africa Nettie finds the ultimate source of all this grief in the colonial road that crushes a people.

The building of the African road is what brings Nettie home. All the women are shown walking symbolic roads home that finally converge on Celie's house which is a metaphorical projection of her completely transformed self. The conceptual meaning of houses in a film shot as a fable is perhaps the best refutation of critics who complained that the proportions and decor of the house settings lacked realism. The houses were, in fact, based on pictures of Alice Walker's grandparents' houses, and the critics' desire to see shacks instead revealed to Spielberg, as he expressed it in an interview, 'their own inclination for racial stereotyping'.[11]

Throughout the film Celie is ruled by men who sit in judgement on tribunal porches. Spielberg represents the porch as a stage of execution, in the parting of the two sisters and the razor-scenes. Often he uses a low camera-angle to emphasize the men as looming or views them through a subjective eye looking out of the window from within. That is how Nettie and Celie first view Mr —— and how Celie and Shug know that Mr —— will not interrupt their reading of Nettie's letters. Exterior space is masculine, interior feminine. Spielberg's gift for representing tight spots of entrapment and secret spaces of privacy is used in this film to convey the gender war. By taking letters from the mailbox and hiding them in the floorboards Mr ___ perpetuates the frightening rhythm of Celie's life: violation, followed by loss. In a single gesture of the shorthand used in *Raiders of the Lost Ark* (USA, 1981) to suggest alien space, film editor Michael Kahn, who also worked on *Raiders*, makes a spider pop up out of a floorboard, frightening the audience as it does Celie with the ominous nature of the house. Lenses that elongate and deepen rooms, as in the upstairs hall, make interior space – which should be natural to her – overwhelming to Celie. This happens less as Celie grows powerful. In sequence she is shown first to clean and order Mr ___'s house, then locate its secret spaces where the letters are hidden and finally take control of the dinner-table. In her own house at the end of the film she is shown, significantly, stepping out of the light interior to preside over the porch. For an instant she stands with Shug and Squeak, registering Nettie's approach with a pose of transfixed awe reminiscent of *Close Encounters of the Third Kind* (USA, 1977).

This mood would seem completely at odds with slapstick, and indeed many critics of the film were bothered by the tone of crude comedy in two particular segments: Mr ___ bumbling about the house, cooking and dressing up for Shug; and Harpo falling through his roof and explaining the beating he took from Sofia. Both scenes undercut male power in the house and show men under the spell of women. The last is told as a shaggy-dog story and the other delivered with the broad gestures of incremental repetition, that belong to folk-play and are faithful to the novel. Walker's 'Womanist' theory represents laughter as the natural counterbalance of tears. In the film this translates into a tragicomic tone which is most acutely felt in Sofia's disturbing, cosmic laugh.

Actors and personnel

Oprah Winfrey got the part of Sofia after Quincy Jones saw her on Chicago television where she hosted a talk-show. His conception of the film was that it should, as quoted by Susan Dworkin, provide 'top visibility of black experience', so it is easy to understand why he was attracted to a media personality whose hallmark was empathy. Winfrey, who studied speech and drama but had never acted in films before, might have approached the role through her personal history of childhood sexual abuse, but she chose rather to generalize it, as she explained to Joan Barthel,[12] through the black female legacy inherited from Fannie Lou Hamer and Sojourner Truth. The effect is of a character elevated to the role of allegorical chorus.

Whoopi Goldberg first wrote to Alice Walker asking to play Sofia. In the nightclub routine that gained her a reputation as a comedian, she specialized in the morality-play tragicomedy of women's lives. But Spielberg, after seeing her perform, wanted her for Celie. The flexibility of her body-language and facial gestures enabled her to assume every archetypal mask of black portraiture; she had, moreover, universalized the black experience of suffering, identifying with the holocaust both in her monologue on Fontaine, the Junkie, at the house of Anne Frank and in her adopted name. For Spielberg, who had related the novel to his experience of growing up as an isolated Jew in Arizona, she was the perfect actress to carry what she took to be Walker's message about the spirit of survival. Like Spielberg, she has a special gift for identifying with human trials through the point of view of childhood wonder. Since many of her own stand-up characters are children, she effected an easy transition from Desreta Jackson's portrayal of young Celie to what Jill Kearney described as 'a child's-eye view from a child in a grown-up's body'.[13] In her comic routine, moreover, she had acted white personae as in Surfer Chick, the Valley Girl. Thus she was sympathetic to Spielberg's desire to go beyond a black movie into a universal story, making her the perfect character-actress for a film complimented by Armond White as the 'first true racial crossover movie'.[14]

Goldberg's archetypal sense of character also made her perfectly compatible with a director called by Mona Gable 'The Aesop of White Suburbia'. The epithet was levelled with implied contempt that became characteristic of the split between audience and critic response. *The Color Purple* was called an 'infantile abomination' (John Simon), 'Disney Rape film' (David Ansen) 'Cinderella fairy tale', 'greeting card' and 'self-help book' (Gerald Early), in abusive name-calling that showed not only many critics' hatred of Spielberg but also their loathing of the Hollywood sentimentality that Spielberg defends: 'In my work everything is melodrama', he said, 'it's heightened drama, taking things to histrionic extremes.'[15] Though some critics like Armond White understood how

Spielberg's melodrama leads him to the 'mythic, general terms' of 'lucid fable', much more was written to deny that *The Color Purple* had anything to do with folk-culture. Yet the truth is that Spielberg and Walker are both fabulists in the mainstream of the American tradition, which is to convert ominous folk-tale to escapist fairy-tale hinging on wonder, love and the happy ending. Their perspective both uses and transforms folk-culture.

Keith Byerman, who has shown how Celie in the novel is a composite of Snow White, Cinderella and Sleeping Beauty, grafted to Brer Rabbit and African tradition, concludes significantly that 'to live "happily ever after" ', as the folk characters do in *The Color Purple*, is, ironically, to live outside the folk world.[16] Thus Celie in the novel is economically liberated from the pastoral world and becomes an entrepreneur whose house is designed by an Atlanta architect. In place of this detail, the film uses titles to identify its time-frame, 1909–47, and simply shows close-up portraits of women who have over these years become middle class. This is most apparent in the last head-shot of Shug.

Margaret Avery was Spielberg's own choice for this role. Tina Turner was Whoopi Goldberg's idea, but the singer turned it down because the theme of marital abuse was too close to her own experience. Gerald Early, in a scathing denouncement of the film,[17] objected that Avery's Shug (including her singing voice, over-dubbed by Tata Vega) is neither raw enough nor faithful to early jazz. It is, however, sweet and subtle, like the costume and make-up transformations that allow her to modulate among the several female roles for which she is a model: lover–sister–teacher–confidante. Michael Seitz called her 'too Wellesley [College] looking'[18] but that is precisely the message of Spielberg's fable: she signifies the upward mobility of black rural generations.

This same mobility is what critics seem to have against the music of Quincy Jones, which was called 'ubiquitous', 'obtrusive', 'inauthentic' and 'saccharine' by critics as obsessed with his commercial success as they are with Spielberg's. Jones's programme score includes the work of a tremendous number of prominent black musicians. Only Lynn Norment called the film 'enriched with Jones' African, gospel, blues and jazz musical compositions'.[19] As a musician who has crossed over into composing for film and television, he appears to have aroused tremendous jealousy in the industry. Originally, Walker agreed to the film because Jones represented for her a black artist who had become rich and famous and still had a strong social conscience. His music for the film illustrates the mainstreaming of grass-roots music into middle-class media sound, which parallels the transformation of the film characters. His 1991 Grammy award for the 'Back on the Block' LP is a belated acknowledgement of his contribution to American music. Like Spielberg and Goldberg, Jones was nominated but failed to get an Oscar for *The Color Purple*.

The film was, in fact, nominated in eleven Academy Award categories but received none. Its exclusion by the Academy was interpreted as a personal slight to Spielberg by the Director's Guild of America, who gave him their award. Whoopi Goldberg won a Golden Globe and the film did win the National Board of Review of Motion Pictures Best Film Award for 1985, but amidst political antagonism. At the same time that reviewers for the popular black magazines *Jet* and *Ebony* and the *New York Amsterdam News* reviewed it as generally free of racism, the opening was boycotted by the National Association for the Advancement of Colored People (NAACP). This was in spite of the fact that most of its cast and more than half its crew were black or third-world people. Controversy centred on the film's portrayal of black men, which spilled into reviews, public debate and numerous editorials in the black press particularly.

The most interesting extention of this was the involvement of the cast. Against accusations that the film slandered black men, Danny Glover defended his portrayal of Mr —— as an archetypal abuser of any race whose behaviour is a response to feeling abused by the world. 'I can't deny that there are Misters. There are homes for battered women, children being molested and incest happening not only among Black people, but White people.'[20] In his own background, by contrast, he pointed to the strong marriage of his grandparents. And one interviewer used Glover himself as the very model of a middle-class happily married black professional man, an extension and proof of the film's message.[21]

The association of the actors' lives with the 'novel images' they portrayed on film is even more pervasive with respect to Oprah Winfrey and Whoopi Goldberg. Through their performances in *The Color Purple* both rose to national prominence, their personal lives interpreted as equivalent to the transformations of Sofia and Celie. The Oprah Winfrey Show was broadcast nationally and showed the fairy-tale achievement possible for a woman once victimized by abuse. Typically she generates emotional discussion on the most controversial dimensions of race, gender and sexual issues and has continued Sofia's reputation as a strong figure who can handle and ameliorate the pain of others. 'You have helped the way that people watch television', Whoopi (both women are first-name household words in America) told her on camera, 'the hue, the colour'. In September of 1992 Whoopi followed suit, becoming host of her own late-night television talk show.

Whoopi appeared on The Oprah Winfrey Show in April 1991, just after she won the Academy Award Oscar for her role in *Ghost* (USA, 1990). The achievement made them reflect together on *The Color Purple* and its failure to win awards, an issue Whoopi took up earlier in the year in her acceptance speech for the NAACP Image Award in which she openly accused the NAACP of undermining the film's recognition and costing the actors work. The NAACP, in fact, reversed its position and gave Spielberg the Image Award in 1986. From the first, the actress had defended Spielberg as the right director and the film against racial exploitation. Having overcome an abusive marriage, welfare dependence and dope addiction, she has retained the strongest possible identification with her performance in *The Color Purple*, which Steve Erickson called a 'rageful mix of experiential pumice and psychic hot springs'[22] that comes from neither Walker nor Spielberg but from herself. To Oprah she commented that the Oscar meant 'I wouldn't have to be picked on any more'. That was the same image she projected at the end of the film, a woman wizened more than aged. Already politically assertive when she played Celie, Whoopi has gone on to develop iconic roles of black female identity, such as in *Serafina* (SA, 1992). One recent motion picture, *The Long Walk Home* (USA, 1990), paid tribute to the women who stood together in the historic bus-boycott in Montgomery, Alabama in 1956 which triggered the Civil Rights Movement. The fact that survivors who actually took part in the boycott acted as extras in the church-sequence makes a particular point about the thin dividing-line between history and fiction in America.

For the mass American audience media-heroes like Whoopi Goldberg and Oprah Winfrey are folk-heroines whose roles in fiction have validated their political credentials. Though *The Color Purple* was criticized by its detractors as a sanitized white version of a black text, the heroines created by the film became role-models of black and feminist self-imaging who now have a national, multiracial following for their continued exploration of controversial issues. Thus *The Color Purple*, despite Spielberg's reservations, turned out to be a 'populist' film that transformed Alice Walker's characters, by transference, into living myths.

NOTES

1 David Breskin, 'Steven Spielberg', *Rolling Stone* (24 October 1985).
2 *In Search of Our Mothers' Gardens: Womanist Prose* (San Diego: Harcourt, Brace, Jovanovich, 1983), 356–8.
3 'Celie's Short for Cinderella: Alice Walker Takes on European Myth', Division on Afro-American Black Women Writers, Popular Culture Association Convention, San Antonio, 28 March 1991.
4 ' "Show Me How to Do Like You": Didacticism and Epistolary Form in *The Color Purple*', in Harold Bloom (ed.), *Alice Walker* (New York: Chelsea House Press, 1989), 185–94.
5 '*The Color Purple*: Revisions and Redefinitions', in Bloom, *Alice Walker*, 67–80.
6 ibid., 78–9.
7 Darryl Pinckney, 'Black Victims, Black Villains', *New York Review of Books* (29 January 1987), 174.
8 Susan Dworkin, 'The Making of *The Color Purple*', *Ms.* (December 1985), 68.
9 *Anatomy of Film*, 2nd edn (New York: St Martin's Press, 1990), 186.
10 Mona Gable, 'Author Alice Walker Discusses *The Color Purple*', *Wall Street Journal* (19 December 1985), 27.
11 'Steven Spielberg', *American Film* (June 1988).
12 Joan Bartherl, 'Here comes Oprah: From *The Color Purple* to TV Talk Queen', *Ms.* (August 1986), 49.
13 Jill Kearney, 'Whoopi Goldberg: Color Her Anything', *American Film* (December 1985), 26.
14 Armond White, '*The Color Purple*', *Films in Review* (February 1986), 113.
15 *American Film* (June 1988).
16 'Walker's Blues', in Bloom, *Alice Walker*, 59–66.
17 Gerald Early, '*The Color Purple* as Everybody's Protest Art', *Antioch Review* (Summer 1986), 265, 268.
18 Michael Seitz, 'Pop Purple', *The Progressive* (February 1986), 40.
19 Lynn Norment, '*The Color Purple*', *Ebony* (February 1986), 150.
20 '*The Color Purple* Brings New Black Stars to Screen in Shocking Story', *Jet* (13 January 1986), 61.
21 Trudy S. Moore, 'Danny Glover: Villain in *The Color Purple* is a Kind Family Man', *Jet* (17 March 1986), 38.
22 Steve Erickson, 'Whoopi Goldberg', *Rolling Stone* (8 May 1986), 90.

10

A PLAY FOR ENGLAND

The Royal Court adapts *The Playmaker*

Jim Davis

THE NOVEL

Thomas Keneally dedicated *The Playmaker* 'to Arabanoo and his brethren, still dispossessed'.[1] The novel is constructed around the first production of a European play in Australia, George Farquhar's *The Recruiting Officer*, performed by convicts in Sydney in 1789, which becomes a catalyst for the exploration of possession and dispossession, themes that reverberate throughout the narrative. At the heart of the novel are the aboriginal people, eventually to be dispossessed of their land, their gods, their culture; in turn we have the British, both officers and convicts, displaced from their native land and from European so-called 'civilization'. The British settlers, possessing and colonizing a new land, are in themselves 'possessed' – by strange dreams, strange passions, strange gods and, perhaps strangest of all, by playmaking. The theatre's ability to 'possess' becomes one of the novel's central metaphors; for, just as colonization can mean the imposition of alien cultures and new order on a subject people, so the play itself is something that colonizes life, imposing an order, a pattern, a structure on intractable material. 'A play', says Governor Phillip in the second act of *Our Country's Good*,[2] 'is a world in itself, a tiny colony we could almost say' (p. 25). Playmaking is a form both of possession and of possessing. It is paradigmatic of the attempt made by Governor Phillip to impose European notions of culture, civilization and social organization, on both the convicts and the aboriginal, Arabanoo. High culture imposes itself on presumed 'low' culture, on the assumption that its redemptive and transforming potential can only be for the good.

Ralph Clark, the officer designated responsible for the production of *The Recruiting Officer* in Keneally's novel, is darkly aware of the disparity between art and life:

> And so as Ralph's version of *The Recruiting Officer* neared its end . . . the players and the playmaker Ralph himself were left with the sense that life could be easily amended, that love was an easy play, and that everyone really intended the best.
>
> Ralph considered that in the real world it might also be the case except that there was always too much hidden, and too much to take into account. It was only within the circumference of a play, and particularly of a comedy, that all characters could be so deftly delivered from their meanness . . .
>
> As Ralph would soon have it proved again, though art perpetually improved itself, society went its reckless and complicated way.
>
> (p. 254)

Indeed, the classically derived sense of order that Governor Phillip attempts to impose upon the colony is constantly threatened by a sense of otherness, whether it be the dark, brooding hinterland, 'unseen and unguessable' (p. 35); the unfamiliar world of the native inhabitants; or the concealed alternative world exemplified by 'the Tawny Prince' of the criminals. The orderly world epitomized by plays and playmaking is undercut by these glimpses of unknown and unknowable worlds. Keneally describes Australia as the 'anti-Europe' (p. 28); by implication, a threat to the established order of things and therefore a prime candidate for colonization.

In the hangings forever threatening the criminal community Keneally has located the anti-play. Robert Hughes describes the public hangings in eighteenth-century England as 'a saturnalia of death', 'an expiatory theatre';[3] Harry Brewer, in Keneally's novel, also recognizes that 'hangings are a sort of theatre' (p. 16). Even Governor Phillip in the novel, for all his liberalism, sees hangings as a sign 'that society had arrived here and was asserting its order' (p. 90). Hangings, in this context, are a form of discipline to which playmaking offers an alternative. The production of *The Recruiting Officer* is almost undermined both by the threat of hanging hovering over Nancy Turner, the perjurer, and by the capture and threatened execution of Black Caesar during the actual performance. The novel seems to offer a balance between playmaking with its impulse towards order based on a harmonious society and punishment, which imposes order on a divided people through flogging and hanging.

THE PLAY

In 1988 a free adaptation of Thomas Keneally's novel, in a version by Timberlake Wertenbaker, was presented at the Royal Court Theatre in London. Entitled *Our Country's Good* and directed by Max Stafford-Clark, it was presented in tandem with a production of *The Recruiting Officer*, performed by the same cast. Max Stafford-Clark first had the idea as a result of reading Keneally's novel; he commissioned Timberlake Wertenbaker, whose earlier work had used both colonization and the eighteenth century to explore the limitations imposed by gender and patriarchy on self-determination, to dramatize the novel. This was to be her first experience of building a play through the workshopping process that Stafford-Clark often uses with his actors and dramatists. Consequently, the play reflects more than one voice, although its use of history to highlight contemporary issues is an already-established practice in Wertenbaker's work. In a note to *The Grace of Mary Traverse*,[4] which is set in the London of the Gordon Riots, she writes:

> Although the play is set in the eighteenth century, it is not a historical play . . . I found the eighteenth century a valid metaphor, and I was concerned to free the people of the play from contemporary preoccupations.
>
> (p. 57)

Max Stafford-Clark also observed this tendency in *Our Country's Good*:

> Timberlake is very concerned that her play should be a contemporary play, as well as a history one, and that it should have something to say about the history of the theatre in the twentieth century . . . the parallels between the situation the convicts were in and our own society don't have to be looked for, you stumble across them every moment.[5]

However, whilst Wertenbaker's play draws heavily, if freely, on *The Playmaker*, the focus changes considerably. Keneally's novel emphasizes loss and dispossession and a struggle to find order and meaning, but the world he creates is ambiguous and unknowable. Wertenbaker is more concerned with empowerment and self-determination, focusing on the production of *The Recruiting Officer*, whilst excluding equally pertinent issues. Keneally explores the forces that lie behind the making of modern Australia; through Ralph Clark's tentative playmaking he allegorizes its beginnings. For Wertenbaker Ralph Clark is not so much a playmaker, one who creates and constructs, but the rather more authoritarian, powerful (and anachronistically titled) figure of the Director, one who controls and imposes. According to Stafford-Clark:

> Part of Timberlake's thesis is that theatre has a power – not the power of redemption, but the power to change people's lives, the power to bring out the best in people.[6]

Keneally's novel concedes this as a possibility; Wertenbaker's play states it, somewhat ironically, as a triumphant fact.

Prisoners and players

Wertenbaker's play is in many ways as much a response to the Britain of the late 1980s as to Keneally's novel. It stresses the possibility of rehabilitation within a society still (in the 1980s) obsessed with punishment and law and order; it stresses the value of education as an instrument of enlightenment and personal development in a society about to undergo the Draconian imposition of a National Curriculum within the state education system; it stresses the value of art and theatre in a community beleaguered by funding cuts and a complacent belief in market rather than creative forces. The British prison system has long been considered one of the worst in Europe; indeed, the British place a higher percentage of their population in prison than any of their European neighbours. Tessa Blackstone writes:

> Britain's prisons are institutions of which we should be ashamed. They are absurdly expensive, yet scandalously inhumane . . . . They are overcrowded and unhygienic.

> They enforce idleness and encourage helplessness. They certainly punish; they hardly reform.[7]

Those who are sent to prison are predominantly young, male and unemployed, largely from poor, urban backgrounds. The imprisonment of women in Britain has also increased since the 1960s, with a disruptive effect on their personal life, since over half the women imprisoned have to leave behind dependent children. As part of their research for *Our Country's Good* the Royal Court actors talked to male and female criminals: they found many analogies between the motives, needs and circumstances of those that they interviewed and the convicts they were playing.[8] Tessa Blackstone, whose study implies that attitudes to punishment have not changed much either, suggests that prisons

> ought to provide some challenge to prisoners to set themselves objectives, to master skills and to acquire new knowledge. Above all they should help prisoners become less dependent and more self-disciplined and as a result acquire a more positive self-image.[9]

Her argument, in a year when the conditions in Britain's prisons sparked off extensive rioting in a Manchester prison, stresses self-respect and empowerment rather than punishment and degradation.

In *Arguments for a Theatre* Howard Barker describes a performance by life-prisoners of his play *The Love of a Good Man* at Wormwood Scrubs on 7 July 1988:

> In the performance they affirmed the drama as freedom. They asserted the superior life of the imagination. In the moment of performance they were not in custody. . . . They felt gratitude for the existence of speech and metaphor, and made it their own . . . . They wished to inhabit other life.[10]

Arscott, one of the convict actors in Wertenbaker's play, also recognizes this need to 'inhabit other life':

> I don't want to play myself. When I say Kite's lines I forget everything else. I forget the judge said I'm going to have to spend the rest of my life in this place getting beaten and working like a slave . . . I don't have to remember the things I've done, when I speak Kite's lines I don't hate anymore. (p. 31)

Stafford-Clark, Wertenbaker and the actors also saw this production of Barker's play whilst working on *Our Country's Good.* Stafford-Clark describes how he was moved by this occasion, which left him 'optimistic about the power of theatre and its ability to transform people's lives'.[11] In so far as the theatre was a liberating force for the convicts, within an atmosphere of repression and restraint, it brought home to Stafford-Clark the tremendous 'sexuality' of the theatre, a quality he saw as analogous with the convicts' experiences in *Our Country's Good.* The experience of the Wormwood Scrubs performance may well have contributed more than anything else to the positive and optimistic thrust and eventual focus of the Royal Court's production.

The issues of crime, punishment and rehabilitation become closely linked with the world of playmaking in both novel and play. Questions of balance predominate in Keneally's novel, whether of hanging versus playmaking or of punishment versus rehabilitation. Wertenbaker's adaptation does not lose the sense of punishment forever hovering in the background – the beating of Arscott during one of the rehearsals makes the antithesis theatrically vivid – but the power of the theatre to transcend is strongly affirmed. When Major Ross, the officer least kindly disposed to playmaking and most entrenched in his views on the punishment of prisoners, abuses some of the actors in rehearsal, the play itself enables them to re-establish their autonomy, as they marginalize his provocation by breaking once more into their lines. There are many officers like Ross, however, who doubt whether change is possible. In a scene entitled 'The authorities discuss the merits of the Theatre' Watkin Tench suggests that criminality is ingrained, an 'innate tendency': 'Many seem to have been born that way (they start as children). It is in their nature' (p. 8). Governor Phillip, however, is convinced of the educative and regenerative power of the theatre:

> The theatre is an expression of civilization. We belong to a great country which has spawned great playwrights. . . . The convicts will be speaking a refined, literate language and expressing sentiments of delicacy they are not used to. It will remind them that there is more to life than crime, punishment. And we, this colony of a few hundred, will be watching this together, for a few hours we will no longer

> be despised prisoners and hated gaolers. We will laugh, we may be moved, we may even think a little.
>
> (p. 9)

Governor Phillip draws on the Greek notion of theatre as an obligatory and unifying element within society, but the use of culture as an instrument of colonization is also implicit in these lines. Later the Governor extends his argument in conversation with Ralph, taking Plato's *Meno* as an instance that proves that 'human beings have an intelligence which has nothing to do with the circumstances in which they are born' (p. 24). Intelligence, in the Governor's view, is closely linked to humanity and he encourages playmaking as a means of redeeming humanity. 'How do we know', he says to Ralph, 'what humanity lies under the rags and filth of a mangled life?' (p. 25) Interestingly, the published text of the play is prefaced with a quotation from R. Rosenthal and L. Jacobsen's *Pygmalion in the Classroom*, which recounts an experiment in an elementary school where 20 per cent of children were deemed as showing unusual potential for intellectual growth. These children, unknown to their teachers, were selected at random, but nevertheless began to fulfil the expectations the teachers had been led to have of them.

Language and transformation

The possibility of change and transformation is at the heart of much of Wertenbaker's work. The expressive potential of language is often a key factor in the liberation her characters undergo or to which they aspire. David Ian Rabey has suggested that

> We witness the explosion of institutionalized terms of reference (identified with the dispossession and restriction of human potential) by public experience, and individual communication of that experience . . . .Characteristically, she locates the seeds of crisis in consequences of patriarchal-imperial impositions of definition . . . . Wertenbaker depicts paternalistic restrictions of responsibility, as manifested in the dispossession of speech as a right to selfhood, and the contrary reactions of marginalized characters, sometimes childlike in their eagerness and initial naïveté, attempting to construct and express their own senses of import and possibility in imaginative terms.[12]

An early play, *Case to Answer* (1980), concerns a woman who feels colonized by her partner (a Marxist writing a thesis on imperialism) who imposes his own world-view on her, but will not acknowledge her perceptions or her language. In *The Grace of Mary Traverse* Mary leaves the confinement of her father's home and the limitations of her role as his daughter in order to discover her own identity and her own language. She reappropriates the world for herself as she learns to think, to see and to speak in her own terms. She redefines relationships: 'The father I want cannot be the father of "your" daughter. And yet I had a father. Could you not be "my" father? Could you not try?' (p. 99). In confronting the need for change she dreams of 'new worlds', but comes to realize that this must not be the inherently male dream of power – of conquest and rule over the future – but a process of self-liberation and shifted perceptions. More recently, in *The Love of the Nightingale* (1988), Philomele who, like Mary Traverse, yearns for knowledge and experience, loses the power of language when she berates Tereus for raping her. His response is to cut out her tongue. In the words of Niobe, Philomele's servant: 'Now truly I pity Philomele. She has lost her words, all of them. Now she is silent. For good . . . the one alive who cannot speak, that one has truly lost all power' (p. 36). Procne, Philomele's sister, has already experienced the deprivations caused by loss of language, for as the wife of Tereus she is exiled in an alien land. 'Where have all the words gone?' she asks. 'There were so many. Everything that was had a word and every word was something. None of these meanings half in the shade, unclear' (pp. 6–7).

The loss of language may lead to the loss of one's right to self-determination, but its acquisition can be equally disempowering. Words can be treacherous, as Wisehammer and Mary demonstrate in *Our Country's Good*: 'Country can mean opposite things. It renews you with trees and grass, go rest in the country, or it crushes you with power: you die for your country, your country doesn't want you, you're thrown out of your country' (p. 17). Later the convicts stress the extent to which thought and identity are dependent on language:

LIZ. You have to think English. I hate England. But I think English . . .

CAESAR. I don't want to think English. If I think English

> I will die. I want to go back to Madagascar and think Malagasy . . . . If I die here, I will have no spirit.
>
> (p. 23)

In this context deprivation of language is spiritual death; yet acquisition of language, although often interpreted as redemptive, is also a form of colonization. Liz Morden is one of the most difficult women in the colony, 'full of loathing, foul mouthed, desperate', in the words of Governor Phillip (p. 25). Threatened with hanging for perjury, she answers her accusers with silence, but is finally persuaded to speak and save herself 'for the good of the colony' and 'of the play' (p. 35). She subsequently replies to the Governor's hope that she will be good in her part: 'Your Excellency, I will endeavour to speak Mr Farquhar's words with the elegance and clarity their own worth commands' (p. 35). Language has reclaimed her; she has succumbed to the discipline of playmaking rather than the discipline of the scaffold. Yet her reclamation is a form of dispossession, for she has acquired a language that does not allow her any definition of self.

Dispossession and colonization

If underlying Keneally's novel is a sense of the dispossession of the aboriginal people, underlying Wertenbaker's play is a sense of the dispossession of women. Farquhar's play in itself provides a masculine view of the world, in which male behaviour is largely excusable and females are little more than property, both sexually and financially. Stafford-Clark suggests that 'the drive of the play is to make us side with the lads and see things from Plume's point of view'.[13] In a scene entitled 'The meaning of plays' this issue is touched on by Dabby Bryant, who gets to the heart of *The Recruiting Officer's* mores when she says 'Love is the barter of perishable goods. A man's word for a woman's body' (p. 30). She is critical of the play's rewriting of female experience: 'I could write scenes, Lieutenant, women with real lives, not these Shrewsbury prudes' (p. 30). She considers *The Recruiting Officer* 'a silly play': 'I want to be in a play that has more interesting people in it . . . . I want to play myself . . . . I want to see a play that shows life as we know it . . . . Why can't we do a play about now?' (p. 31). Her experience and her language, as a woman and as a convict, are denied by the imposition of the play and its values. As Arscott speaks Kite's lines about his early life, Dabby interrupts: 'That's about me . . . . That's my story. Why do I have to play a silly milkmaid? Why can't I play Kite?' (p. 32). She suggests that gender should not be considered an impediment to her taking the role; indeed, by her intervention, she brings into question the way in which gender is constructed and presented in Farquhar's play. She also raises the problem of the limitations imposed on female experience by gender, a theme explored by Wertenbaker in a number of plays. In *New Anatomies* (1981) Isabelle Eberhardt is only able to experience the world as she wishes in the male Arab persona of Si Mahmoud; her possibilities and those of other women in the play who cross-dress are contrasted with the restricted horizons of those women who accept the female role imposed upon them by society.[14] In Farquhar's play[15] Silvia also chaffs at the restrictions imposed on her by gender: 'In short . . . I think a petticoat a mighty simple thing, and I'm heartily tired of my sex' (I.ii) – and longs for the masculine right 'to know the world'. Eventually, through cross-dressing, she briefly escapes such restrictions, but her motives turn out to be very conventional: 'I altered my outside because I was the same within, and only laid by the woman to make sure of my man' (V.vii). In Keneally's novel the courtship of Ralph and Mary Brenham concludes with Mary's capitulation as she utters these lines. Significantly, although Wertenbaker dramatizes this episode in the play, she excludes the sentimental and submissive lines favoured by both Farquhar and Keneally.

The situation of the women convicts contrasts strongly and ironically with the women they play. In *Our Country's Good* Mary's qualms about playing Silvia – 'she's brave and strong' – are assuaged by Dabby's remark, 'She didn't spend eight months and one week on a convict ship' (p. 13). For the women convicts dispossession meant loss of both physical and sexual liberty; they endured a double colonization in fact. Harry Brewer, possessed by dreams and jealousy, epitomizes the restrictively colonial nature of such relationships, in both play and novel, through his possessive attitude towards the convict woman, Duckling. Although Harry saved her from being hanged, she says in the play: 'Why didn't you let them hang me and take my corpse with you, Harry? You could have kept that in chains' (p. 12). In contrast, Ralph, who commences a sexual liaison with Mary Brenham, tries, in the words of Keneally, to create a household that is a willing commonwealth rather than a tyranny (p. 287). Wertenbaker recreates this in theatrical terms when Ralph asks Mary to undress before him, in a scene replacing the capitulation of Mary through the utterance of Silvia's speech, which Keneally had used in the novel:

RALPH. I've never looked at the body of a woman before.
MARY. Your wife.
RALPH. It wasn't right to look at her. Let me see you.
MARY. Yes. Let me see you.
RALPH Yes.
[*He begins to undress himself.*]

(p. 33)

Despite the inequality of the situation here, Mary arguably re-appropriates some dignity through her request to Lieutenant Clark and his acquiescence. She also exemplifies Wertenbaker's view that desire is an active as well as passive aspect of female sexuality and that, as in the majority of Wertenbaker's plays, the acquisition of knowledge and the expression of sexuality are irrevocably linked.[16]

Within the colonial context the relationship of Mary Brenham with Ralph Clark is nevertheless ambiguous; in the novel it is paralleled by the Governor's relationship with Arabanoo. Keneally implies that one possible interpretation of the Governor's relationship with Arabanoo (which he hints may be sexual) is that of an assault by a high culture upon a low (p. 236). Arabanoo, along with the convict Black Caesar, is marginalized by Wertenbaker's play. Black Caesar's rape of Mary Brenham is ignored by Wertenbaker, as is his capture at the end of the novel; in the play he is turned into a peripheral and comic figure. The token aboriginal who appears briefly in the play significantly fails to embody the intended weight of meaning and demonstrates how the Royal Court's appropriation of the novel has failed to grasp, perhaps intentionally, the centrality of this issue.[17] 'Capture a man', says Harry Brewer in the novel, 'and you capture his gods' (p. 266). As Robert Hughes shows, this is particularly pertinent in regard to the colonial intrusion of Europeans into Australia:

> Take away this [the aborigines'] territory and they were deprived, not of 'property' . . . but of their embodied history, their locus of myth, their 'dreaming'. There was no possible way in which the accumulated tissue of symbolic

> and spiritual usage represented by tribal territory could be gathered up and conferred on another tract of land by an act of will. To deprive the Aborigines of their territory, therefore, was to condemn them to spiritual death – a destruction of their past, their future and their opportunities of transcendence.[18]

Keneally describes Ralph Clark's reaction to Arabanoo's capture as sensing that some sort of violation had taken place. Like many of the convicts Arabanoo has been torn from his family: like them he is expected to conform or adapt to the requirements of the dominant class or culture, although his innate reactions sometimes lead us to question the values that this class represents. Interestingly, he fails to 'absorb the social meaning of flogging' (p. 141), which distresses him, but he is instinctively drawn to the rehearsals:

> Arabanoo was somehow aware that these were not the convicts in their normal persons, but in their transformed persons, and given that ritual was not unknown among the Indians themselves, Arabanoo seemed to take some comfort from the rehearsals. It was possible, thought Ralph, that he considered the reading of the lines and the rehearsal of the actions to have religious meaning, and Ralph was beginning to wonder himself if it were not so.
>
> (p. 126)

The idea of the play as ritual – as a rite of passage – is implicit in these lines.

Max Stafford-Clark has written that he was drawn to Keneally's novel because:

> it catches people at a moment when there's a possibility of change. Performing the play becomes, for Keneally's convicts, a way of re-establishing a relationship with humanity and civilization.[19]

Keneally certainly acknowledges the potential of the theatre to transform. He describes the desperate first readings by the criminals 'as if they sensed . . . that their best chance out of hunger and lovelessness and a bad name was to capture the first primitive stage of the earth' (p. 8). The eight-month voyage to Australia is seen as transforming in itself – 'nearly as absolute a change as death', (p. 18) – and as giving rise to the notion that one might become 'a different sort of being from the one you had been in that world of rational starlight from which you had now been excluded' (p. 34). Ralph's experiences of rehearsing the play lead him to a sense that the otherness of the convicts' world might be broken down. Yet, in so far as playmaking does bring together the two worlds, it sounds an ominous note for the future:

> Seen from the immensity of time, Ralph's play might appear a mere splutter of the European humour on the edge of a continent which, then, still did not have a name. This flicker of a theatrical intent would consume in the end the different and serious tribes of the hinterland. In the applause at the end of the evening, in the applause, whether of H. E. or of Will Bryant, Arabanoo – had he still lived – might have heard the threat.
>
> (p. 305)

Moreover, Keneally reminds us that the world of hunger, disease and insecurity, experienced by the first settlers, whilst distanced historically, has not disappeared. 'The Sichwanese, the Eritreans or the Masai would understand better than us the destinies which befell some of our players' (p. 306).

Wertenbaker's play lacks these perspectives. It appears to be a celebration of empowerment through playmaking, disregarding the dark and ironic implications built into Keneally's novel. One senses from the novel that playmaking in itself may be a strategy for coercion, an imposition of discipline; that it is the state, rather than the individual, that stands to gain through the play's paradigmatic equation with social control. Wertenbaker is not unaware of this: indeed, colonization is a recurrent theme and metaphor in her work. Yet, whilst Keneally's novel allegorically explores the imposition of colonial power, Wertenbaker's plays have consistently concerned themselves with strategies for liberation. In adapting *The Playmaker* she has been placed in the ambiguous position of dramatizing a novel that uses the theatre metaphorically to represent the colonizing process. Admittedly, in *The Love of the Nightingale* she actually demonstrates the dangers inherent in theatrical representations and their influence[20] and, in the light of her other plays, it seems reasonable to suppose that she intends the spectator to respond to the empowering possibilities of playmaking in *Our Country's Good* with a certain degree of irony. The fact that neither the Royal Court production nor the critical response to the play recognized this possibility suggests that Wertenbaker herself was ultimately disempowered – exiled like Procne in *The Love of the Nightingale* from her own language – by the colonizing power of the theatre itself.

The production

Both the novel and the play are ultimately appropriated by the theatre, at least as evidenced in the Royal Court production. Max Stafford-Clark's unironic direction of the play as a celebration of the theatre's potential to empower was accepted almost unequivocally by the critics. Catherine Wearing's comment that 'the glib, unquestioning reinforcement of the dominant culture was more than a little unpalatable'[21] is rare in its divergence from the generally enthusiastic critical response. Even Wertenbaker herself complied with the desire to endorse the power of theatrical performance as unambiguously as possible. One of the most memorable features of the Royal Court production was the use of Beethoven's Fifth Symphony, welling up at the end of the play as the convicts are about to perform. Interestingly, in the first edition of the play there is no reference to this, whereas the revised edition actually calls for Beethoven's 'triumphant' music (p. 39). As in the most vulgar of show-business musicals, all obstacles are overcome, the human spirit is shown to be indomitable and the show goes on.

Our Country's Good nevertheless transcended mere vulgarity. In part, this may have been due to Stafford-Clark's use of cross-gender and cross-racial casting, which provided its own ironic comment on some of the play's issues. In production it was a play that made an affirmative statement in a country whose inhabitants and institutions seemed as dispossessed as the convicts of the first fleet. Stafford-Clark wrote:

> Not the least of the play's achievements was the resonant chord it touched in London's beleaguered theatrical community . . . . A play that proclaimed the power and enduring worth of theatre, and that celebrated its centrality to our lives, was of importance in the third term of a government who deemed subsidy a dirty word.[22]

Wertenbaker's play celebrated theatre as an agency of transformation and education. It argued for rehabilitation rather than punishment. It also asserted the right to language, as a means of self-expression and self-determination. It highlighted the plight of women in a patriarchal and transactional society. Yet, in so effectively colonizing Keneally's novel, it dispossessed the novel of its centre. *The Playmaker*, a novel for Australia, had been turned into *Our Country's Good*, a play for England.[23]

NOTES

1 (London, 1987). All page references to *The Playmaker* are printed in parenthesis within the text.
2 Timberlake Wertenbaker (London, 1988). A revised edition of the play was printed in 1989. All references to *Our Country's Good* are taken from the 1989 text. Page references are printed in parenthesis within the text.
3 Robert Hughes, *The Fatal Shore* (London, 1987), p. 31.
4 *The Love of the Nightingale and The Grace of Mary Traverse* (London, 1989). An earlier version of *The Grace of Mary Traverse* was published in 1985. All page references, taken from the 1989 edition, are printed in parenthesis in the text.
5 Max Stafford-Clark, 'Poised for Change', *Plays International* (August 1988), 25.
6 ibid.
7 Tessa Blackstone, *Prisons and Penal Reform* (London, 1990), 1.
8 Max Stafford-Clark, *Letters to George: The Account of a Rehearsal* (London, 1989), 77, 115–16.
9 Blackstone, *Prisons and Penal Reform*, 40.
10 Howard Barker, *Arguments for a Theatre* (London, 1989), 68–9.
11 Stafford-Clark, 'Poised for Change', 25.
12 'Defining Difference: Timberlake Wertenbaker's Drama of Language, Dispossession and Discovery', *Modern Drama*, 33/4 (December 1990), 518.
13 Stafford-Clark, *Letters to George*, 43.
14 *Plays Introduction: Plays by New Writers* (London, 1984), 297–339.
15 All references to *The Recruiting Officer* are taken from Peter Dixon's *Revel's Plays* edition (Manchester, 1986).
16 Timberlake Wertenbaker's views on these topics are briefly expressed in Susan Carlson, 'Self and Sexuality: Contemporary British Women Playwrights and the Problem of Sexual Identity', *Journal of Dramatic Theory and Criticism*, 3/2 (Spring 1989), 157–8, 169–70.
17 An alternative reading is that Timberlake Wertenbaker has shown great sensitivity in not attempting to give theatrical expression to aboriginal experience. The omission of this aspect of the novel might then be seen as tact rather than evasion.
18 Hughes, *The Fatal Shore*, 18.
19 Stafford-Clark, *Letters to George*, 1.

20 Tereus in part blames his rape of Philomele on a play he has seen enacted at the court of her father.

21 *What's On* (6 December 1989); in *London Theatre Record* I/ix, (19 November–2 December 1989), 1645.

22 Stafford-Clark, *Letters to George*, 189.

23 Not long after the completion of this chapter Ann Wilson's article '*Our Country's Good*: Theatre, Colony and Nation in Wertenbaker's Adaptation of *The Playmaker*' appeared in *Modern Drama*, 34/1 (March 1991), 23–34. Despite a difference in emphasis, I find myself in agreement with many of her findings.

11

ADAPTING *NICE WORK* FOR TELEVISION

David Lodge

For a novelist, the most challenging aspect of adaptation is not the formal difference between the two media – the fact that a book communicates by words alone, whereas film communicates by a combination of words, images and music – but the different status of the writer in the production of the artefact. These two differences are, however, connected.

The novelist has total control over the production of the work. He may, if he so wishes (I usually do), compose it in complete privacy and secrecy, showing it to no one until it is finished. He may then invite suggestions (from spouse, agent, publisher, friends) for cuts, additions and revisions, but publication is not normally conditional on acceptance of such advice, at least in the case of established writers. Indeed, some distinguished novelists are known to insist that their work be printed exactly as delivered, with not a single comma changed. I am not sure such self-confidence could ever be well founded, but my point is that not even the most highly esteemed screenplay writer in the world would expect the first script submitted to be the final one. On the contrary, it is a basis for discussion, negotiation and revision.

The reason is simply that whereas prose fiction is an individualistic medium (it is hard to think of a really good novel written by more than one person), film is a collaborative medium, involving many different people with distinct creative skills – producer, director, cameraman, casting director, actors, designers, lighting and sound supervisors, editor – all of whom contribute to the creation of the artefact; and the method of production itself is, compared to writing and publication, complex, expensive and cumbersome, involving a small army of other collaborators responsible for such tasks as budgeting, location hunting, property purchasing, set-building, timetabling, and so on, all of which have some bearing on the creative enterprise. The evolution of a film, or television serial, from the words on the page of the screenplay, to the finished product on the screen, is therefore subject at every point to a multitude of determinations, some aesthetic, some personal, some practical, that are outside the writer's consciousness and to a large extent outside his or her control. Working under such constraints can be very frustrating; but it can also be very rewarding when it leads to the discovery of new meanings and effects in familiar material. In this chapter I shall endeavour to illustrate these points by an empirical and anecdotal account of my experience of adapting my novel *Nice Work* as a serial for BBC television.

I finished writing the novel in the winter of 1987–8. Not long before, I had made the acquaintance of Chris Parr, a television drama producer based at the BBC's Birmingham headquarters, Pebble Mill, working under the general supervision of Michael Wearing, a producer with a distinguished track-record, especially in the field of realistic, socially relevant drama series like *The Boys from the Black Stuff* and *Blind Justice*. They expressed an interest in my writing something 'regional and topical' for production at Pebble Mill. I told them I had the very thing, and gave them the typescript of *Nice Work*. They liked it, and after one meeting, in April 1988, commissioned me to write the screenplay. Unusually, the contract was for the complete script, and did not stipulate approval of a treatment or first episode. This was an encouraging act of faith in a writer with no proven ability to write a screenplay, and a warrant of their serious commitment to the project. But we all recognized that it was important to broadcast the television version of the novel while its picture of Thatcher's Britain was still recognizable; and the winter–spring calendar of the story meant that the serial would have to go into production in the following March, or be postponed for another year. I had, therefore, to produce the complete script by the end of 1988, but I did not begin work immediately. The novel was still at the proof stage. I waited until I had corrected the proofs and seen the revises, and the text of the novel was irrevocably fixed, before beginning the screenplay. It was as if the story was having two different 'lives', and I wanted the first to be over, as far as I was concerned, before the second one began.

TIMING

The most important single component of a television writer's brief is the temporal format of the drama, especially if it is a serial. No narrative medium is as precisely timed as an episode of a television series. When transmitted, it must fit a preordained slot measured in minutes and even seconds. Such precision can only be achieved in the editing, rather than in the writing process; but the writer must turn in a script that will fit the programme slot at least approximately. This is an exceedingly difficult matter to judge, especially for a beginner; and the rule-of-thumb that a page of script equals a minute of screen-time is a very rough guide indeed.

With a serial there is the additional problem of dividing up the whole narrative into a number of blocks of equal duration, each of which will have a satisfying dramatic structure and end with some kind of 'lure' (to borrow Roland Barthes's term) to encourage the audience to watch the next episode. The production of *Nice Work* was hampered, and perhaps ultimately impaired, by exasperating changes of mind concerning its format by the powers in the BBC who determine programming.

At my initial meeting with Chris Parr and Mike Wearing, Mike suggested a format of two parts of 75 minutes each. By the time the contract was drawn up, this duration had been redistributed as three episodes of 50 minutes. Later it was expanded to three episodes of 60 minutes; and, after much cutting and rewriting, that was the form in which I delivered the 'final' script in December 1988, and the form in which it was subsequently typed up as a rehearsal script. In the course of filming,[1] the Director, Christopher Menaul, became increasingly concerned that he would end up with too much material to fit into three hours. This was partly the consequence of his own highly creative visual imagination, which was continually adding effects not envisaged or required by the script.

He pressed Chris Parr to ask the higher echelons of the BBC for permission to divide the series into four episodes of 50 minutes each, giving us an additional 20 minutes in all, but the word always came back: no, three by 60 minutes is what it has to be. In consequence, already pushed for time, the two Chrisses decided to cut or abbreviate several scenes in the screenplay – scenes that everybody liked very much – because they were quite certain that they would not be able to include them. Some small adjustments to other scenes were required by these cuts.

A few days after shooting had finished, and the actors and crew had irretrievably dispersed, the word came from London that, after all, a series of four episodes of 50 minutes was required – shortly afterwards expanded to four of 55 (in which form it was eventually transmitted). In Birmingham we had mixed feelings about this volte-face. On the one hand, we were delighted to have the additional 30 minutes of screen-time, because it was already evident, from the early editing, that much of what had been recorded would have had to be drastically cut to fit a three by 60 format. On the other hand, what we had in the can only just filled the newly available time, and it was bitterly frustrating to think of the scenes we had needlessly sacrificed. In particular, I mourn the loss of (1) a scene (not in the novel) in which Charles refuses to accompany Robyn to Sunday lunch at the Wilcoxes – his first rebellion against the force of her will in their relationship, a relationship which could have done with a bit more detail in the television version; (2) a sequence in the swimming-pool and gym of the German hotel where Vic and Robyn have their brief affair, which would have made this development seem a little less abrupt; and (3) a scene in which Vic, changing out of his business suit on returning home in the late afternoon, absent-mindedly puts on his pyjamas and gets into bed – a scene both amusingly expressive of his emotionally traumatized state and one that would have provided a smooth transition to the nightmare sequence that immediately follows.

One consequence, of course, of the last-minute change of format, was that my carefully worked-out climaxes for episodes One and Two had to be scrapped, and three new episode-endings created in the editing room. There is a scene in the second episode as transmitted, where Robyn is in bed with Charles, who challenges her about returning to the factory; if the acting and direction seem a little over-emphatic it is because this was originally going to be the final scene of Episode One. My Episode Two had ended with Robyn in bed with Vic in Germany, saying 'I prefer to be on top.' Now it ended rather inconclusively with Vic and Robyn returning from their walk after Sunday lunch, followed by a wordless sequence in which Vic drives to work listening dreamily to Jennifer Rush singing 'The Power of Love'. At Chris Menaul's request, I wrote some additional dialogue in which Robyn urges Vic to address the work-force at the factory about his rationalization plans, thus providing a link to the first scene of the next episode, and the principal actors were recalled to record these lines, which were dubbed over a rear-view shot of them re-entering the Wilcox house. There were, it has to be said, some dramatic gains from the reformatting of the series. The superbly acted morning-after scene in Germany, for instance, is all the more effective for coming immediately after the scene in bed the night before, rather than separated by an episode-break.

EXTERNAL CIRCUMSTANCES

The German part of the story provided perhaps the most striking example of how external circumstances can condition the form of a television drama. In the novel, Vic Wilcox goes to a trade exhibition in Frankfurt to buy an expensive machine-tool for his foundry, taking with him his Industry Year 'shadow', Robyn Penrose. Through her knowledge of German, she protects him from some rather sharp practice by the German businessmen with whom he is dealing, and this action precipitates their brief affair. Very early in the process of turning *Nice Work* into a television serial – before, indeed, the contract with the BBC was even signed – Chris Parr and I had what we thought was an amazing piece of luck in this connection: we discovered that the principal foundry trade-show in Europe, which is only mounted once every four years, was to be held in Düsseldorf in May 1989, exactly the time when we would want to shoot the German scenes in *Nice Work*. The organizing body, GIFA, readily agreed to let us film inside their exhibition. A participating company agreed to let us use their stand. I accordingly wrote the screenplay showing Vic and Robyn, as in the novel, making their way through a crowded hall in which massive machines are in simulated operation. It promised to be a spectacular scene of a kind which could not possibly be faked. It seemed too good to be true, and it was.

In February 1989, when *Nice Work* was already in production, alarm bells rang. Someone had sent to Germany the script, not only of the scenes in the Exhibition hall, but also of a subsequent scene in a restaurant, in which the German businessmen are shown trying to pull the wool over Vic's eyes. GIFA had immediately withdrawn their permission to film, not only inside, but anywhere near the show, on the grounds that we were portraying German businessmen in a dishonourable light.

We pleaded that our film also showed British businessmen indulging in deception – but to no avail. We appealed to GIFA's sense of humour – it did not apparently exist. Desperately we offered to make the offending characters Swiss. No dice. In the end I had to rewrite the episode so that Vic visits a German factory to appraise and purchase his automatic core-moulder. There was no time to find a suitable factory in Germany. The location we used was a factory in Stourbridge that made core-moulders under licence (another irony here, since I thus discovered that in reality Vic would not have had to travel to Germany to buy his machine). German-language notices were put up on the walls, and German actors imported to take part in the scene. Efforts were made to tidy up the factory floor, though it still, I'm afraid, fell well short of German standards in this respect. Visually, the scene was much less spectacular than the one I had originally envisaged in my screenplay. But, dramatically, I believe it was an improvement. Deprived of spectacle, the scene had to be more carefully researched and imaginatively written. The technical discussions were more convincing in the new scene and the comedy of Robyn's pretending to be Vic's dumb bimbo was much enhanced. It also helped that by the time I wrote the new scene I had observed the actors, Warren Clarke and Haydn Gwynn, in rehearsals and knew what they were capable of.

CONDENSATION

Turning a novel into a film, even a serial film several hours long, is inevitably mostly a matter of condensation rather than expansion. This is because, very simply, it usually takes longer to perform an action, including a speech act, than it does to read a written report of the same action. But there is another reason: novels contain a great deal of information that is superfluous in film. In adapting a novel for film or television, there is a natural temptation to try and incorporate as much as possible of the information in the original text in the form of dialogue, but this is nearly always a temptation to be resisted. The information should as far as possible be translated into action, imagery, gesture – or dispensed with altogether. The realistic novel, in particular, is bound by a code of plausibility based on cause and effect; and since the reader is in control of his or her reception of a text – can stop and ponder and re-read and check back – this code requires from the writer a great deal of explanation, covering of contingencies, anticipations of the reader's possible objections, and so on. Much of this apparatus is unnecessary in film, because the presentation of events in motion pictures does not allow the viewer time to analyse their plausibility, and sweeps aside scepticism by its vividness and immediacy. The fundamental narrative device of film (one that modern novelists have, of course, borrowed and exploited) is the cut, which moves the story instantly from one spatio-temporal context to another without explanation.

I can perhaps illustrate these points, and the essentially collaborative nature of film-making, by describing the evolution of the first part of the first episode of the televised *Nice Work*. Readers of the novel will recall that the first chapter consists of a leisurely description of Vic Wilcox waking on Monday 13th January, 1986, getting up, getting dressed, having breakfast and driving to work, combined with a fairly detailed account of his biography and family background. Chapter Two does the same for Robyn Penrose; and reference is made in it to a one-day strike of University staff, planned for the following Wednesday, in which Robyn intends to take part. Chapter Three describes the activities of these two characters at their respective work-places later the same day, alternating between the University and the factory, and also introduces, via the character of Philip Swallow, the Shadow Scheme which will bring them together. At the end of the day, both are pressured into participating in the scheme, which is due to start the following Wednesday. Vic is mistakenly informed that the shadow is a male 'Robin'.

These three chapters make up Part One of the novel, covering Day One of Week One of the action, which is also the first week of the University term. Chapter One of Part Two picks up the story ten days later, on the Wednesday of Week Two, when Robyn makes her first visit to the factory. We learn that she postponed her visit for a week because she would have been 'strike-breaking' if she had gone on the Wednesday of Week One. On this second Wednesday, she is delayed by a heavy snowfall. When she finally arrives, Vic recognizes her as a participant in a demonstration outside the University gates that delayed him on his way to work the previous Wednesday. This provokes a discussion about the strike which sets them at odds at the very beginning of their acquaintance.

At the first moment of thinking about adapting *Nice Work* for the screen I decided to use the essentially cinematic cross-cutting device of my third chapter from the very beginning of the screenplay. Episode One therefore begins with a sequence of short scenes alternately set in Vic's and Robyn's houses, showing them getting up and preparing for the day's work at roughly the same time. In the novel, the processes of washing and dressing afforded opportunities for detailed descriptions of the physical appearance of each character, but in the television version this information is of course continuously transmitted by every shot in which the actors appear. Conversely, the detailed biographical data provided about the characters in the novel had to be reduced to a few vital pieces of information that could be spoken or shown. This led me to have Robyn's boy-friend, Charles, present in the first scenes of the screenplay (in the novel he had returned the previous evening to his own University of Suffolk) to show rather than refer to their relationship, and to provide an interlocutor for Robyn.

My first draft screenplay followed the sequence of events of Day 1 in the novel; but it then showed in chronological order what was reported retrospectively (via the interiorized rendering of Robyn's consciousness and Vic's consciousness) in Part Two of the novel: her participation in the union demonstration outside the University on the Wednesday of Week One, which delays him on his way to work. And in the screenplay I sent her to the factory later that same day. I simply dropped her scruple about strike-breaking, and made her picket duty the reason for being late for her appointment with Vic. This moved the story on more quickly. It also provided a convenient explanation for her lateness to replace the snowstorm in the original novel (since it would have been prohibitively expensive to cover all the relevant locations with artificial snow).

The change had important consequences for the effect of the narrative when Robyn finally arrives at the factory. What is an enigma in the novel (Vic feels he has seen Robyn somewhere before, but cannot immediately remember where or when) becomes an irony in the screenplay (the viewer will have already seen Robyn on the picket-line that delays him). There is an additional irony in the picket-line scene itself, since the viewer knows, as neither character does, that their fates are already entwined through the Shadow Scheme.

Chris Parr's reaction to the first draft screenplay of Episode One was generally encouraging, but he said it was too long, and too leisurely in following the main characters as they got up and went to work on the first morning of the action. He suggested using a split screen to present some of these scenes simultaneously. This seemed like a good idea, which I implemented. (Later it was dropped, and split screen used instead for some of the many telephone conversations in the story.) I also made some cuts, but essentially the second version of the episode was structurally the same as the first.

While I was working on Episodes Two and Three, Chris Menaul was appointed as Director, and at another conference about the script of Episode One he suggested that the union demonstration should happen on Day One of the action, so that Robyn gets up and goes straight to the picket line that delays Vic on his way to work. In this way the ideological opposition between the two main characters is established dramatically in the first five or six minutes of the film. Instead of just ironically juxtaposing them, the screenplay now showed them in conflict or potential conflict. This was neatly underlined by Chris Menaul's direction of the scene when it was finally shot: Robyn approaches Vic's car with a leaflet, and almost speaks to him, before she is distracted by a cheer from her fellow-pickets.

These changes, however, entailed others. If the University staff were on strike on Day One, then the Shadow Scheme could not be discussed and settled on that day. So Robyn's interviews with Swallow about her job and about the Shadow Scheme, and other University scenes, were postponed to Day Two, along with several scenes in the factory. In the novel Robyn and her colleague Bob Busby have an argument with Swallow about the efficacy of the strike on Day One, before it happens. This was incorporated in the film by having Swallow challenged by Busby and Robyn as he drives through the picket line – again, a more dramatic handling of the topic.

These changes were a huge gain in cinematic terms, but they entailed some improbabilities that would have been unacceptable to me in a novel. First of all, they violate the facts of history. The novel makes reference to many current events, taken from the newspapers of the day, and the realism I was aiming at in it is partly created by the documentary accuracy of this dimension of the story. There actually was a one-day strike by University staff on Wednesday 15th January 1986. It is highly unlikely in any case that the union would ever hold a demonstration on the first day of term – it would be too difficult to organize. The one-day strike was a national event, raising the question of why Charles is lingering in Rummidge instead of taking part in the strike at his own University: I solved that one by making the Rummidge strike a local day-of-action. Some of my university colleagues may have been bothered by these implausibilities and inconsistencies, but I am quite sure that the vast majority of the audience will not have been bothered by them, or even noticed them.

Condensation – cutting out superfluous material, accelerating the tempo of events – and dramatization – translating narration and represented thought into speech, action and image: these are the fundamental tasks of the adapter. But it is not always easy, especially for the author of the original novel, to see what is essential and what is not. It seemed to me, for instance, that the episode in which Robyn goes to lunch at the Wilcoxes, and afterwards for a walk through the University halls of residence with Vic, was not essential to the development of the plot, and so I cut it out of my first draft screenplay, in order to save time. The two Chrisses persuaded me to put it back – and, of course, they were absolutely right: it is one of the most effective scenes in the whole serial, expressing, through beautifully played comedy of manners, all the conflicts and contrasts between the various generations and classes portrayed in the story. One of Vic's children, his daughter, did, however, disappear in the course of the various rewrites. Her part became so abbreviated by the exigences of overall timing that we thought it was better to cut her out of the story altogether. Robyn's friend, Penny, also disappeared. Her function as confidante, useful in the novel, seemed unnecessary in the screenplay and made for rather static scenes. One such scene in the first draft screenplay had Robyn reading out to Penny extracts from Charles's letter announcing his intention of becoming a merchant banker. This was my attempt to 'dramatize' the letter in the original novel. Letters, so at home in prose fiction (some of the earliest classic novels were written in the form of letters), are, however, clumsy devices in film. At the prompting of the two Chrisses, I wrote a new scene in which Charles waylays Robyn at the University to announce his change of career and make a proposal of marriage (the subjects of two separate letters in the novel). This is much more effective visually and dramatically. We see Charles in his sleek yuppie suit, already transformed from the rumpled don of the earlier scenes. His special pleading and Robyn's response are acted out in terms of her getting into her car and driving away, resisting his attempts to detain her or follow her.

NEW MATERIAL

Adapting *Nice Work* consisted mostly of reducing and re-presenting material in the original novel. However, a few new scenes were added, not just to solve problems created by the processes of condensation, but to convey additional meaning. These were the dream sequences, in which Vic sees Robyn transformed into the figure of the goddess Diana. The origin of these scenes in the novel was a passage describing Vic's thoughts, as he sits in his office one evening after an excursion with his 'shadow'. She has just revealed to him that she has a lover (Charles) and he finds himself surprisingly disturbed by this information.

> She was the most independent woman he had ever met, and this had made him think of her as somehow unattached and – it was a funny word to float into his mind, but, well, *chaste*.
>
> He recalled a painting he had seen once at the Rummidge Art Gallery on a school outing – it must have been more than thirty years ago, but it had stuck in his memory, and arguing with Shirley the other day about nudes had revived it. A large oil painting of a Greek goddess and a lot of nymphs washing themselves in a pond in the middle of a wood, and some young chap in the foreground peeping at them from behind a bush. The goddess had just noticed the Peeping Tom, and was giving him a really filthy look, a look that seemed to come right out of the picture and subdue even the schoolboys who stared at it, usually all too ready to snigger and nudge each other at the sight of a female nude. For some reason the painting was associated in his mind with the word 'chaste', and now with Robyn

> Penrose. He pictured her to himself in the pose of the goddess – tall, white-limbed, indignant, setting her dogs on the intruder.

This is very characteristic 'novel-discourse', the interiorized rendering of a character's thoughts, using free indirect style, and a very literary kind of irony at Vic's expense, appealing over his head to the educated reader to supply the missing information that explains why Vic associates Robyn with chastity and with the painting: the subject of the painting was Diana, the goddess of chastity, something he was told by his teacher but has forgotten. The technique of the passage is antithetical to film and has no essential narrative function in the book. It did not occur to me to try and incorporate it into my screenplay. But Chris Menaul, at a fairly late stage in the evolution of the screenplay, was still looking for some way of expressing the turmoil of Vic's inner emotional life as he becomes romantically infatuated with Robyn, and he saw this passage as a possible key: in dream and reverie Vic could picture Robyn as Diana, the chaste, forbidden, angry, unobtainable object of his desire. His actual acts of voyeurism – spying on her through the peephole when she first arrives at the factory, and involuntarily glimpsing her naked breast when he first calls at her house – provoke visions in which he re-enacts watching Diana bathing with her nymphs and is pursued by the huntress and her hounds. As the BBC at Pebble Mill has considerable resources for studio-based set-design and special effects, which were not otherwise bespoken at the time, Chris Menaul was able to stage these scenes on a lavish scale. A large warm-water pond, complete with waterfall, was constructed in order to produce a *tableau vivant* of Titian's famous picture of Diana surprised by Acteon. Lasers were used to cast an eerie light over Haydn Gwynn's impersonation of Diana as huntress in the other Titian painting of this mythical story.

The main problem for me as screenplay writer was how to convey to the audience the reason for the associations between Robyn and Diana in Vic's mind. These associations could be mysterious up to a point, but eventually they would have to be explained. The solution I arrived at, in discussion with Chris Menaul, was to have a flashback scene in which Vic recalls himself as a boy looking at the painting in the Rummidge Art Gallery, then another scene set in the present in which he revisits the gallery to track down the picture and overhears an art historian lecturing some students about it, relating the myth of Diana. A large painting in the style of Titian, in which Diana bears a faint resemblance to Haydn Gwynn, was produced by the Pebble Mill design team, and the gallery of the Birmingham Royal Society of Artists was hired for the two scenes.

When the serial was well into production, Chris Menaul asked me to write some additional lines for the art lecturer to cover the camera movements he had planned for the second of these scenes. I promised to do so, but there was some confusion about the deadline. One morning, just as I was leaving my house to go to London, I received a telephone call from Chris at the Art Gallery, saying he was about to start shooting the scene and had not got the extra material. I raced down to the Art Gallery where, standing in the lobby in my raincoat, I wrote several lines of art-historical jargon about the nude and voyeurism and the male gaze, using a ball-point pen and the back of a discarded page of script, before rushing off to catch my train to London. Whatever the quality of the lines (actually, I thought they came across rather well in performance), writing a novel was never so exciting.

NOTE

1 Strictly speaking, I should say 'recording', since *Nice Work* was made on videotape, not celluloid. There are differences between these two media and the techniques that go with them which are of great interest to professionals, but they have little bearing on the subject of this chapter. The director uses a single video camera much as a movie director uses a film camera, and although the editing processes for each medium are technically different, they use the same 'grammar'.

INDEX